GREEN BEAT

The Forgotten Era of Irish Rock

Daragh O'Halloran grew up in Dún Laoghaire, County Dublin, after the beat group era had already come and gone. The Velvet Underground, The Doors and 1960s rock in general saved him from the plastic mediocrity of mid-80s pop music. This is his first book.

GREEN BEAT

The Forgotten Era of Irish Rock

Daragh O'Halloran

THE BREHON PRESS
BELFAST

First published 2006 by The Brehon Press Ltd

1A Bryson Street, Belfast BT5 4ES, Northern Ireland

ISBN: 1 905474 10 5

Design: December Publications

Printed and bound in England by J.H. Haynes & Co. Ltd, Sparkford.

CONTENTS

For my parents Jimmy & Joan

ACKNOWLEDGEMENTS

The sole name of the author on the cover of this book conceals behind it a wealth of assistance generously given to me by a large number of people in order to make the story of Ireland's beat scene come to life. I must first thank both Sean Reynolds and Joe Dodd for trusting me with unlimited access to their incredible archives of Irish pop magazines from the 1960s. I don't think the project would have really got off the ground without all those important names and dates. The following is a list of people who kindly donated their valuable time to either talk with me, respond to my queries via e-mail, send a DVD, pass on another phone number, or lend precious photographs, records and memorabilia: Peter Adler, Roger Armstrong, Paul Ashford, Tony Boland, Smiley Bolger, Brendan Bonass, Tony Bradfield, Paul Brady, Terry Brady, Rab Braniff, Robbie Brennan, Murielanne Butterworth, John Byrne, Patrick Campbell-Lyons, Ted Carroll, Ditch Cassidy, Paul Divito, Mick Cox, Alan Dee, Rod Demick, Jerry Dennon, Johnny Duhan, Kevin Dunne, Jimmy Dunne, Tommy Dunne, Pat Egan, Roy Esmonde, BP Fallon, Jimmy Greeley, Len Guest, Cha Harren, Shay Healy, Danny Hughes, Bob Kelly, Francis Kennedy, John Keogh, Sjef Kolen, Robert Lamrock, Caroline Lewis, Dave Lewis, Brian Lynch, Larry Lynch, Dave McAnaney, Henry McCullough, Ian McGarry, Ray McDonald, Gil McWilliams, Maxie McEvoy, Jaye Malone, Mike Niblett, Mick Molloy, Dave Moore, Quintin Oliver, Deke O'Brien, Oliver O'Toole, Larry Page, Alec Palao, Chris Phelan, Jim Phelan, Maria Phelan, John Ryan, Jonathan Ryan, Aidan Scannell, Matt Sheffe, Brush Shiels, Bill Sommerville-Large, Sam Smyth, Chris Stewart, Richie Unterberger, Pat Ward, Pat Whelan, Ian Whitcomb, Benny White, and Peter Yeates.

Special thanks to Brian Harris for his unstinting help and enthusiasm during the course of my research. I would also like to mention Colm O'Ríagáin for encouraging me to put together the original proposal and for making that proposal reach Damian Keenan of The Brehon Press, who bravely took on this novice writer and supported me in my work over the last fourteen months or so. I am grateful to my editor Nicola Keenan, who smoothed out the rough edges, improved the overall quality, and brought her expertise to a manuscript which I had become far too familiar with to look at objectively.

Pictures have been kindly contributed for reproduction from the following sources: Ted Carroll (pages 22, 24, 26 and 28); Maxie McEvoy (pages 36 and 81); Ian Whitcomb (pages 39, 42, 45, 46, 49, 50, 51, 56, 58 and 65); Paul Ashford (page 71); Jaye Malone (pages 72, 73, 94 and 95); Brian Harris (pages 83, 86, 87 and 88); Robbie Brennan (pages 91, 105 and 203); Alan Dee (pages 99, 103 and 213); Brendan Bonass (page 104); Sean Reynolds (page 110); Alec Palao (pages 111 and 146); Rod Demick (pages 113 and 119); Mike Niblett (pages 121 and 134); Caroline Lewis (pages 126 and 131); Maria Phelan (pages 138 and 141); Sjef Kolen (pages 149 and 152); Bill Sommerville-Large (page 166); Mick Cox (page 187) and Benny White (page 196). The front cover photograph is reproduced by kind permission from Roy Esmonde. Additional illustrations have been reproduced from the hallowed pages of two legendary Irish music periodicals of the 1960s: *Spotlight* magazine (pages 13, 29, 31, 64, 77, 101, 107, 116, 122, 124, 129, 148, 162, 164, 167, 172, 177, 179, 185, 193, 199, 200, 206, 210 and 218) and *Hitsville* magazine (pages 90, 115, 118, 170, 174, 176, 191, 204, 209 and 211).

PREFACE

You could be forgiven for thinking that 1960s popular music in Ireland meant one thing – showbands. The dinosaurs from that era still regularly pop up on the comfy sofas of chat shows to tell us how great *their* era was, how everyone danced the night away to Dickie and Butch and Eileen, how the halls didn't even serve a drop of drink, and how you might have been lucky enough to meet your future wife in a ballroom if you worked up the courage to cross the floor and invite some 'young wan' out to waltz.

In the late 1990s, specialist record labels began to re-issue highly obscure cuts of 60s pop, garage rock, folk-rock, soul, rhythm 'n' blues and psychedelia by bands from across the globe that no one outside of exclusive collectors' circles had ever heard of before. It was clear that the influence of The Beatles, Stones, Kinks, etc – and later their US imitators – had spread worldwide at breakneck speed during that decade. The presence of 7" singles that sounded like animated rip-offs of the new Brit groups (but nevertheless thrilling and brilliant in their own way) from such far-flung outposts as Australia, Uruguay and Cambodia was proof that rock 'n' roll had given birth to the global village long before the internet did. So why had I never heard about Irish groups doing the same thing? Surely with our close geographical proximity to Liverpool and our economic dependence on the UK during that era we could not have escaped the onslaught of the new pop music? Well, we didn't.

Irish rock wasn't born at the Dandelion Market, where U2 gave some of their earliest performances. And just because it took the rest of the world until the 1970s to recognise the thrilling talents of Thin Lizzy and Rory Gallagher doesn't mean that these artists sprung fully formed from a void. After a little digging around, I discovered that out on the margins of the mainstream entertainment industry – where, let's face it, the good stuff is always found – during the 1960s existed a small but vibrant community of young groups who were very much aware of all the latest developments in the world of rock, and who were busy producing their own Irish version of it.

These groups of young men – and they were always young men: an interesting aspect of the Irish pop scene in the 60s was the almost total absence of female performers; there were no Lulus, Sandie Shaws or Dusty Springfields on this island, the closest equivalent perhaps being unfashionable mainstream singer, Clodagh Rodgers – existed side by side with the deep-rooted showbands and its big money-spinning wheeze. They created their own hip world of (literally) sweaty underground clubs packed with clued-in fans, where they presented cutting edge musical styles which the showband 'heads' wouldn't dream of touching, too afraid of alienating the ballroom punters who paid their high wages.

Little has been written about the Irish 'beat scene', as it came to be known, up until now. It is often regarded as an irrelevant aside to the showband scene where the big boys played and where you had to have your hair neatly cut and always wore a suit on stage. Not only did some of Ireland's most talented performers of the last three decades emerge from the beat scene, but plenty more gifted groups and individuals just missed out on the fame and fortune that they so thoroughly deserved. Contained within these pages are the stories of those successes and failures. It is high time that the pioneers of Irish rock music during that exciting time are given their due.

Daragh O'Halloran
Dublin, July 2006

Part One

Adolescent boys and girls in early 1950s Ireland had very little choice available to them for musical entertainment. In fact, as this sub-culture of young teenagers had yet to be specifically defined and catered for, it was a slightly older crowd who flocked to see the live music attraction of the day, the dance band orchestras. These were large unwieldy aggregations of musicians dressed formally in black evening wear, seated meekly in a row on wooden bandstands, sheet music propped up on stands in front of them, methodically going through their pre-arranged set as dancers waltzed or did the foxtrot on the large polished floor in front of them. In the drab days of the decade following the Emergency (World War 2) in Ireland, these dances usually took place under the strict supervision of the parish priest in cold, functional parish halls, and along with the local cinema served as one of the few meeting points of the sexes.

The Clipper Carlton Showband, formed in 1950 in Strabane, County Tyrone, was the first act to break away from the strict confines of the dance band set-up. They kicked away the music stands, eschewed the traditional black suit and bow tie in favour of formal outfits in a variety of colours, and popularised the usage of the hand held microphone, gaining widespread fame by freeing up the hitherto physically restrained deportment of the band. They also helped to coin the name 'showband' bringing variety, comedy and choreographed dance steps to their routine. Showbands played *to* the audience rather than just *for* them, becoming an attraction in themselves instead of merely supplying anonymous background music for the assembled dancers. Unlike the orchestras, who relied on a rotating set of numbers that in many cases had been in their repertoire for years, new bands like The Clipper Carlton included up-to-the-minute pop hits in their set, amongst a wide variety of tunes ranging across the genres of country 'n' western, ballads, Dixieland jazz and light rock 'n' roll.

As the 1950s turned into the 1960s the phenomenon of the showband grew massively, spurred on by a radically new social and economical environment sweeping the country. When Seán Lemass took over the running of the government in 1959 Ireland began to shake itself free of the isolationist ideals of the previous Eamon de Valera-led administration. The

Irish began to look outside their national borders for a much needed process of modernisation.

In his 2005 book, *Noisy Ireland: A Short History of Irish Popular Music*, Gerry Smyth argues that the showbands were central to this modernisation, importing and showcasing for the first time some of the sounds of American pop to a culturally starved population. On the back of the sudden increase in the popularity of this new live music, large imposing ballrooms sprang up in countless rural and urban locations across the country to cater for the masses of bands touring nationwide. Not much consideration was given to the comforts of the paying punter. Opportunistic ballroom owners constructed basic, concrete, hangar-like halls with wooden benches stretched along opposite walls and a low wide stage at the top, all the better for squeezing in a couple of thousand people for a night's alcohol-free entertainment. Starved of any real alternative, particularly in rural areas, these ballrooms became hugely popular in every part of Ireland, and at the height of the showband boom in the mid-60s there was enough demand for approximately 500-600 bands to fill them on any given night. Sunday was the most popular night of the week, as mass-going obligations seemingly hindered young people from letting their hair down too much on a Saturday evening. The oppressive influence of the Catholic Church was also felt in the stricture that prevented any dancing or showband performances during the six week religious period of Lent (most bands took off for venues in Great Britain or the United States at this time, where they played to halls packed with enthusiastic Irish emigrants).

In April 1963, in order to cater for this booming industry, *Spotlight* magazine was published for the first time in Cork. It became a hugely important vehicle throughout the decade for disseminating information on home-grown talent (the names of such popular acts as The Royal, The Capitol and The Dixielanders appear in the first issue), and for reviewing new records and reporting on international artists – child star turned country pop queen Brenda Lee was the cover artist in the inaugural edition and a prescient article entitled 'Is Elvis Slipping?' took up a full page inside. This first issue was just eight pages long and sold less than its 1,000 copies print run. By the start of 1965 with a change to a (limited) colour press and an updating of the name to *New Spotlight* (but forever known amongst purchasers as just *Spotlight*), circulation increased to 20,000 copies per month.

In June 1963, national broadcaster Telefís Èireann took the step of airing a weekly programme to capitalise on the popularity of the showband movement, imaginatively called *The Showband Show*. This gave many bands the opportunity to promote their name in a much more visceral and forceful way than by simply taking out a small print ad in *New Spotlight*. The TV programme occasionally featured touring artists from the UK who were in Ireland to promote their latest release. The 7" single was also viewed primarily as a promotional device for showbands rather than an artistic statement in

The well-groomed Clipper Carlton Showband, 1966

itself. The Royal Showband (featuring Brendan Bowyer) was the first to take the plunge in 1962, releasing 'Come Down The Mountain Katy Daly'.

Whilst the showbands drew huge crowds up and down the island, and served as an important social bond particularly in remote country areas, musically they were less than innovative. Technically, the ability of musicians in the top showbands was hardly in doubt, honed by daily gigs which lasted up to four or five hours, though any notion of straying from exact covers of the day's popular tunes was never considered. In a way, the showbands created a strait jacket situation for themselves which they then found impossible to break out of, if they ever wanted to. They were bound by an audience expectation that they had helped to foster – stick to the big tunes of the day – not to mention the desire of the ballroom managers for the band to only satisfy that expectation.

> **JOHN KEOGH** (piano and vocals, The Greenbeats): In the same way as the bands were cover bands, the ballroom owners were

> house facilitators. They had a shed or a warehouse which they rented out and they got well paid for it. They weren't in the business of trying to create a new scene. It had nothing to do with the music. If someone had said to them, I could give you the same money week by week by displaying Massey Ferguson tractors every Friday and Saturday, they'd have knocked the side wall down and had a tractor stand in there.

Apart from snippets of crackly broadcasts on Radio Luxembourg sneakily listened to beneath the bedcovers at night, or the odd shilling thrown into a jukebox at a local café, there were precious few opportunities to hear pop music in Ireland in the late 50s and early 60s unless you actually went out and purchased the records. For many young people still in school or with limited employment prospects and, particularly in non-urban areas, a dearth of record selling outlets, the showband was the only way to hear their favourite sounds.

The received wisdom regarding the history of popular music in Ireland is that Dickie Rock, Joe Dolan, Butch Moore and their ilk were the only gigs in town during the 1960s, and that it wasn't until the early 1970s after the showband boom had peaked and was on the wane, that the country developed its own indigenous rock music scene. While the popularity and success of bands such as the Miami, Plattermen and Cadets cannot be denied it is inaccurate to assume that musically there was no alternative. Firstly, away from the crowded ballrooms, there were pockets of dedicated aficionados listening to other popular forms of music such as jazz and folk. The more accessible folk scene coalesced initially around places like the Coffee Kitchen in Molesworth Street, the Auld Triangle on Mount Street and subsequently O'Donoghues Pub on Merrion Row, and was influenced as much by a fascination with the American folk revival of the time as a renewed interest in traditional Irish forms.

With the drab 1950s receding and a period of self-assertion emerging The Clancy Brothers' timely return to Ireland re-introduced a ballad tradition that had slipped into the background. Comhaltas Ceoltóirí Éireann, established in 1951, was responsible for keeping alive the indigenous traditional music of the island through the numerous fleadhs it staged up and down the country, hosting a particularly popular one in Thurles in 1964 which really kick started the folk boom. Many key names of Irish folk that came to prominence in the latter part of the decade could be found at impromptu sessions in the city in the early 1960s such as musicians from The Dubliners and founding members of the influential Sweeney's Men. By the middle of the decade pubs and lounges throughout the city and suburbs were holding ballad and folk sessions nightly and it wasn't long before the ballrooms decided to get in on the act. Both Sweeney's Men and folk-pop group The Johnstons found themselves playing interval slots for showbands at various points during their careers, such was the widespread popularity of the folk boom.

> **SHAY HEALY** (folk music journalist for *New Spotlight* in the 1960s): I was MC at thousands of shows all over Dublin, and all over Ireland. The show would always have a showband and a folk act and a trad musician all on the one bill, there were no lines of demarcation at all, it was just entertainment.

The Emmet Spiceland, a young folk trio with a hip contemporary image (denoted by dandy-ish ruffled shirts, John Lennon glasses and a casual approach to the length of their hair), scored an Irish number one hit in March 1968 with 'Mary From Dungloe', and managed to attract a sizeable young following, crossing over temporarily into the pop mainstream.

The more erudite jazz music lovers could be found huddled around tables in the Quo Vadis Club, Rob Roberts coffee shop on Grafton Street or the long-established Green Lounge on St. Stephen's Green, nodding their heads appreciatively to both modern and trad sounds produced by the likes of brothers Dara and Ruan O'Lochlainn, noted kingpins of the Dublin jazz scene. This was a smaller, less inclusive and more sophisticated environment than both the folk and showband worlds, drawing much of its older following from the college campuses and middle-class salaried communities; many restaurants employed jazz trios as background music for their diners. Although showbands featured a few swing and trad numbers in their sets, the scene here was never quite as big as the trad jazz revival sparked in the UK by Acker Bilk and Chris Barber.

These days it has become fashionable and commonplace to criticise the showband scene and downplay its contribution to Irish life and the evolution of the domestic music scene. However, the disdain shown by some modern Irish rock stars and cultural commentators for that era is not simply the result of a contemporary revisionist standpoint. For a substantial section of Irish urban youth in the 1960s the showbands were viewed as out of touch, irrelevant, unadventurous and doused in schmaltz. Antiquated serious folk idioms and aloof jazz combos did little to pique their interest either. These kids decided to look to another more exciting type of music, which in its myriad offshoots throughout the decade and beyond would prove far more durable and influential than the boys in the ballrooms could ever hope to be.

In the early 1960s, Ireland, like the rest of the world, was in rock 'n' roll terms dozing sedately and completely unaware of huge cultural changes around the corner. The jumped-up rockabilly beat of the greasers and teddy boys had been sanitised by record company moguls, always on the lookout for ways to earn a fast buck from the teenage market. The suits were quick to produce an assembly line of clean-cut pop crooners like Neil Sedaka (who completed a ten-night tour of Ireland in August 1963), Pat Boone and Bobby Vinton – watered down acceptable Mom-and-Pop versions of the original white rock rebels, singing smooth assembly line pop numbers that were cranked out by dedicated song-writing teams in New York's famous Brill Building. There *had* been a noticeable sub-culture of brothel-creeper-wearing 'Teds' in Ireland in the late 1950s, upsetting parents and authorities with their oily quiffs, drape coats and curled-up lips. At the back of the Lido fish and chip shop–cum–ice cream parlour in Blackrock, South Dublin, thrived a joint called The Alligator Club which drew crowds of teddy boys and their gals on Sunday nights, throughout 1956 and 1957, to play rockabilly 78s on the jukebox and lean against the wall looking sullen and mean. Years before he gained fame with The Miami Showband, Dickie Rock played there with his rock 'n' roll group, The Blackbirds.

> **JOHN KEOGH** There was a running battle between the heavies from Blackrock/Dún Laoghaire and the guys from Ringsend. And when you got Dickie Rock and his band there'd be a massive *mêlée* in the main street in Blackrock outside the Lido.

The threat of the Teds was not taken lightly by ballroom managers – to keep out undesirables jiving was banned in popular venues like The Olympic and The Crystal ballrooms, on the pretence that its free-flowing and unpredictable movements would interrupt the regimented steps of couples sedately making their way around the shiny dance floor like crowds at an ice rink. At a screening of the 1956 teenage movie *Rock Around The Clock* in Dublin's Carlton Cinema (an attempt to actually rebut accusations of delinquency aimed at its predecessor *The Blackboard Jungle*), the authorities' fears were realised when the pent-up frustration of the local 'hoodlums' burst forth in an orgy of dancing in the aisles, singing in the streets and seat slashing in the auditorium. When unlikely rock 'n' roll hero Bill Haley and his Comets played the 4,000 seater Theatre Royal in Dublin the following year, the crowds couldn't resist repeating their Carlton performance.

> **TED CARROLL** (beat group manager, rock 'n' roll fan and club promoter): It was incredible; they did two shows, an hour each set. At the time Bill Haley was the peak of what you wanted to see. They looked fantastic, the sound was fantastic, nobody had seen anything like him. People were so high when they came out that they rioted, turned over cars and all sorts of stuff.

By the early 1960s even the original global rock 'n' roll star, Elvis Presley, had been segregated away from the switchblade set. After military service in Germany he found himself submitting to the increasingly authoritarian rule of his manager Colonel Tom Parker, resulting in a succession of bland saccharine Hollywood movies accompanied by a slew of insipid soundtrack tunes. In Britain, Cliff Richard and Adam Faith reigned as the teen idols supreme. In Cliff's case, the outrage that greeted his first forays into the charts had subsided as he suppressed the sexuality of his early performances in order to pursue a more middle-of-the-road direction. Adam Faith caused something of a stir when he played the Top Hat Ballroom in Dún Laoghaire in November 1963. Newsreels show distraught teenage girls being dragged out from the mass of bodies in front of the stage where a be-suited Faith struts his stuff. However it was Cliff Richard's backing group, The Shadows, which was the biggest influence on young Irish musicians, particularly after they broke away from the pop star and set out on their own in 1960. Their crisp, clear and simple riffs were an inspiration to young musicians kicking around in various non-professional combos before Beatlemania hurtled into view in late 1963.

> **BRUSH SHIELS** (bass guitar, The Uptown Band and Skid Row): The Shadows started everything. I think they sold more guitars than The Beatles. The Shadows were the start of the whole guitar band thing – three guitars, singer out the front and a drummer. The type of hits they had would be easy enough to play. At that particular time, the sax and trumpet and trombone were the biggest things, and trad jazz [was] taking over. But once The Shadows came along it changed everything. It's always hit records that creates what's going to happen next and they were the guys with all the number ones.

A few years earlier, future beat group members had also been enthralled by that peculiar English take on American roots music invented single-handedly by Lonnie Donegan – skiffle. One of the key attractions of this now anachronistic musical form was its rudimentary and affordable instrumental set-up. An Irish showband at the time almost always consisted of seven or more members, at least three of whom made up the brass section. Now, with a battered acoustic guitar (or a cheap electric plugged into the back of a radio for basic amplification), a snare drum and cymbal and an upright bass, scores of teenage boys could attempt to recreate the sounds of the rock 'n' roll singles that they spun on their record players and listened to on the 'wireless'. Soon, a few lucky groups such as the cleverly named Young Shadows from Ballyfermot, The Hootenanys from Artane and The Strangers from Balbriggan were playing relief to the professional showbands in the city's ballrooms. Clever (or lazy, depending on your viewpoint) showbands would organise for these young inexperienced beat groups to play to the relatively small crowds in the ballrooms from 9pm until pub closing time, at which point the main dancing crowd would flood in. These groups were accommodated on the bill as long as they didn't overshadow the headliners and stuck to playing commercial chart fodder. They also gave showband members a well-earned break during long sets, as their description would suggest.

Some writers, including Vince Power in his account of the showband phenomenon *Send 'Em Home Sweatin,* claim that Ireland's beat group scene evolved out of the scraps thrown to the four-piece line-ups from the table of the professional bands. Although these support dates were a welcome opportunity for beat musicians to play to a live audience rather than eternally rehearsing in an empty room or repeatedly playing to their local fanbase, inroads made by these few groups into the ballrooms were the exception rather than the norm. Alternative venues for the burgeoning beat scene needed to be found.

> **TED CARROLL** Groups couldn't do the ballroom circuit because people wanted a band and they wanted more versatility. Showbands were basically a jukebox, these guys would come and recreate the records they heard on the radio *exactly*.

There was a circuit of small tennis and rugby clubs in Dublin's suburbs in the early 1960s where fledgling beat groups found themselves more welcome – although the name 'beat' had yet to find general acceptance as a catch-all term for the new sound. That particular word, used to describe all manner of groups playing in Ireland in the mid-60s, be they soul, R&B, rock 'n' roll or Hollies-type pop, had become a commonly accepted appellation by fans and the few journalists reporting on the scene by the beginning of 1965. Loosely, it referred to a type of rhythm heavy music played by young people *for* young people in small clubs, quite distinct from the professional showbands in the ballroom circuit. The word stuck to the scene in Ireland long after its usage had expired elsewhere. In fact, the term 'beat' never really gained much currency in the United States, as the UK bands that burst into the American charts in 1964 were all gathered under the umbrella term 'The British Invasion'. The initial response by American teenage musicians to these marauding armies was their own 'garage rock', an exciting short-lived phenomenon which featured two influential Irish musicians to be discussed later.

Even in the early 1970s, after all manner of niches and sub-genres in the pop/rock realm such as psychedelia, sunshine pop, folk-rock *et al* had come and gone, the term 'beat scene' still applied to Irish bands working outside of the showband/showbusiness domain. Included were acts that could be classified as heavy rock or even progressive rock, that over-elaborate style of music forever talked about with slight embarrassment after the onslaught of punk in the late 70s. Undoubtedly, the emergence of Merseybeat (a phrase coined by the appearance of a Liverpudlian entertainment magazine of the same name in 1960) as a distinctive musical form in the early 1960s had a lot to do with the adoption of the term by Irish commentators for the entire teenage rock and pop field. The German music fans also had appropriated the phrase as a label for the scores of British combos infesting their club circuit at the time.

Spotlight reported on 'The Biggest Thing Since Rock – The Fabulous Liverpool Beat' in May 1963, naming Gerry and The Pacemakers, The Big Three, Billy J. Kramer & The Dakotas and The Beatles ('distinguished by a somewhat off beat hair style and a zany sense of humour') as being in the vanguard of the new sound. The following month in *Spotlight* Tim Horgan speculated on the popularity of groups from both the US (The Drifters, The Cascades, The Shirelles) and Britain (the aforementioned Liverpool groups as well as Freddie and The Dreamers, The Spotnicks and The Shadows amongst others) and wondered, 'are these groups ousting the solo artists? It is unlikely that they will take over from Elvis, Cliff, Del Shannon etc. but it must be admitted they are playing a very big part in the charts today.' They certainly were.

The beat scene came to be recognised as the underground musical movement during the 1960s in Ireland, the definitive alternative to the highly visible middle-of-the-road showband mainstream championed by most sections of the national media. Its moniker also referenced the somewhat derogatory phrase 'beatnik' which had been widely used (although perhaps not always fully understood) since the early 1950s after coming out of the modern literary scene involving such American greats as Jack Kerouac and William Burroughs. Although the image of beret-clad bebop hipsters with goatees and dark glasses listening to cool jazz in dingy coffee bars has now become a comical stereotype, the beatniks were most definitely the alternative youth culture of their time. Long before rock 'n' roll adopted a similar mantle they represented all things counter-cultural, anti-authoritarian and subversive. Somewhere between the popular Merseybeat sounds of 1963 and the residual cultural (rather than strictly musical) influence of the jazz-loving beatniks was born the term 'beat scene', and it stuck.

There was one key event, devastating in career terms for some and hugely galvanizing for others, that occurred in November 1963 and defiantly announced the arrival of beat music to these shores; indeed as part of a greater cultural movement it did nothing less than signal the re-birth of rock 'n' roll itself across the western world. At midday on 7 November John, Paul, George and Ringo stepped onto the tarmac at Dublin Airport to be greeted by a crowd of over three hundred eager fans, for their first and only visit to Ireland as a foursome.

Beatlemania was a term already familiar to many in Ireland and the moptops' singles had been enjoying phenomenal success here. In the preceding months teenage boys had been crowding barbers' shops demanding haircuts in The Beatles' unruly style. The pages of *Spotlight* in autumn 1963 were still dominated by smiling showbands, country and western crooners, trad jazz buffs and clean cut solo singers. The new group from Liverpool was beginning to create quite a stir yet the snooty staff writers at the Cork-based publication weren't quite sure whether to take the young band seriously or not. In a review of their latest single, just two months before the trip to

Dublin, an anonymous writer sniffed: 'The Beatles hoarsely shout She Loves You, throw in a few yea yeas for good measure and then they're uninhibitedly yelling their way through a typical Liverpudlian number…no change in the hit making style of this odd looking, raw sounding quartet who are the golden boys of today's British "pop" world.'

Already aware of the pandemonium caused by The Beatles on recent live dates in England, Harry Lush, manager of the Adelphi Cinema (where the group were to play their two shows) made additional security arrangements, including preparing a phalanx of Gardaí to keep the peace on Middle Abbey Street. They were immediately needed to restrain the crowds that gathered outside the cinema for the afternoon press conference, and were an essential presence later that evening as hundreds of fans, many of whom didn't have tickets, swarmed over cars and smashed shop windows in the vicinity. The now forgotten supporting bill was more suited to a Sunday night at The Palladium variety show than an era-defining rock 'n' roll concert. The gig opened with The Vernon Girls, a Liverpool girl group who had started out with approximately seventy (!) members in the mid-50s and who were sponsored by a UK football pools company. They were followed by the British equivalent of The Everly Brothers, The Brook Brothers from Hampshire, chart-toppers in Italy in 1960. Next were the outmoded seven-piece group Peter Jay and The Jaywalkers who served up soon to be obsolete numbers from the likes of Acker Bilk and Russ Conway; and finally just before The Beatles were The Kestrels. They were a vocal harmony group styled on light American R&B acts such as The Platters, who would also find themselves bulldozed into oblivion by the very group they were playing second fiddle to that night. The reaction from the capacity crowd in the Adelphi was the same that had greeted The Beatles on their recent dates in Sweden and England – absolute mayhem.

> **JONATHAN RYAN** (guitar, The Rootzgroop): The Beatles were there with just two Vox amps, two microphones. I didn't hear a damn thing because the girls never stopped screaming. I remember my ears were sore, it was actually hurting. The only thing I remember is Lennon over on the right in the grey suit with his Rickenbacker shouting, 'Shut fucking up!' They wanted to be heard. But they were playing all sorts of crap then, stuff from musicals. The only one I heard was the last one, 'Twist and Shout', and they cranked everything up. Anytime Paul went 'oooh oooh' the girls went berserk.

Evening Press journalist Donal McCann, writing about the gig in next day's newspaper, described the feeling in the auditorium with barely concealed relish, 'The atmosphere was hot and sharp; full of powder and perfume and a frightening excitement.' The set was very short by modern day standards, as so much of the show was taken up by unnecessary support acts supposedly on the bill to give value for money. The Beatles played just nine numbers – 'I Saw Her Standing There', 'From Me To You', 'All My Loving', 'You Really Got A Hold On Me', 'Boy', 'Till There Was You', 'She Loves You', 'Money' and 'Twist And Shout'.

> **TERRY BRADY** (drums, The Chessmen): I remember I couldn't hear a bloody thing. The big deal was that they were touring with the loudest equipment that could possibly be purchased at the time, those huge Vox 100 Watt amplifiers. I was three rows from the front and I couldn't hear a thing, it was amazing.

At the finale, with the crowd baying for encores, any semblance of control that the ushers had disappeared when scores of fans rushed to the front of the auditorium, hurling programmes and anything else they could lay their hands on at the stage. Hundreds of Beatlemaniacs burst through the doors of the cinema, swarming through the 2,000 strong horde already queuing impatiently for the 9pm performance. The 250 Gardaí tried vainly to control the seething masses and could not stop a mini-riot breaking out which spilled over into O'Connell Street, with cars being overturned and set alight. People were crushed in the *mêlée*, and many fans had to receive treatment from staff of the St. John's Ambulance. Restless hoodlums hissed the well-dressed couples who fought their way to a dance at the Metropole Hotel. The cat and mouse game between the teenagers and police continued until the Beatles' second performance ended, just before 11pm, whereupon hundreds more fans spewed out of the Adelphi, causing further crowd control problems and resulting in several arrests.

Already well used to this kind of scene whenever The Beatles played, the group's assistant manager hatched a top secret escape plan with Harry Lush. A dispatch van from the headquarters of the *Evening Herald* newspaper (located directly next door to the Adelphi) had been arranged to idle inconspicuously at the side door about half an hour before the end of the performance. Although there were scores of excitable teenagers buzzing around outside, the van drew little suspicion from the mob. Within seconds of the final bars of 'Twist and Shout' the Fab Four were safely ensconced in the back of the battered van and making their way to the Gresham Hotel where they were staying before travelling up to the North. There were still a few eager fans to dodge at the hotel's rear entrance as the group made a dash through the kitchens, eventually reaching their rooms unscathed and unharmed. A similar scenario would be played out the following night when they appeared at the Ritz Cinema in Belfast. After those encounters and many more like them it is perfectly understandable why the group would later give up touring for good. Meanwhile their visit to Dublin and the concomitant media coverage had indelibly made their mark on the hearts and minds of

Ad for TV appearance by The Viscounts

Irish teenagers, announcing that the new music was here to stay and accelerating the onslaught of the growing domestic beat group scene.

Originally Dublin's live music scene of the early 1960s centred around the middle class suburban tennis and rugby clubs, and the odd parochial hall, which were the preserve of 'swing' jazz type combos and proto-beat rock 'n' roll bands. The jazz bands played something a bit more modern than the popular trad sound, infusing their set with the jump blues typified by Louis Prima and Louis Jordan, but stopping well short of the bebop improvisations pioneered by artists like Charlie Parker and the cool jazz stylings of Miles Davis. They didn't dress as formally as the showbands, although the more professional groups did make something of an effort by wearing Ivy League button-down shirts, smart jackets and buffed shoes. The sports clubs were a popular social meeting point around the outskirts of the city, and every Saturday night the club committee would book a four-piece group (generally featuring piano or guitar, bass, sax and drums) to entertain the dancers. Popular groups included The Vic Mellows Quartet, The Four Kees and The Viscounts, a group remembered by many non-music fans as well as enthusiasts alike, led by charismatic drummer Paul Russell. Tighter than the cumbersome showband line-up The Viscounts consisted of one saxophone, two guitars, piano and drums. Such was their immense popularity that they played to appreciative audiences up to seven nights a week throughout the country and were regular guests on Ireland's domestic radio station, Radio

Éireann. They were also the first group, apart from the showbands, to appear on national television and gave a lot of encouragement and support to young groups attempting to offer an alternative to the well-drilled acts in the large ballrooms.

> **ALAN DEE** (beat musician): I was a great fan of The Viscounts, I thought they were really smooth. Paul Russell used to drive a blue metallic Jag, and he'd have a blue metallic Ludwig drum kit on the roof rack with no cases.

What was missing from The Viscounts' set though was the hot rhythm 'n' blues sound of urban America personified by the music of performers like Ray Charles and Chuck Berry. The group also tended to stick to the polite side of rock 'n' roll, covering the likes of Bobby Darin and the other teen idols.

> **SHAY HEALY** The Viscounts were a bit old for us, they were kind of Dads almost at that point. Because they wore suits they represented a safe side of music. They were never dangerous.

In the days before permanently housed clubs opened to cater for the rapidly expanding popularity of the rock and pop groups of the mid-60s, many scenes across the water in the UK grew out of improvised venues run by enterprising devotees of the new sound. So it was that The Rolling Stones played some of their first gigs, with the famous five man line-up, to hot and sweaty crowds in the back room of a hotel at Giorgio Gomelskey's club the Crawdaddy in Richmond, southwest London. In a similar fashion, The Animals were legends in Newcastle's Club A Go-Go before setting off for bigger rewards down south in the English capital.

In May 1962, Ted Carroll opened Ireland's first regular club dedicated to giving groups, not showbands, a place to play their rock 'n' roll sounds. He found a small dance hall attached to some tea rooms, which were originally built in the 1920s, at Killiney Beach on the south coast of County Dublin. Minimal alteration was required to convert it into a simple live music venue. After a slow start Ted soon had 150 paying customers through the door of the White Cottage every Sunday night to be entertained by arguably Ireland's most important early group, The Caravelles.

> **TED CARROLL** We called it the Rhythm 'n' Blues Club because it made it sound a bit like jazz, a bit arty. Rock 'n' roll was a dirty word basically, and it was kind of on the way out even though loads of people still loved it. If you were going to play rock 'n' roll you'd be getting gigs in dodgy rough parochial halls in places like Crumlin, Phibsboro and the North Circular Road.

Site of the Rhythm 'n' Blues Club, Killiney, pictured in the 1980s. The building is now gone

The Caravelles were formed in 1960 in the Dún Laoghaire area by Ted (on bass, which was actually an old Spanish guitar with the top two strings removed and the instrument tuned down a few octaves), Des Bonner (guitar and sax), Paul Williams (guitar), John Keogh (piano) and Ken Healy on drums. Leader of the group John Keogh had taken up the piano after seeing outfits like Dave Kane and The Whispers play at local tennis clubs, and got together with a few friends to form a small knockabout group called The Five Frets. They quickly learned to play Buddy Holly numbers in rehearsals but rarely got the chance to play to a live audience. The Caravelles, however, turned into a much more serious proposition.

After choosing an aeronautical name in deference to The Viscounts, The Caravelles rehearsed solidly for four months before setting out on a cyclical tour of the local tennis clubs such as the Green Road in Blackrock, and draughty church halls like The Barn in Mount Merrion. The popularity of the group amongst Ted Carroll's co-workers at the Ulster Bank ultimately contributed to his decision to quit The Caravelles mid-1961 to concentrate more on the business side of things. The group had played at Mount Pleasant Tennis Club in Ranelagh and some of the younger female staff from the bank had attended. Word got back to Ted's superiors about his extra-curricular activities and the conservative management worried that their young employee was putting more energy into his outside interests than into his work. A friend of the group, Brian Lynch, was invited to come in on bass to replace him.

By Ted's own admission Brian was technically more accomplished than himself and the musical competency of the group moved up a notch. At around the same time it was decided Ken Healy wasn't quite up to scratch on the drum kit and an audition was secretly held to try out the bespectacled Maurice 'Mog' Ahern. Ted Carroll had spotted him down at Monkstown Rugby Club playing solo on the drumkit as an interval act for The Viscounts. 'We discovered he was a big Ray Charles freak,' recalls Ted, 'that was it, IN!' Des Bonner went back to college in September 1961, got bored of academic life after a month and headed off to Sweden to live the life of a beatnik. He wasn't seen for another five years.

It was this classic line-up of The Caravelles – Mog Ahern (drums), Paul Williams (guitar), Brian Lynch (bass) and John Keogh (piano) – that played the summer residency at the White Cottage in Killiney in 1962 and would stay together until mid-1965. On only their second date at the Rhythm 'n' Blues Club, guitarist Paul Williams was unable to play due to the pressing matter of an exam the following morning for his degree course in entymology, so The Eblana Jazz Band were summoned to substitute for the young foursome. This more sophisticated combo brought a big crowd of eager punters in with them, many of whom turned up the following week mixing with The Caravelles fans, both enamoured with the bubbling pot of scorching songs on offer.

> **KEVIN DUNNE** (who used to carry out roadie duties for the group and later took over management from Ted Carroll): It was fantastic fun. It couldn't happen now. There was no drink in the ballrooms or tennis clubs then. There were fourpenny bottles of minerals. Although you'd always the get the loonies who came along half tanked, falling around the beach. On lovely summer nights half the crowd would be dancing on the beach. We didn't make a lot of money from it because they didn't have to pay in, they could just hang around and hear the sounds.

Although the club proved extremely popular with teenagers looking for something looser and less formal than what was on offer in the showband ballrooms, the Sunday night sessions had fizzled out by the end of the summer. Even today, the old site of the Rhythm 'n' Blues Club on Killiney Beach is not directly accessible by bus, the form of transport most of the attendees would have used in 1962. The nights were closing in, the kids were starting to drift back to school and The Caravelles returned to the familiar surrounds of the suburban tennis club circuit.

The following summer the club was revived, but demand wasn't as strong as the previous year and by mid-August Ted Carroll was casting around for another venue to book his old band mates in. Ted and two of his friends were all due to turn twenty-one on 22 August 1963 so they hired out the Longford Tennis Club in Monkstown, a few miles north of Killiney along the same stretch of coastline, to throw a party. The wooden pavilion at the tennis club had burned down a few years earlier and then been rebuilt in brick with the insurance money. There was no stage to speak of, so the three friends built a temporary structure using drinks crates and plywood. Through his job with Aer Lingus one of the budding young promoters got his hands on some travel posters to cover the bare walls, and a few red light bulbs were strung along the ceiling to take away the starkness of the small room and create some kind of club atmosphere. The Caravelles were booked to entertain the partygoers and when the night turned out to be a huge success the owners of the tennis club were approached by the eager entrepreneurs to hire the venue on a more permanent basis.

Mog Ahern, The Greenbeats

In September 1963 the Rhythm 'n' Blues Club was reborn and proved even more successful than the original one by the shore in Killiney. Over the next year and a half the club would play host to the young up and coming beat groups that were crucial in the development of Dublin's beat scene – The Cyclones, The Creatures, Bluesville, The Kult, The Kingbees and The Mad Lads from Belfast to name but a few. Originally it was just The Caravelles that played every Sunday night as the resident group, their popularity increasing by the week. The four-piece were paid £12 per night at the beginning of their residency, quickly moving up to £40 as they became more widely known. A few months after the club had been established, the group's new manager, Kevin Dunne, approached Ted Carroll and asked that his boys be excused from the coming Sunday's slot as they had been included on a bill at a charity gig in Cork, playing support to the mighty Royal Showband, an engagement that would be instrumental in the spread of the group's popularity outside the capital city. Worried that the take at the door would drop, Ted got local boys The Semitones to fill in, paying them half of what The Caravelles were earning, so that despite a small decrease in the number of customers at the door the promoters still came out in the black! A pattern quickly established itself whereby The Caravelles would play every second Sunday with a myriad of beat groups taking their place when they weren't around. The foursome led by John Keogh had by now developed an extraordinary set, stretching across numerous musical styles and incorporating up to fifty songs or more by the likes of Jerry Lee Lewis, Chuck Berry, Little Richard, James Brown, The Isley Brothers, The Coasters, Billy Fury, Elvis, Clyde McPhatter and Ray Charles, and also including instrumentals by The Ventures and The Shadows.

> **TED CARROLL** I've never come across another band that played it like that. The punters lapped it up. One minute they'd be playing something really bluesy like 'The Night Time Is The Right Time' with Mog [Ahern] doing the Margie Hendrix screams, and then the next thing they'd be doing something like 'Pretty Woman' by Roy Orbison, which was in the charts at the time.

> **JIMMY DUNNE** (beat group manager and promoter): It was a ramshackle wooden place, you wouldn't be let even look at a place like that now. But it swung; they queued from all over to get in.

Songs by popular UK groups such as The Searchers and The Rolling Stones were also incorporated into The Caravelles' set, which generally lasted from 8pm until 11.45pm with a twenty minute break, when a local group would sub for them. The Caravelles were well known for having every new Beatles' release, which came out on a Friday, learned off perfectly within forty-eight hours for the Sunday night engagement.

> **TED CARROLL** The band would be there, set-up, ready to start at 8pm on the dot. The punters would start queuing up from 7.15pm. We'd start to let them in at around 7.55 and at 8pm the place would be full. After about twenty minutes you could get 'pass outs' [cards which allowed re-entry], so people would go off down to [local bar] the Purty Kitchen to have a few drinks which made room for more people to come in. Forty or fifty would come back about 9.30pm by which time it was more or less full so as they were coming in it was beginning to get quite packed and hot. Then couples would start going out and disappearing into the shrubbery.

'You had the best looking birds in Dublin at that thing,' said [one] punter 'and it was the easiest place to pull because it got so hot they just wanted to get out!'

Local residents complained about the noise from the teenagers hanging out on the veranda that ran the length of the hall on one side, so an ad-hoc canvas covering was purchased from a nearby yacht club, enclosing the

The Greenbeats on Curtain Up. *Centre picture John Keogh*

narrow space and jacking up the temperature a few degrees more. With a four shilling entrance fee, 500 excitable teenagers crammed in, a band that charged £40 for a night, £6 to hire the hall and £2 slipped into the pocket of a local policeman moonlighting as bouncer on the door, Ted Carroll was making a lot more money than the £7 he got each week from the bank.

The Caravelles' career really took off in 1964, with a change of name, exposure on Telefís Éireann's *Showband Show*, and their first single release propelling them into the national limelight. The group had previously boosted their profile with an appearance on the Sunday night variety show *Curtain Up*, broadcast live on television, alongside the usual middle-of-the-road serving of jugglers, mime artists, comedians and polite pop acts. In September 1963 at the invitation of Paul Russell they also toured Ireland as the backing band to The Springfields, featuring Dusty and her brother Tom, which greatly enhanced their reputation, especially outside Dublin.

JOHN KEOGH We were warming up in the Crystal Ballroom when [the Springfields] walked in. They were standing down the end in the dark; we were jamming away playing all sorts of Chuck Berry numbers. They were happy enough and we got up and rehearsed with Dusty. After that their guitar

> player said, 'Do you know there's an awful lot of young bands in the north of England, around Liverpool and Manchester, all playing what you're playing in tiny clubs and little holes?' That was exactly the parallel, Little Richard, Chuck Berry, and for the same reasons – pissed off with Brian Highland, Cliff Richard, the softy-softy rock 'n' roll. We couldn't believe that other people were dragging back the music I had heard on the radio, and that was the music that meant something to me.

Ted Carroll remembers a fortuitous visit to the Rhythm 'n' Blues Club from a trendy young scenester and regular panellist on RTÉ's *Pickin' the Pops* show, which would set in motion a series of events that would transform the group into domestic stars. 'BP Fallon turned up one night at Longford Tennis Club and he said, "Hey man, this band is really cool. You should go and play in The Cavern, I'll sort it out."' '[I] rang the owner of The Cavern, Ray McFall, in Liverpool one afternoon after school,' recalls Fallon, 'and said they were great and he said, "Bring me over a bottle of whiskey and they're on."' In the first week of April The Caravelles travelled to Liverpool to play in the club made famous by the biggest beat group of them all.

> **JIMMY DUNNE** John Keogh had one great desire in his life and that was to play in The Cavern, the same piano that John Lennon played. I went on a boat from Dublin to Liverpool overnight and all the gear was put on the deck covered with tarpaulin. When we got to The Cavern Bob Wooler [the manager of the venue] said, 'Panic stations!'

BP Fallon, mid-60s

There was a problem. The group were booked to play a number of lunchtime and night-time sessions at The Cavern, sharing the bill with three or four other acts. At the time, a girl duo going by the name of The Caravelles had scored an international hit with a song called 'You Don't Have To Be A Baby To Cry' and were making inroads into the British charts. In order to avoid any confusion the management of the club suggested the Irishmen come up with an alternative moniker. After rejecting a number of alternatives including the trite and mildly offensive Leprachauns, Shillelaghs and Shamrocks, they spotted a more appropriate name on the list – The Greenbeats. A musical style known as 'bluebeat', the forerunner to reggae and ska, was gaining currency in England at that time. Furthermore the adjunct 'beat' was a popular choice for many new groups (The Beat Boys, The

Fourbeats, etc), and the addition of 'green' left little doubt as to the group's geographical origin.

After completing a few more dates at another Liverpool club, the Iron Door (home of The Searchers), the newly christened Greenbeats returned home to Ireland where they were soon offered a slot as resident group on *The Showband Show*, occasionally playing behind Paul Russell of The Viscounts and also performing current pop hits on their own each week, sandwiched between the big showband names of the moment. They popularised songs like 'Pretty Woman' by Roy Orbison and 'I'm On Fire' by Jerry Lee Lewis, so much so that the former became as inextricably linked to the indigenous Irish group as it was to the black-clad US country pop singer.

> **JIMMY DUNNE** This was at a time when needless to say, [RTÉ] was the only station you could get. The only pop programme was *The Showband Show* and they became huge stars in a very short period of time.

> **JOHN KEOGH** We made an impact after the first show but the sound was appalling. They realised it was bad, and they jacked it up for the second show and from show two it just went bananas. I went into town to go to the cinema and had to leave the queue. We were attacked, our hair was cut, cops had to get me out of Henry Street, it was crazy stuff.

In November, The Greenbeats, all aged just twenty-one and enjoying their new found fame, released their debut single on Pye Records, chosen from a selection of numbers cut at Regent Sound Studios in Denmark Street, London's own 'Tin Pan Alley'. The A-side was a slow, slightly maudlin ballad written and sung by pianist John Keogh called 'If This World Was Mine', a song at odds with many of the more upbeat numbers in their live set. Up until this point, Pye Records' expertise was in releasing safe ballads by showbands that could be enjoyed by all the family, and were unfamiliar with the type of material that The Greenbeats were interested in recording. As a result, they insisted that the group put out the original number as an A-side. In an interview with *New Spotlight* in January 1965, The Greenbeats' piano player was diplomatic about the unpopular decision.

> **JOHN KEOGH** We went to London to record a few numbers, and when we had done the others we had a bash at 'If This World Were Mine'. When we got the sample discs back in Dublin it turned out that this was the best number on record, so we decided to go ahead and release it, even though we knew that people would expect a beat record from a beat group. (*New Spotlight*, Jan 1965)

Today the group's leader is a little more frank about the choice:

> **JOHN KEOGH** [It was] the wrong thing to do. A band that was known for me with my foot on the piano on television, jumping up and town, tearing the place apart, and you come out with a ballad?

A more interesting up-tempo R&B style track was to be found on the B-side, 'You Must Be The One', credited to a duo going by the names of Jagger and Richards. This track was taken from that cache of original songs penned by the scruffy pair when The Rolling Stones' brash young manager Andrew Loog Oldham locked the pair into the kitchen of their flat in Edith Grove to force them to come up with their own material in order to move their group away from an over-reliance on blues and rock standards. Like some of Mick and Keith's other initial attempts at song-writing it pales in comparison to anything they came up with subsequently. It was Oldham himself who provided The Greenbeats with a stack of acetates comprising demo versions of Jagger/Richards songs played by the Stones (including 'As Tears Go By'), out of which they chose the B-side for their debut release. He was also credited as producer on these tracks, ably assisted by a talented young multi-instrumentalist called John Paul Jones, who had a reputation as being the top

The Greenbeats, 1965. L-R: Brian Lynch, John Keogh, Paul Williams, Mog Ahern

arranger/musical director in the business at that time and would go on to mega-stardom in the late 60s and 70s with rock behemoths Led Zeppelin. 'The Stones were in recording and John was working on that session,' Tony Boland, a friend of Oldham's, claims, 'and we were waiting for the Stones to walk out and then we moved in. They went on lunch.' Andrew Oldham shrewdly and unscrupulously registered the publishing of both sides under his own company's name.

This first commercially successful single by an Irish beat group was voted number eight in a list of the best Irish records of 1964 in *New Spotlight*, drawn from a poll of nationwide promoters. The Greenbeats had been doing their utmost to create a high profile for themselves around Ireland, getting booked to appear with big name showbands and following up their mini-tour with The Springfields by supporting wholesome English duo Peter and Gordon during August 1964. Beat fans north of the border were also beginning to see a lot of the Dublin group through regular gigs in Belfast in early 1965. Encouraged by the reception that the single received, the group flew across the Atlantic in April and were paid handsomely to play a few dates in a New York club (billed as the 'Irish Beatles'), just prior to releasing a second single, 'So Sad' b/w 'I'm On Fire' in May.

> **KEVIN DUNNE** We were over there for about ten days. We saw Dizzy Gillespie, Gerry Mulligan, Gene Krupa, just wandering around New York into pubs and bars, all these amazing jazz players. John and Mog had quite a jazzy background.

In an interview given to *New Spotlight* that month, drummer Mog Ahern was less than enthusiastic about the potential of the group's new single, an Everly Brothers' hit from 1960 (the flip was a 50s rock 'n' roll rave-up), expressing instead a desire to record a live album which would capture his group's true sound. Indeed, there was some internal turmoil in the group around this time. In mid-1965 after increasing pressure from associates in the music scene the group crossed the line in the sand and officially became a showband, much to the dismay of Brian Lynch who departed the group after almost four years. Mog Ahern wasn't interested in the new direction either and also bowed out that August, eventually turning up the following year with the avowedly commercial Aesop's Fables (with St. John Connolly who co-wrote their debut single 'Why Don't You Love Me?' on lead guitar), and later still putting together a jazz band called, deliberately or not, The Never Greens.

Phil Solomon, a well-respected but feared manager from Belfast, who had Van Morrison, The Bachelors and The Dubliners in his stable, offered John Keogh a contract as a solo musician along with the tempting offer of a financially lucrative tour with Tom Jones. Although Keogh wasn't keen to leave the group he had been with for such a long time, the prospect of international touring and better pay was tempting. Suspicious of Solomon's less than saintly reputation amongst other musicians, he had an acquaintance check out the fine print in the contract and was advised that he would have no rights or protection under the deal as it stood. He rejected the offer.

The decision to metamorphose into a showband was not a happy one, and within three years The Greenbeats would be finished, never having recaptured the spontaneity and enjoyment experienced in the Rhythm 'n' Blues Club in Monkstown or on RTÉ's *Showband Show*. The tragic death of their guitar player Paul Williams in a road accident in 1967 contributed to the dissipation of enthusiasm within the band. 'The way it was put to me was,' says John Keogh today, 'if you want to stay in the business, you'll never make any money in Ireland unless you become a showband.' The new Greenbeats' line-up hoped they might be able to change the predictable routine of the country's top acts. They adopted a format similar to that of Tom Jones and The Squires, with a brass section limited to saxophone and trumpet, still featuring quite a bit of their R&B material, especially that of their hero Ray Charles, who John Keogh had actually seen in the Gaiety Theatre when the father of soul was shooting a film there in 1964. Despite the transformation The Greenbeats found it difficult to infiltrate the tightly closed fortress of showband land and actually ended up on a much lower wage than the one they were receiving as a beat group.

> **JOHN KEOGH** We weren't getting the work because I had opened my mouth and slagged off the showbands and the Reynolds ballroom group said they would never have us back again. I don't know any businessman who would turn down a band that was bringing in the cash for simply saying something in the papers. It coincided with a number of attempts to shunt Kevin Dunne as manager, and I was told to get rid of Kevin and I'd be taken into a group of managers where you'd be guaranteed work.

Dunne stayed on as manager for quite a while after, which may not have helped with getting those essential bookings in the ballrooms. However, he was not short of novel ideas and schemes to get recognition and money for his band. A report in *New Spotlight* in June 1967 announced that a new record label had been set up by The Greenbeats to self-release their next single, and that another trip to the US was in the pipeline, this time including a not-yet-confirmed invitation to the Monterey Pop Festival in California. It is fascinating to consider what could have been if this Irish group-cum-showband had played to the fields of idealistic young flower children alongside the likes of Jimi Hendrix, Jefferson Airplane and The Mamas and The Papas at the era-defining festival. Alas, it never transpired.

Ted Carroll's Rhythm 'n' Blues Club ran into some trouble of its own during the spring of 1965. The owners of the tennis club had originally been granted a license to hold four or five public dances a year, which they had used for private functions. As a result anyone wishing to get in to dance to the stomping sounds of The Greenbeats and the other Dublin beat groups had to become a fully paid up member of the Rhythm 'n' Blues Club, something made expressly clear on a temporary sign posted on the door – four shillings for members, five shillings for members without cards. (Irresponsible youths would forget to bring their membership identification, and were punished with a surcharge for holding up the queue while management checked their name on a list). One night in April the club was raided by a group of policemen and the three young promoters were brought up in front of a judge in the district court. The police insisted that the sign, which Ted and his friends tried in vain to locate at home, read 'five shillings for non-members' and the trio were fined and ordered to shut down.

In these more innocent times, such a non-event warranted coverage in the daily newspapers and an outraged judge was quoted in the popular *Evening Press*, describing the club as the 'Black Hole of Calcutta', despite the fact that he had never set foot in the place. Ted Carroll suspected a devious motive for the abrupt end to his hugely popular venue, although his speculation was never confirmed: '[An influential policeman] had a sixteen-year-old daughter who was bugging him to be allowed to go to Longford [Tennis Club]. He basically shut it down so his daughter couldn't go there.' 'There were nasty accusations made to make a case,' confirms John Keogh, 'when they probably could have got a case for environmental noise or something, or overcrowding although they did try the fire officers as well but the fire exits were there.'

What had begun as a method of ensuring a regular gig for some pals in a shack on the edge of a remote beach on Dublin's south coast, ultimately developed into a fulcrum for the Irish beat group scene, amply demonstrating to groups and promoters alike that there was a huge demand for this type of music amongst the city's teenagers. Just as the life of the R&B Club in Longford Tennis Club was coming to an end, a consortium of businessmen from Liverpool, including the playwright Alun Owen, were planning to open a basement club on the bottom of Harcourt Street, modelled on the famous Cavern Club. As the pre-eminent club owner of the day, Ted Carroll was approached by the Liverpudlians to buy out their interest in the lease for the not inconsiderable sum of £1,200. Having just been shut down by the police on a decidedly flimsy charge, and wary of further run-ins with his employer due to the time and energy he was putting into the devil's music, Ted declined. Two brothers who had a background in the catering business, Tony and Brendan O'Brien, stepped in and started what would become one of Dublin's most important and successful beat group centres, the No. 5 Club. An attempt was made by Ted to recreate the thrilling buzz of Longford Tennis Club when he launched the Bastille Club at the Cliff Castle Hotel in Dalkey some months later, but despite printing up new membership cards and inviting all the old punters to come the club never really took off.

The Rhythm 'n' Blues Club in Monkstown was perhaps the first and best known regular venue for many of Dublin's emerging beat groups (especially on the south side of the city), but it certainly wasn't the only place where the new pop sounds were being heard. In community halls and sports clubs throughout the suburbs, other small bands of musical neophytes were forming independently of each other and getting booked to play weekend nights to scores of teenagers roughly the same age as themselves.

In Balbriggan, North County Dublin, three friends formed the nucleus of a group that would turn out to be the biggest and most versatile pop draw in the city during the mid-60s, hitting a peak in 1967 with two successful single releases, huge crowds paying to see them in both clubs and ballrooms throughout the island, and appearances on the same bill as world famous Californian pop stars The Beach Boys in Dublin and Belfast. Len Guest ran a record 'hop' (a very basic forerunner to the 1970s discotheque) in a hall in Balbriggan during 1962, the proceeds of which went to the purchase of his first Fender Stratocaster guitar. Len and his friend Maxie McEvoy would take short breaks from spinning discs at the hop and strap on their guitars to give their clientele brief renditions of surf and pop instrumentals from the likes of The Ventures and The John Barry Seven. The duo were joined by Vic McNamara who fashioned himself a pair of homemade drumsticks, purchased a kit from local showband The Graduates for £10 and took a few lessons in how to keep a steady rhythm. Len soon invited on board a powerful local singer called Jimmy Fanning who was a big fan of Del Shannon, Cliff Richard and Carole King. Tommy Caffrey, the only non-native of Balbriggan, hailing from the wilds of Drogheda, County Louth had recently acquired a spanking new AC30 amplifier and he was brought in on rhythm guitar, with Maxie switching over to the bass. Len took the name of his new group from a Shadows tune and by late 1963 the five-piece Strangers were born. The group epitomised the commercial side of the Irish beat scene, their repertoire leaning towards more accessible numbers from the British pop maestros rather than the gutsier fare served up by the Stones, Animals and the US R&B groups.

> **RONAN COLLINS** (broadcaster and early beat fan): The Strangers had the perfect line-up, they could be Cliff Richard and The Shadows, they could be The Hollies, they could be The Beatles and they were very good at it.

They were occasionally referred to as a mini-showband such was the range of their abilities, their professional versatility and the ease with which they moved from local tennis club to city centre basement dive to cavernous ballroom. Furthermore, they did what few beat groups had the temerity to

The Strangers at the Apollo Cinema, Dundrum, 1964

consider – they wrote and recorded some of their own material. It was still perfectly acceptable to groups and their fans back in the 1960s to take songs written and popularised by international performers and make local versions of their own. By and large these covers weren't simply pale imitations, indeed quite a few of the singles released were injected with the idiosyncratic personalities of the beat groups in question. There was also an emotional connection with the material that was lacking in the showbands who played whatever was popular at the time, regardless of personal taste. In a country with a distinct lack of broadcast and retail outlets for teenage popular music it was an unusual and brave step for a group to play their own compositions live and even to take the next step and put them out on record. Vic McNamara and Maxie McEvoy were the songwriters for The Strangers, splitting lyric writing and music writing between the two.

> **MAXIE MCEVOY** If I was in bed and I got an idea for a melody in my head it was like a headache. It wouldn't go away and there was no way I could sleep. So I'd have to get up out of the bed, grab the guitar, sit down and work it out and hope that I'd remember it the next day.

It wouldn't be until July 1967 that one of their collaborations would appear on a single ('Daytime Turns To Night', a jaunty celebration of teenage love) as the B-side to the shimmering summer sounds of 'You Didn't Have To Be So Nice', written by John Sebastian of The Lovin' Spoonful. In the meantime, The Strangers were building up a considerable fan base, especially of young females, throughout the northern parts of the city, showing up at youth halls in Donabate, Portrane, Fairview and Clontarf. They also carved out a residency at Glasnevin Tennis Club, playing support to The Teenbeats, where future Taoiseach Bertie Ahern would regularly go to see them play. Southsiders weren't immune to their sweet harmonies and sharp playing either, and the group's popularity was further consolidated with a number of well received relief slots for the big showbands. Quite a few of the punters began to come to ballrooms early if they knew The Strangers were on the bill, something that didn't sit too well with the jealous headliners.

> **LEN GUEST** Showbands used to sabotage your gear. [One well-known band] did it to us [once]. We were using their gear one night, doing a double gig with them. They set the volume levels all different on the mics and they turned the treble off on some of the mics. They robbed two pairs of sticks as well. After the first song we stopped.

Despite a hostile antagonism from their musical colleagues and the early curt dismissal of the media establishment, by the end of 1964 the beat groups' own scene had solidified out of the various disparate threads of activity taking place across Dublin over the previous couple of years. Inspired by the highly regarded Viscounts, The Greenbeats had shown (initially at least) that you didn't have to sacrifice your musical passions to become, simultaneously, a nationally famous draw and an artistically satisfied group. Years of listening to the US Armed Forces Network charts on Radio Luxembourg and the onslaught of the British beat boom had inspired hundreds of Irish kids to learn how to play instruments and form groups. There is a well worn rock 'n' roll cliché which states that everyone who bought the first Velvet Underground record went on to form a band. It might be equally valid to claim that every young Irish male dancing to The Beatles, in the aisles of the Adelphi cinema, was either already in a beat group or just weeks away from forming one. The Irish beat scene blossomed fully from the beginning of 1965 until the end of the decade, growing and evolving rapidly in a wealth of different directions with countless groups emerging from all over the country, north and south of the border. Eventually this early promise would lead onto considerable artistic and commercial success at home and abroad for the more talented and driven participants. Everyone was surprised when out of nowhere, the first to achieve such fame was a group of *jejune* beat musicians from Dublin's Southside, ably led by Ian Whitcomb, the 'Father of Irish Rock'.

Part Two

'The Father of Irish Rock' is the self-applied moniker of Englishman Ian Whitcomb – public schoolboy, Irish beat group trailblazer, twentieth century music historian and latter day ukulele expert – whose claim to this grandiose title is validated somewhat by his appearance on the very first home produced slice of vinyl to hit the US Billboard Top 10, in July 1965. It is doubtful that his progeny in Irish rock music of the 1970s and beyond would have been aware of their forefather. Destined to be consigned to that overflowing bin of one-hit wonders of the 1960s, Ian Whitcomb's name means nothing to fans of Irish rock today, and perhaps little more to music scholars of the golden decade of popular music. Decked out in seersucker suit and deerstalker hat for his lip-synching appearances on US TV in 1965, he was accompanied by an absent R&B band of gifted Irish musicians going by the name of Bluesville.

What Bluesville were doing in early 1960s Dublin was not all that different from what The Rolling Stones were doing in London – reinterpreting the sounds of the electric blues and early rock 'n' roll, injecting it with their own energy and vitality and showcasing it to audiences who had never been exposed to sounds like that before. With a mixture of chutzpah, opportunism and no mean musical talent Ian Whitcomb and Bluesville grabbed onto the coattails of the armies of the British Invasion and wrote themselves into the annals of Irish rock history.

In the autumn of 1961 Ian Whitcomb registered at Trinity College Dublin to do Modern History and Political Thought at the suggestion of the wealthy and well-known Le Broquy family, who had a business connection with Whitcomb's uncle. Fresh faced and naïve, he arrived in Ireland to find a city quite different from what he was used to in England. Dublin was teeming with colourful characters, lively pubs, movie theatres showing old classics and cafés with outlandishly dressed commissionaires beckoning customers inside. Ian had experienced a comfortable upper-middle class childhood in the south east of England. Like many children of the post-war generation he was transfixed by American culture – music and films of the 'New World' were a romantic escape from the grey austerity of 1940s-50s Britain. In particular he was captured by the sounds of rock 'n' roll and the electric blues, that urban

An impish Ian Whitcomb during his early days at Trinity College

evolution of rural Mississippi Delta folk blues which had developed in the black ghettos of cities like Chicago and Detroit. In a rebellious move, he was the first boy in his public school to purchase a copy of Bill Haley's 'Rock Around The Clock', and the first to form a DIY skiffle group.

Excited to find scholars of varying nationalities and philosophical persuasions amongst his peers at Trinity, Whitcomb unsuccessfully tried to share his love of blues with some of the African students, gauchely assuming they would have an innate appreciation of the form. He soon found that girls were more receptive. Sensing an opportunity to combine his studies with pleasure, Ian wasted no time signing up to the college jazz club, joining their jazz band on piano. Some of their early gigs were not quite up to the required professional standards. One fan recalls an appearance at the internationally flavoured Carnival of Nations show, at St. Anthony's Hall on Merchant's Quay, where the band squabbled loudly amongst themselves as the curtain was being raised. While playing in various combos outside of the college walls Ian met fellow English student and American music enthusiast Barry Richardson, who was in a showband called The Crickets.

Initially the duo cobbled together a quasi-blues band called Warren Whitcomb and His Bluesmen, in homage to Ian's then American screen idol Warren Beatty. As an entity they only ever played one gig, the Trinity Jazz Band Ball at the Shelbourne Hotel on St. Stephen's Green. Their performance didn't go down well with the local trad heads who preferred their musicians to stick rigorously to the jazz standards. Undaunted by the reception, Ian and Barry pressed ahead with their dream of forming Ireland's first R&B group and invited some of The Crickets to participate. Out went the clarinet and banjo and in came electricity and amplification courtesy of Barry's bandmates.

At this time there were no tailor-made venues in the city suitable for a group of this nature – such an exclusively R&B oriented band had rarely been seen or heard around Dublin at the time. As a result the developing group ended up playing mostly to bemused crowds at protest marches and rugby games as well as to the raucous hordes in Trinity's Buttery Bar. However, as the band's reputation spread they got to showcase their sound in more sophisticated and impressive venues – showband ballrooms and tennis clubs – allowing the band to whip up a rhythm 'n' blues frenzy to the now receptive crowds. Ian took up duties on piano and vocals, Barry honked the sax and the showband moonlighters filled out the sound with bass, drums and electric guitars.

In the summer of 1963 Ian took off for the USA on a 'Union of Students of Ireland' charter flight to find the source of the American music that had so transfixed him from an early age. As a quest to tap into this rich musical heritage the trip fell some way short of being a success. But there were other benefits. Displaying the kind of initiative that would serve him well in the near future, Whitcomb strode into a Nashville radio station one afternoon and simply announced that he was British. Cue a frenzy of activity by the staff who had him featured on the news bulletin as… well, an Englishman. A brief stop off in New Orleans gave him a taste of the swamp city's trad jazz culture while in California he was fortunate enough to arrive as the surf music craze was riding its popular crest. Further up the coast in Seattle, after casually tinkling the ivories of a coffee shop piano, he was offered a two week stint, entertaining the customers with a mixture of blues, rock 'n' roll and native ragtime. His musical education was further enhanced by seeing the white bread folk hootenannies there, although he was put off by their clean cut wholesomeness and earnest political concerns. It reminded him a bit too much of Trinity.

Returning to London in the late winter, Whitcomb found the UK in the grip of Beatlemania. He had missed the pandemonium of the Adelphi concerts in Dublin that November, and still steeped in the sounds of America he was bemused at the hysterical reception that the Mersey beat groups were receiving in the press and amongst the general populace. The authentic grit of The Rolling Stones was more to his liking, closer to that well of indigenous blues from the Mississippi Delta and Chicago that his Irish bands had been drawing their inspiration from. He decided to christen his Dublin collective Bluesville Manufacturing, a name inspired by Blues Incorporated, the pioneering English group formed by Alexis Corner and Cyril Davies in London in early 1962. More used to the traditional set up of the showbands, the reference was lost on the people of Dublin, who took to referring to the group as simply The Bluesvilles. Barry Richardson drafted in some new members to the group courtesy of another showband he played with, The Alpine Seven, solidifying the line-up into the core that would stay together until the middle of 1965 – Ian McGarry (drums), Deke O'Brien (rhythm guitar), Mick Molloy (lead guitar), Gerry Ryan (bass), and the triumvirate of Trinity students from England – Ian Whitcomb (piano and vocals), Barry Richardson on harmonica, and Peter Adler, son of famous harmonica player Larry Adler, on saxophone.

Deke O'Brien and Mick Molloy had become close friends whilst attending school at Christian Brothers College in Monkstown. Deke discovered his passion for music after purchasing a cheap guitar and taking a crash course in the basic rock 'n' roll chords of E, A and D. Mick Molloy took an interest in music from an early age. He grudgingly learned piano at home before being introduced to the hypnotic sounds of the guitar by his friend, and future member of The Greenbeats, Brian Lynch. Mick was given an acoustic guitar of his own one Christmas and was soon playing with various skiffle combinations formed from a group of young enthusiasts in the Dún Laoghaire and Blackrock area, many of whom would soon become involved with groups in the vanguard of the early beat scene. Deke and Mick would regularly bunk off school and head down to the Irish Federation of Musicians on Gardiner Street. Here, touring showbands would look to pick up temporary players for their bookings, piling everyone plus their equipment into a VW microbus on trips which sometimes took the young novices to the distant ballrooms of Kerry and Donegal.

On Sundays in the summer of 1963 the duo played some Little Richard and Jerry Lee Lewis covers at the White Cottage on Killiney Beach, Ted Carroll's club. They were asked to join The Alpine Seven by Crickets' roadie Mick Cummins towards the end of 1963 where they encountered most of the future line-up of Bluesville.

> **DEKE O BRIEN** There was more American country than what you would call 'Country 'n' Irish', a little bit more tasteful. We were

good enough to get away with not playing the schmaltz, there were good players and a lot of energy in the band, so we got away with playing a better class of music.

Deke was struck by Ian Whitcomb's star quality when he met him shortly after.

DEKE O BRIEN This guy looked like Mick Jagger. Good looking lad. Enormous stage presence, you couldn't say no to him. You'd

Ian Whitcomb on stage

have a little giggle at his accent, because he had a few affectations, but he was a lovable guy.

As a schoolboy, Ian McGarry wanted to join an accordion band, but his family couldn't afford such a luxurious item, so he had to settle for the much more affordable pair of drumsticks. He initially studied in the School Of Music on Chatham Street before going on to play in a number of different showbands, one of which was The Alpine Seven. The normal brass line-up of the showband in those days was trumpet, trombone and saxophone. In order to play their cherished rock 'n' roll sounds The Alpine Seven chose to perform with just two sax players. As it happened one of the saxophonists became ill, and according to Ian McGarry, the group were told of a chap in Trinity College called Barry Richardson, who was first and foremost a very accomplished blues harmonica player ('the best I ever heard in my life,' attests Ian), but who was quite adept on the saxophone as well. As it turned out, it was Richardson who managed to poach the rhythm section of The Alpine Seven for *his* band (at this time centred around the three Trinity Students, Ian Whitcomb, Peter Adler and himself), and Bluesville were born.

Strolling along the streets of Dublin in early 1964, Ian Whitcomb was stopped by curious passers-by to inquire if he was The Rolling Stones' 'vulgar' lead singer, Mick Jagger (photographs show some similarity between the pair, two fine cherubic English boys, a lock or two of hair crawling disobediently over the collar). Impressed by the attention that he was receiving from young girls over this resemblance and mindful that his groups had always lacked a certain drive, Whitcomb decided to point Bluesville in a more commercial direction. Abandoning some of the more esoteric material and throwing in the odd Roy Orbison song, Bluesville began to attract a dedicated crowd, more in tune with the happening raw aggression of the Stones and the cheeky insolence of The Beatles.

IAN WHITCOMB I had come to Trinity from school as a fat boy and I always thought women had no interest whatsoever in me. Then suddenly one day someone told me, 'You're one of the sexiest guys on campus', and I thought, Jesus that's incredible, I had no idea. I knew that the only way we could succeed was not just playing pure rhythm and blues but we had to have the Jagger appeal as well, because the Stones were coming through at that time. I knew we had to have some sort of sex appeal so that's when I started throwing myself around on the stage. I noticed when I did it, whenever I shook my hair or wiggled a bit, the local colleens [sic] would scream and shout so I knew there was something going on there.

Bluesville's live act was a fresh and exciting revelation on the Dublin scene, particularly for those youngsters beginning to sense a move away from the showbands with their choreographed dance steps and subdued physical demeanour. As well as a sprinkling of hard-edged chart hits Bluesville's set included classics from old blues masters like Howlin' Wolf, Muddy Waters and John Lee Hooker, combined with early soul standards.

> **JONATHAN RYAN** (Bluesville fan, and guitarist with The Rootzgroop): The first time I saw Bluesville I think [it] was in a place called Marian Hall [in Milltown]. Everyone just went mad at the response to them, because we had never heard anything like that. The Greenbeats were one thing, they were very enthusiastic, but Bluesville had the extra dimension of their appearance.

On stage the group were certainly a most striking sight. Peter Adler exuded an exotic cool, with dark glasses constantly propped up on the bridge of his nose, a piece of sellotape holding them delicately together at the side. Whitcomb would stand up at the piano wearing oversized American football jerseys, stomping his huge basketball sneakers to the incessant beat, drainpipe trousers pasted to his skinny legs. A large floppy tweed Tamoshanter hat topped off the bizarre ensemble. In contrast, the tall and stoical Barry Richardson would appear in evening dress, as if he had wandered in from a wedding party. In the corner, Deke O'Brien sported a rockabilly leopardskin print shirt, collar turned up in a gesture of sullen rebellion. Beside him stood Mick Molloy wearing a simple white shirt, sleeves rolled up to the elbow, ready for the work ahead. Deke was a favourite of the females in the crowd, gripping a Gibson 335 Cherry with his initials carved onto the body. His partner in the dual guitar axis was expressionless and enigmatic, cradling a brown Gibson 345 TD, and more often than not stood with his back to the audience. Bass guitarist Gerry Ryan hovered quietly beside Ian McGarry, Bluesville's very own Charlie Watts, immaculately decked out in sharp suit and tie, a pin slotted carefully in between the collar, performing his patented 'skip beat' pattern on the gleaming white bass drum.

> **JONATHAN RYAN** The great contrast of the band was this sort of bohemian look about three or four of them and then the others looked very serious. They were visually so interesting to look at, but [they also had] this amazing sound. It was a mixture of rock 'n' roll and blues and Ian Whitcomb's music hall [influence], all mixed up. It was a heady brew and we were all knocked out by it.

> **TERRY BRADY** (drummer with showband The Chessmen): They were fabulous. Whitcomb was great, he was a real performer.

> The band were excellent musicians too, really interesting to listen to because they were doing a lot of blues stuff out of the US and really making it sound authentic. It wasn't like a cheap copycat version of a John Lee Hooker song. They were certainly the antithesis of the showbands at the time.

Bluesville on stage. L-R: Barry Richardson (harmonica), Deke O'Brien, Ian Whitcomb, Peter Adler

The group were building up a large word-of-mouth following around Dublin, from regular appearances at the Apollo Cinema in Dundrum, frequent shows on the Trinity campus and the occasional substitution for the absent Greenbeats at the buzzing Rhythm 'n' Blues Club. They were popular enough to headline a rowdy 'R&B Spectacular' in the Crystal Ballroom on South Anne Street in October 1964, on a bill that included The Semitones, The Inmates and The Greenbeats.

> **IAN WHITCOMB** (regarding The Greenbeats): That was a helluva good band. Musically they were actually much more proficient than us. They didn't quite have our charisma and our unusual look and maybe our sex appeal, but certainly as far as musicians are concerned they were better than us technically, and certainly John Keogh knew his rhythm 'n' blues.

One particular night Bluesville were appearing at a charity function in The Barn, a little church hall in the suburb of Mount Merrion, soon to be a popular residential area for beat groups from Dublin's Southside, many of whom secured residencies across the road at the Stella House pub. (Van Morrison and his band, Them, would come down the odd time to play at Stella House. Bluesville were always proud of the fact that they could pack more of a crowd into the spartan surrounds of The Barn than their Northern counterparts could under the expensive lighting rig across the road). The stage set-up that night was impressive – humming amps positioned all round the performing area twinkling with little red lights, guitars scattered left and right, and Ian Whitcomb fired up and raring to go at the decrepit church-hall piano. The combination of electrical energy and copious amounts of alcohol proved to be an incendiary rhythm and blues mix.

Ian Whitcomb on piano, Ian McGarry in background

IAN WHITCOMB I was really getting into the songs, really feeling mad, when WHAAM! I fell into a city of black-coffin amplifiers and the amps and I all collapsed together onto the stage floor of Mount Merrion. What a mess! What a foul up! But wait! While I lay on the floor I heard a scream – a girlish one – then more, excited with sexual anticipation. My bottom touched a loose

> amplifier wire and the shock sent me into the air, jack-knifing in the Jagger manner. A huge howl of ecstasy from the audience. After that I limped around the stage in agony (and ecstasy) while the band played on, though their instruments were now acoustical. But the thump thump of the drums was enough to accompany my agonized dancing and the crowd joined in with claps and yelps. I realized I had happened upon my innate sex appeal… it was a revelation. I determined to work on it and, after the gig, I returned to my rooms at the college and went to bed – after tossing out the usual comparative strangers I'd found in there. (Ian Whitcomb, *Rock Odyssey*, pp119-120)

Whitcomb had stumbled, literally, upon the magic formula that the power and attraction of rock 'n' roll is built on. Before the year was out another unplanned and fortuitous occurrence would propel him into the American Top 10 singles chart and herald a short-lived stardom that he could hardly have dreamt about during those cold nights in university digs back in 1961.

Inspired by the British Invasion in the US – those heady months in 1964 when acts such as The Animals, Kinks, Beatles and Stones were assaulting the hearts and minds of American youth – Whitcomb sat down to channel his energy into writing his own tunes while his fellow students continued with their studies around him. A request from the left-leaning head of Trinity College's drama group resulted in a truncated version of Bluesville entering a recording studio for the first time. Although 'recording studio' is probably too fanciful a description for the damp basement on Merrion Square where Ian, Barry Richardson and an unknown drummer (remembered only as Brian) congregated with engineer Pete Selwood to cut a song called 'Pall Me Mantle' (the deliberately incomprehensible title was also the title of the college revue). The tune was little more than a harmonica solo, formed around a simple Chuck Berry riff, with no vocals. The full band also laid down a ragged and exciting version of the Larry Williams' rock 'n' roll standard 'Bony Moronie' around the same time.

> **IAN WHITCOMB** 'Bony Moronie' is the best example of the real Bluesville. It's got two saxophones, Barry is playing one sax, Pete Adler is playing the other and it's got a terrific garage [sound].

Despite its primitive nature 'Pall Me Mantle' was well received and Ian even had an American visitor to Trinity College inquire about its availability on record.

Sensing the opportunity to use the connections made on his previous US trip and to exploit America's fascination with his British heritage, Whitcomb brought the crinkled reel-to-reel tape of 'Pall Me Mantle' with him on his next journey across the Atlantic that summer. Preparing for adventure he purchased some Beatle-esque fashions (Cuban heeled boots, turtle-neck sweater, leather jacket) and grew his hair even longer. In Seattle, he flipped open the Yellow Pages to R, for record companies, and made an appointment with Jerry Dennon, head of local label Jerden Records. Jerden were responsible for unleashing that timeless frat-rock classic 'Louie Louie' by The Kingsmen onto the music world in 1963. A combination of decidedly amateur playing, slurred and unintelligible vocals and youthful ebullience has ensured its legendary status, inspiring thousands of punk bands down the decades, countless cover versions, a radio airplay ban in Indiana and even an FBI investigation into the supposedly salacious lyrics.

> **JERRY DENNON** I'm an enterprising young American kid in the record business, the British Invasion [has] just happened and I'm a little stunned because of my rock 'n' roll record, which I knew was a biggie, was being beaten up by this funny named group out of England with a sound I'd never heard. So, obviously when I heard there was somebody from England who I can actually talk to who was an artist, I had great intrigue and great interest in him. Ian just looked like the image I had of an English rock artist!

Leaving his tape of the Bluesville song with Dennon, Ian returned to playing piano at the coffee shop where he had encountered the folkies the previous summer, but they were nowhere to be seen. The Americans had taken the Beatles and all things Anglo to heart and Ian found himself the object of lavish attention from the local girls, who were intrigued by his accent and exotic aura. One particular night, he found himself alone with an excitable nymphette while her parents were away.

> **IAN WHITCOMB** She purred, 'Talk pretty to me. You talk so vurry pretty.' I had stopped talking because I was planning devilish fun. Then, 'Ian, baby – you're turning me on!' What a vivid phrase! You turn on a tap, a television, a stereo, but a person? I rushed to the nearest pad and pencil without delay. (Ian Whitcomb, *Rock Odyssey*, p133)

He may have left his companion rather puzzled and dismayed, but by jotting down the phrase Whitcomb ensured it could be used again 4,500 miles away, back in the cramped surrounds of a Dublin recording studio. Meanwhile, Jerry Dennon had made contact and was prepared to offer him a record contract, releasing 'Pall Me Mantle', shrewdly retitled 'Soho' (emphasising its bogus 'Swinging London' origin) as a 7" with 'Bony Maronie' on the flip side.

Back in Dublin, the British Invader was understandably proud of the disc bearing his name, showing it off to anyone he could. The rest of Bluesville were not quite so thrilled, wondering why the band's name wasn't on the label too. Whitcomb was certain of his priorities. 'I knew the only way we could have success was by having a hit record, otherwise you just remained a local group, and that was always my drive.' By this time Barry Richardson had graduated from Trinity and left the band. Ian suggests that his partner was a little unhappy with the direction Bluesville was taking.

> **IAN WHITCOMB** Bluesville had to get our own sound, not copy American R&B, but do it our own way. Barry and I parted company because he was more of a purist, and he wanted to keep it pure R&B, copy Muddy Waters and so forth and I said no, we really gotta get our own sound.

The lead vocalist preferred to build on the music of his idols, infusing it with a more personal and commercial touch. Inspired by The Animals' pop update of folk classic 'House Of The Rising Sun', Ian dug into his store of old skiffle tunes and came up with the blues-meets-music hall of 'This Sporting Life', which became Ian's second (and Bluesville's debut) release. Notwithstanding his love of American rock and blues, Whitcomb never forgot the indigenous musical heritage of his British upbringing, something that would inform his initial forays into song-writing and future career direction. The band's first recording of 'This Sporting Life', at Pete Selwood's studio in winter 1964, was unsatisfactory. In order to fill out the sound, Ian invited Bill Sommerville-Large, Trinity student, part-time engineer at Eamonn Andrews Studios and accomplished jazz pianist, to play his Farfisa organ on the track. Bill suggested they do the new recording at his employers' more professional location on Henry Street since there was the prospect of offers, from the studio owners, of live dates on the cabaret circuit. More a collaborative band effort than 'Soho' the line-up for the session consisted of Ian on piano, Mick Molloy and Deke O'Brien on guitar, Brian Lynch of The Greenbeats standing in for Gerry Ryan on bass (a function he served at many of Bluesville's live engagements when Ryan was not available), Ian McGarry on drums and Sommerville-Large on organ.

The Trinity trio of Bluesville kick loose

If there had been frequent flyer points awarded in the 1960s Ian would have earned a free trip to Las Vegas, as he was back in Seattle at Christmas, ardently presenting Bluesville's new song to Jerry Dennon. In order to give the track that extra kick, Gerry Rosalie of Northwest proto-punks The Sonics was drafted in to smother the Farfisa with the deep swirling sounds of the Hammond organ and Ian stirred in some additional spice by shaking the maracas. It is a shame that Rosalie didn't also sing, as his famous vocal chord-shredding screams would

Whitcomb outside Eamonn Andrews Studios

have added a much-needed dirtier edge to the polite tones of Ian's delivery. Producer Tom Wilson once said that the combination of electric guitar, gospel-like organ and piano on 'This Sporting Life' was an influence for the sound he was looking for whilst overseeing the sessions for Bob Dylan's era-defining 'Like A Rolling Stone'.

> **IAN WHITCOMB** Everybody thought [this record] was going to be huge. I remember Sonny Bono, whom I met later on, saying 'Man, that was an incredible sound, we never heard any sound quite like that before.' It was different to 'House of the Rising Sun', especially when I went up into a high voice at the end. It was covered in England by Mickey Finn, produced by Shel Talmy. They ripped me off, copied my sound and they got it out in England just before [mine].

The single ('This Sporting Life' b/w 'Soho' which was now re-titled 'Fizz', no doubt to entice those who had already purchased the first platter) was released regionally in the Pacific North West at the beginning of 1965, and nationally on Tower Records in March of that year. Tower was a brand new subsidiary of Capitol Records based in Hollywood, set up to release material by minor artists while the parent company busied itself promoting the big boys (it also had Brendan Bowyer and The Royal Showband on its books, and released their most famous tune 'The Hucklebuck' Stateside). Although a minor hit on some local charts (hot local station KJR made it Pick of The Week and set it on hourly rotation, propelling it into the top ten in Seattle) the record failed to set the Billboard Top 100 alight. Tower Records were impressed with the first couple of weeks' sales however and were willing to put some investment behind Jerden's discovery.

> **JERRY DENNON** I get a call within days after Tower Records put out the single, saying what else do you have on Ian Whitcomb, this thing is going to be a hit and we need to get an album ready.

Excited at the prospect of visiting the land of his ancestors and with his wife in tow, Jerden's record mogul decided to travel to Dublin in March, to record an album with Ian Whitcomb and Bluesville. The group were consolidating their popularity around the beat scene in Dublin, still wowing the crowds in tennis clubs and local halls as well as playing in some of the new venues opened specifically to cater for the popular teenage sound. There was now a definite distinction between the philosophy of the beat groups and the

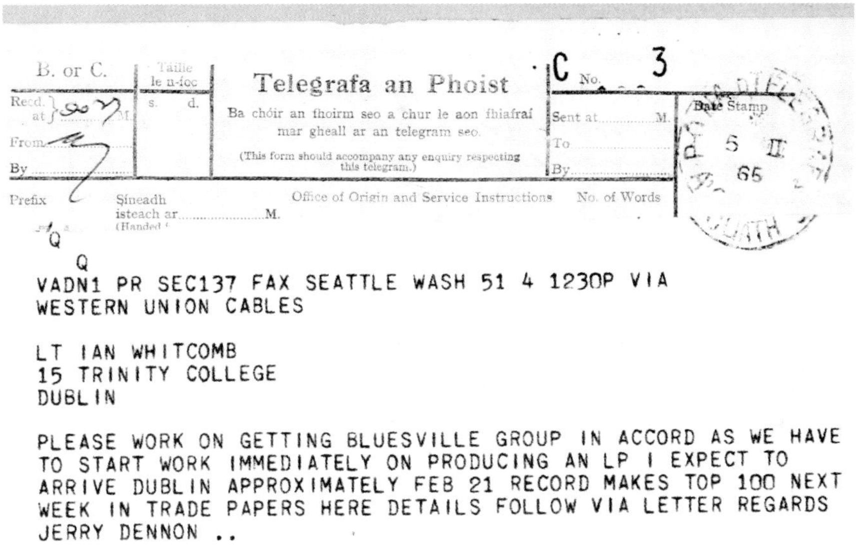
B. or C. | Táille le n-íoc | Telegrafa an Phoist | C No. 3

Recd. at ... M. | s. d. | Ba chóir an fhoirm seo a chur le aon fhiafraí mar gheall ar an telegram seo. (This form should accompany any enquiry respecting this telegram.) | Sent at ... M. | Date Stamp

From ... | To ...

By ... | By ...

Prefix | Síneadh isteach ar ... M. (Handed ...) | Office of Origin and Service Instructions | No. of Words

5 II 65

Q

VADN1 PR SEC137 FAX SEATTLE WASH 51 4 1230P VIA WESTERN UNION CABLES

LT IAN WHITCOMB
15 TRINITY COLLEGE
DUBLIN

PLEASE WORK ON GETTING BLUESVILLE GROUP IN ACCORD AS WE HAVE TO START WORK IMMEDIATELY ON PRODUCING AN LP I EXPECT TO ARRIVE DUBLIN APPROXIMATELY FEB 21 RECORD MAKES TOP 100 NEXT WEEK IN TRADE PAPERS HERE DETAILS FOLLOW VIA LETTER REGARDS JERRY DENNON ..

Jerry Dennon informs Whitcomb about Bluesville's success Stateside

showbands in Ireland, as far as Ian Whitcomb saw it, a fact expounded on by the Trinity student, albeit anonymously, in the *TCD Miscellany* published in December 1964. His comments caused consternation amongst the showband fraternity in Dublin, and aptly demonstrate the growing divide between the mushrooming beat group scene and the established ballroom world.

Most of us probably imagine the Irish pop music scene to be exactly the same as the English. Maybe, but not quite. Take the Showbands, which appear to dominate business over here. Brendan of Murray's Record Shop told us that there are 8,000 showbands in the country, which sent us into ecstasies of gleeful calculation about the number of showbands per head of the population. Unfortunately more sober sources chopped off one of the noughts; but that still left us with one band for every 2,500 people. Once a week the showbands display themselves through a flurry of 'Evening Press' adverts; a line of pork butchers arranged as for the school photo with a couple of saxophones to look convincing and the breathless slogan 'Dance with the Jolly Cretins Showband recently back from Boston, USA'. A good sale for any record in Ireland is 3,000; Dicky Rock and The Miami Showband's 'Candy Store' sold 10,000 – some gauge of showband popularity.

How could it be anything else? Imagine a horde of fancy-jacketed showbanders, kicking their legs in unison, swinging their saxes, trumpets and ceili pipes in the sort of intimate clubs that house British rhythm and blues. The Showband with it's essentially chameleon nature will never be popular with the British teenager. By concentrating on the visual, vaudeville aspect and not developing a musical style the Showbands have lost any potential audience in England. When they pop across… and the Irish press announce with glee 'Clipper Carlton on another epoch-making tour of England' the truth is that the band will be entertaining misty-eyed immigrants in various Irish clubs spotted around the

British Isles. In America it's the same: the drag around the shamrock circuit – green, green everywhere and 'Irish Eyes Are Smilin'; blubbering third generation immigrants telling the band about their grandfather and how he came from Kerry and did they bring over any leprechauns?

On their return to Dublin the evening papers scream 'Showband Conquest of America' and in truth America has never heard them, save a few drunken elks from the Detroit Lodge Shamrock Club. Showband entertainment – the idea that all the bandsmen not only toot horns but also tell funny jokes and are 'characters' – went out with Jack Payne and Roy Fox in the thirties. It's easy to laugh at the absurd antics of the bandsmen – their pinched, blotchy faces; their obsession for the late great Jim Reeves and his slop (this goes with the sentimental Kennedy adulation); their pathetic copying of established band names (Rolling Tones, King Oliver, Young Shadows, Shadows, Crickets) and their lack of musical talent. Rather a shock when you learn that The Royal Showband are the highest paid band in Europe apart from The Beatles.

What sort of material do these Showbands play? Mostly emasculated Country and Western of the very sickly brand. Of course, they're also forced to murder the current chart discs, because the New Pop music has battered down all walls. To watch these Showbanders as they move in unison across the stage and then back again is like being at a tennis match.

Whitcomb finishes his assault with a plug for his own group and others who played with him at the Rhythm 'n' Blues Spectacular in the Crystal Ballroom that October:

There are, however, several groups that play spirited beaty 1964 music. They're a tightly knit bunch and always banging into each other because whenever there's a beat concert or dance these happy few are called upon to perform. This beaty handful should be worth their weight in gold discs. They comprise The Inmates, The Semitones, The Greenbeats and that changeable mob Bluesville. Excepting Bluesville these bands are all four-piece, after the British fashion. Without doubt Greenbeats and Bluesville are the beat kingpins, but as both bands play in quite a different style there's no rivalry.

No doubt part of the impetus behind this stinging attack was to flagrantly boost the profile of the Bluesville collective. In fact Ian Whitcomb was leading a not inconspicuous double life, on occasion donning a 'fancy jacket' and taking up lead vocal duties for The Alpine Seven Showband whenever a few shillings were needed to fill the dwindling coffers. The charismatic singer's more *outré* impulses were reigned in by the showband's manager who insisted that Ian's hips didn't move and that he refrained from doing any of that 'sex stuff'!

IAN WHITCOMB We looked down on [showbands], we thought they were ridiculous, doing all their choreographed steps. Now

> I think they were great! At the time I was filled with a militant zeal.

In early 1965, on the cusp of rock 'n' roll's maturity from teenage diversion to weighty artistic endeavour, 12" albums were not the cohesive and expressive statements they would become in the wake of such epochal releases as Bob Dylan's *Highway 61 Revisited* or The Beatles' *Rubber Soul*. Most pop albums at this time consisted of a couple of hit singles and a generous amount of filler. This was the blueprint that Bluesville's record would adhere to. The band reconvened at Eamonn Andrews' cluttered, pokey studio on Henry Street and laid down the tracks for the album within the space of two days, squeezed in between college lectures. Ian Whitcomb chose the tracks that were to be cut – a mixture of self-penned originals and covers by the likes of The Ronettes ('Be My Baby', with backing vocals from drummer Ian McGarry) and The Coasters ('That Is Rock 'n' Roll'). Barry Richardson and Peter Adler stopped in at the studio briefly to add some saxophone flourishes, although Peter was not always the most welcome of guests.

> **IAN WHITCOMB** We locked the door once or twice against Peter Adler, he was sort of muscling in on the thing. He was kind of pushy, he was trying to out-star me in the band and he was a bit disruptive.

Peter Adler had grown up in a family strong with musical tradition. His father was US-born jazz harmonica player Larry Adler and from an early age Peter trained classically in piano and cello. Whilst attending Dartington Hall public school he immersed himself in jazz, learning tenor sax and double bass, falling in love with the modern proponents of the great American art, like Miles Davis and Dizzy Gillespie. In Ireland he got involved with the jazz and blues performing circuit and contributed to other popular beat groups of the mid-60s.

> **PETER ADLER** I think girls were starting to notice me a bit, which may not have pleased Ian enormously. It was late-teen ego trips going on. I don't think I was trying to muscle in. In fact I very much stayed in the background in those days. It was only after Ian went to America that I took over that lead singer position.

Indeed, there was proof that the attention of a few of Bluesville's female fans was firmly fixed on the sax player with the impressive musical genes. Adler recalls one scribbled note that was thrown up on stage during a gig, 'Dear Peter, I must have intercourse with you tonight. I am wearing a yellow dress, I have blonde hair and I'm sitting in the third row with my sister.'

Although not quite as explosive as their live performances, Bluesville's album still captured the unique contributions each of the band members made to their sound. Mick Molloy's guitar playing was measured and precise, economically offering a screeching note here and there as the rhythm section pounded on behind him. Jerry Dennon oversaw the recording. Brian Lynch, who had played bass guitar on 'This Sporting Life' was absent from the album sessions due to family commitments so Gerry Ryan was on hand to replace him. The main band were each paid handsomely for their contribution, approximately IR£200 which was a huge amount of money at the time when an average weekly wage was around IR£12.

> **IAN McGARRY** We got American session rates. Little did we know at the time we were being bought out, which should never have happened.

> **MICK MOLLOY** We ended up getting a session fee for the work that we did. In other words we were paid off, if you like...We were never offered a part of anything basically.

Deke O'Brien was happier with his 'payoff'. Rather cheerfully, he remembers buying a new guitar, a Vox amplifier, a Ford Cortina and a wardrobe of mohair suits from a tailor on Wicklow Street.

As with many groups, the carefree camaraderie of the early days in Bluesville became a little strained when a slick record producer drifted into town with the attendant prospect of record contracts and stardom.

> **IAN WHITCOMB** I went to [Dennon's] hotel and I signed just as Ian Whitcomb and I'll always remember the band lining up later trying to get a separate contact. Jerry said to me, 'I really only want to sign you.' There was no conspiracy. I don't remember him saying to me we're not going to use these guys.

> **JERRY DENNON** At the time Ian was a person I had a relationship with and suddenly now I'm in Ireland with musicians in the room. Are they band members or are they sidemen that you hire? I had accessed this whole thing as Ian and Bluesville. So you could separate the two, but in reality that wasn't the case, obviously the band and Ian were a package but from my perspective it was a bit different coming from Seattle.

Ian was hoping that his next single would be the serious anti-war protest folk song 'No Tear For Johnny', brought to him by publicist Hal Shaper and included as the last track on the album. After laying down that particular song in the studio the band went into an impromptu shuffle, a whimsical Jerry Lee Lewis-style boogie that they had been showcasing to rapturous acclaim in the venues around the city.

> **IAN WHITCOMB** During the first instrumental chorus an ashtray slid off my baby grand piano and thudded to the floor. Also, the drummer's cymbals were digging into my back. I concluded that this take would be junked, so I had a lark and sang in a campy, high-pitched girly voice, in imitation of The Supremes. I really couldn't hear myself above the clamour of the band. But I made up the words as I went along and stuck a lot of huh, huh, huhs in during the blues 'spasm' breaks. I also plugged the 'Turn On' phrase [in] – couldn't think of anything else to say. And that was that. Nobody expected this joke to ever be released. (Ian Whitcomb, from the liner notes to *The Best of Ian Whitcomb*, Rhino Records, 1985)

Ian McGarry remembers the birth of the song slightly differently. 'I remember playing it distinctly,' he says, 'but after that…it might have been the end of the session…we certainly had to play it a few times to get it right.' The 'Turn On Song', as it was initially called, is a pacy blues romp driven by a punchy rhythm, with the instincts of the group somewhat blunted. In comparison, the comical vocals are up front and grab the listener's attention, most notably the orgasmic stuttering and panting and that kooky phrase Ian had brought back from his Seattle tryst. The effect was somewhat akin to hearing a camp Roger Daltrey of The Who with a public school background singing in high falsetto. Whitcomb altered the song slightly when he was in the US a couple of months later, adding tambourine and shortening the running time.

> **JERRY DENNON** That was not my choice as a follow-up single. When we finished and I had become familiar with all the things we had done I had some favourites. I don't think I got back on the aeroplane thinking we had another hit. I hoped we did, there were a couple of things I really liked, but it was not 'You Turn Me On'.

Pop music by its very nature is immediate, fleeting and ephemeral. Like all successful pop songs, 'You Turn Me On' stays true to these criteria: it has no pretension to high art, it was conceived without much forethought, it is simple and it is *fun*. And it sold in its hundreds of thousands.

Ian Whitcomb began to get an inkling of this in June, 1965. Despite his reservations, Tower released the throwaway single and it began to climb the national charts, overcoming some obstacles on the way – the Mayor of Portland, Oregon, had got the single banned due to its suggestive content. The promotional machine kicked in immediately, ready to milk the single

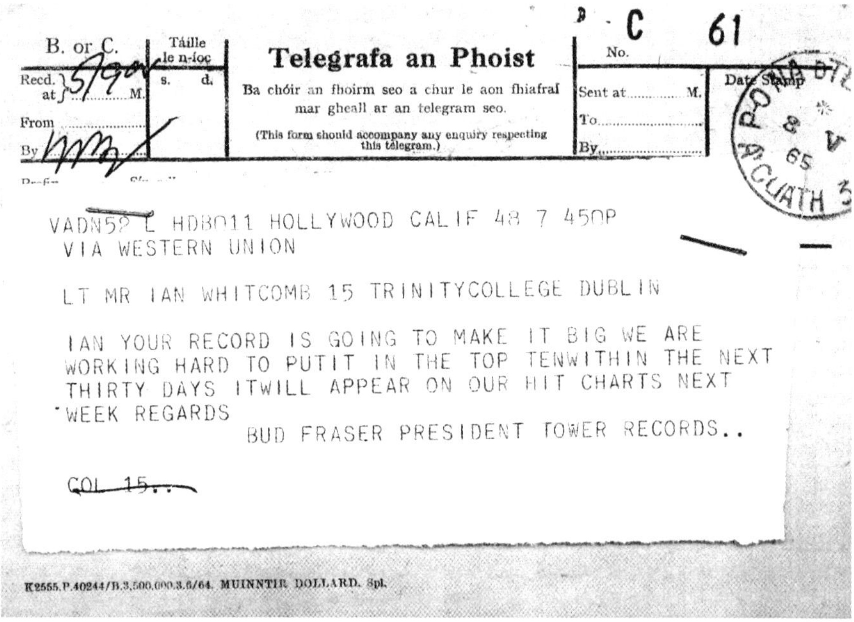

B. or C.
Táille le n-íoc
s. d.
Recd. at
From
By

Telegrafa an Phoist

Ba chóir an fhoirm seo a chur le aon fhiafraí mar gheall ar an telegram seo.

(This form should accompany any enquiry respecting this telegram.)

No. C 61
Sent at ... M.
To
By
Date Stamp

VADN52 L HDB011 HOLLYWOOD CALIF 48 7 450P
VIA WESTERN UNION

LT MR IAN WHITCOMB 15 TRINITYCOLLEGE DUBLIN

IAN YOUR RECORD IS GOING TO MAKE IT BIG WE ARE WORKING HARD TO PUTIT IN THE TOP TENWITHIN THE NEXT THIRTY DAYS ITWILL APPEAR ON OUR HIT CHARTS NEXT WEEK REGARDS
BUD FRASER PRESIDENT TOWER RECORDS..

COL 15..

K2555.P.40244/B.3,500,000.3.6/64. MUINNTIR DOLLARD. Spl.

'You Turn Me On' starts to break big

until its udders were dry and shrivelled. Jerry Dennon arranged for Ian to appear on US network TV show *Shindig*, minus the rest of Bluesville. In his book *Rock Odyssey*, Whitcomb suggests that the head of Jerden was unable to secure visas for the band, who he says seemed reluctant to leave their homeland in any case. Today, Ian claims that there was never any intention of bringing over the others, instead a series of pick-up bands were used for promotional appearances.

IAN McGARRY I don't seem to remember us ever being asked as a band to go to the States. Because I think we would have seriously considered it. Maybe it wasn't financially possible, maybe Jerden or Capitol records didn't want to [take us]. [Whitcomb] tried to put a band together in America, but he could never repeat the sound [of Bluesville].

DEKE O BRIEN I think we were asked to go, because [Dennon] saw the band and liked the whole [set-up]. I couldn't go. Mick would have gone but he wasn't going to go without me. It ended up [Ian] was better off on his own at that stage, financially for Jerry [anyway]. In retrospect had that band gone over there's no doubt it would have been very, very big.

MICK MOLLOY We were pretty young at the time. Certainly Jerry Dennon never asked us, he never offered us anything, to the best of my memory. It was never put on the table to bring the band over to America, because if that had happened I would

> have had to approach my parents and it never got to that stage at all. Looking back on it now that's the kind of opportunity we would have liked to take. As far as Jerry Dennon was concerned Ian [Whitcomb] was the man and that was it, he was dealing with him and he wasn't bothered with us.

> **JERRY DENNON** Getting Ian into [the USA] was not easy. I had to go get work permits for him and green card status and all of that and work with US immigration which was not a lot of fun. The fact that we were able just to get him in the country was amazing enough, but I wouldn't have wanted to even imagine bringing in the whole group. The other issue was economics. The cost of bringing a whole group over, at the level we were functioning at, at that time, would have been prohibitive.

Ian Whitcomb had no doubt that he was deserving of his shot at the big time. 'The fact is that if I hadn't been there pushing and shoving and doing my thing, we'd never have got anywhere, there wouldn't have been any record.'

> **MICK MOLLOY** There's usually a lead singer or focal point in any band, but as often as not it's the band that puts them in a favourable position and invariably they fuck off when they get a few legs up the ladder, away they go and thank you very much and goodbye. So obviously that makes you feel fed up. It's the story of musicians, you're in it for the music and then you end up with nothing at the end of it all.

Arriving first in New York, Whitcomb was briefed in the etiquette of miming on TV, appearing on some local shows with such disparate luminaries as Aretha Franklin and Dizzy Gillespie. In LA, legendary promotions man George Sherlock (immortalised in The Rolling Stones' snide 'tribute' song 'The Under Assistant West Coast Promotion Man') was assigned to plugging duties, initiating Ian into the murky dealings of the Los Angeles music world. That summer, Ian's existence consisted of a weary chain of non-stop lip-synched TV appearances (ABC deemed 'You Turn Me On' too suggestive and insisted he perform 'This Sporting Life' on *Shindig* instead), radio station visits and star-package tours. Initially he felt bemused and ultimately depressed by the whole process – wearing a deerstalker hat in a crass attempt to emphasise his British-ness, shunted around from one studio or sports hall to the next, sleeping overnight on spluttering Greyhound buses as the Mid-West's less cosmopolitan centres flashed past the grimy windowpanes. As a result of all this slog 'You Turn Me On' achieved historical status by becoming the first Irish-produced single to make the American Top 10, eventually reaching

Ian Whitcomb appears on Dick Clark's American Bandstand

number eight in July of 1965. It nestled snugly alongside The Rolling Stones' '(I Can't Get No) Satisfaction' and The Byrds' 'Mr. Tambourine Man'. Back in Ireland, despite the single achieving impressive domestic sales, the rest of Bluesville didn't feel the same level of hysteria as that experienced by their lead singer across the Atlantic. Mick Molloy: 'I don't remember anything particular. I certainly didn't feel famous.'

In the fast moving machinations of the music industry a follow-up single was needed. Bluesville had recorded a song for their album called 'Nervous' that had been going down well in the Dublin clubs, using a similar template to the chart hit – riff cribbed from one of rock's forefathers (this time Chicago bluesman Willie Dixon), simplistic lyrics and quirky vocal tic. (In time Whitcomb would have to settle with the legendary bluesman and split the writing credit. 'Years later I met him,' recalls Ian, 'and he said, "Oh, that's all right man, it's just an old blues thing, I got it from something else as well!"') Over in the United States, Whitcomb thought the original version unsuitable for commercial radio and decided to re-record Nervous at RCA Studios with Stones engineer Dave Hassinger, assisted by experienced session musicians such as James Burton (later to play with Elvis Presley and Gram Parsons) and Delaney Bramlett. This version gives some credence to Ian McGarry's belief that the Bluesville sound couldn't be recreated in America. There is a dry sheen to it that pales in comparison to the unpretentious rawness captured in the Henry Street studios.

No matter, Whitcomb's fifteen minutes of fame were up. The pop music world was evolving into the more erudite rock world, and despite traipsing around the radio stations plugging the life out of the song, the lightweight single barely scraped into the lower reaches of the Billboard Top 50. There was some consolation though, as the faltering heartbeat of 'You Turn Me On' had been revived and proved very popular in the gay bars of California, no doubt due to the camp falsetto and *risqué* sexual content. ('Anybody who was prepared to out themselves at that time, the pink dollar, was definitely on board!' says Deke O'Brien with a chuckle.)

Ian Whitcomb had to make one last trip back to Trinity College in order to sit his final exams, leaving a Dick Clark *Caravan of Stars* tour to be replaced by Welsh sex bomb Tom Jones. The hours he whiled away poring over heavy textbooks on the tour buses evidently paid off as he was awarded a second class degree. His tutors looked kindly on his rock 'n roll antics, taking into account the effect his debauched American adventures must have had on his studies. Bluesville the band were being led by Peter Adler by then, and a replacement singer, later more famous as Led Zeppelin publicist and 'tester of Paul McCartney's grass at Apple records', usurped Whitcomb briefly from his previous position.

> **IAN WHITCOMB** I used to do a song called 'Dinner With Drac' which had been a hit in the 50s for John Zacherle, and I used to wear a cloak [when performing it]. I came back and I went to see the band and I was standing at the side of the stage and I saw BP Fallon doing my act, doing all my gestures and everything. I think he was doing 'Nervous' as well. I got so annoyed and as he came off stage I hit him on the head with a rolled up copy of *Billboard* magazine.

The word amongst the fans was that Fallon had taken over management of Bluesville. There was some acrimony in the ranks over this and he was blamed by some for the split that resulted shortly after. Whatever actually happened, Bluesville did come to an end shortly after Whitcomb returned from the United States, re-uniting for a final one-off performance at The Trinity Ball in 1966. Mick Molloy and Deke O'Brien were asked by Pete Selwood to join a young soul band he was managing called The Chosen Few. Ian McGarry telephoned childhood friend Colm Wilkinson and put together the more jazz influenced Action, with Peter Adler joining the duo in the initial stages.

> **IAN McGARRY** You got the feeling that was the end of an era. Everybody split, went their own way, we made the album yes, but there was no real attempt made at holding the band together. Or even part of it.

Despite the failure of the second single, Ian Whitcomb soldiered on in America for two more years trying to recreate the success of his one smash hit. Someone at his record company suggested that old music hall numbers would be the next happening craze amongst the hipsters, but then again when presented with the chance to sign The Beatles, Decca Records claimed that guitar groups were going out of fashion. Tower Records did release an album of ragtime and vaudeville songs by Whitcomb in 1966 and also a tribute to the original 50s rock 'n rollers, *Sock Me Some Rock,* in 1968 but neither found favour with the record buying public. Both vintage music hall and primitive rockabilly were very much out of the step with the prevailing psychedelic and hard rock scenes.

Since those days, Ian's career has been nothing short of colourful – he produced an album for actress Mae West in 1969; continued his studies into traditional forms of British music to become a renowned expert in the field; hosted the first series of the BBC's *Old Grey Whistle Test*; wrote and recorded music for a Bugs Bunny movie; made spoken word albums, jazz and comedy records and even a disco pastiche. In latter years he became a film soundtrack composer, DJ, voice-over artist and bit-part actor (appearing in *Star Trek's Voyager* TV series). Currently he is a music history teacher employed by the state of California and occasionally gives the odd live performance, although 'You Turn Me On' is not part of his set.

Bluesville's recording career lasted a little longer after the failure of 'Nervous', unbeknownst to the band members in Ireland. A single was put out with the Jagger/Richards composition 'As Tears Go By' as the A-side and Bob Dylan's 'Don't Think Twice It's Alright' on the B-side. It was recorded by Whitcomb and a gaggle of US session players. By his own admission, Whitcomb was never really a born rock 'n' roller. Attired in a black ruffled silk shirt and glamorous fur coat for one promotional photo shoot, he stares at the camera with a mixture of embarrassment and awkwardness. Much more of a music hall vaudevillian he would regularly return to the traditional sounds of his homeland throughout his life in pursuit of a career in music. The legacy of 'You Turn Me On' is still felt in a number of ways, buried in the foundations and communal experiences of rock music. To this day people approach Ian in shops, on airplanes and in the street, nostalgic about that golden summer of 1965 when the song soundtracked their lives, encapsulating what it meant to be young and filled with energy and desire.

> **IAN WHITCOMB** It's all about attitude and rhythm. Like all good rock 'n' roll the words are nonsense, but it doesn't matter. It's about sound and fury. I'm very proud of it; it's still a very exciting record.

It is hardly surprising that forty years later there is still some confusion and a little bit of cagey suspicion about who really benefited, and more to the point who *deserved* to benefit, from the innovative Irish group's success. Furthermore, some of the band feels that the missed opportunity to play to audiences in the United States denied them a chance to progress their careers in directions very different to those that were subsequently followed. None of the members of Bluesville were great financial beneficiaries of the success of the record however.

> **IAN WHITCOMB** The money that I made off that record is made through the publishing, because I wrote the song. But I haven't seen any money from sales of that record since 1965, nothing. Capitol keep re-releasing it and they never pay me, as an artist, anything at all. Somebody at Tower told me Jerry Dennon took most of the money. I don't know what he took but he never paid me the right amount of money. That happened to most rock 'n' roll people at that time.

> **JERRY DENNON** It happens 99 times out of 100, the recording artist doesn't understand their contracts. The record contract says if you're going to be in Eamonn Andrews Studio for a

month and we run up a $10,000 bill that's all deductible from royalties. Everything that had to be paid had to be recouped out of royalties. He got paid very handsomely along the way. Also I gave him his publishing [rights] later which I didn't need to do.

The lead singer is happy to admit that all of the members of Bluesville contributed to the song's triumph.

IAN WHITCOMB One of the main reasons for the success of ['You Turn Me On'] is not my crazy vocals, it's to do with the terrific playing, it's a helluva good rhythm sound. Rock musicians of the time said to me, 'Who's that drummer, he's doing incredible patterns on the bass drum', and nobody had been doing that in rock 'n' roll before.

When Bluesville were formed, the pop/rock music scene in Ireland was primitive and undeveloped, a shabby poor cousin to the showbands' sophistication. Then, budding musicians heard these exotic R&B sounds, realised you could be successful playing this type of music, saved up for the guitars on display in the dusty shop windows and went on to form groups of their own.

IAN WHITCOMB I remember Rory Gallagher saying, 'That was the band that turned me on', and other people have said that was the first band that really gripped me.

PETER ADLER Someone who knew our band back then said, 'Was the film *The Commitments* based on Bluesville?' There was a remarkable similarity in the music, because we were doing that sort of music and probably the first band in Ireland to do so.

DITCH CASSIDY (singer with The Kingbees and The News): Seeing bands like Bluesville gave me a lot more confidence in what I was doing. After the success of 'You Turn Me On' I could see this was the way to go.

PAUL ASHFORD (bass, The Chosen Few): They were the group responsible for me getting into the music business. When I saw them in The Barn I was about fourteen years old and I went right, that's it, that's what I wanna do, because they were the best thing I've ever seen in this country. They were like The Rolling Stones at the time, 1963-64. They were the first real beat group in Dublin. We formed The Chosen Few from seeing Bluesville.

The first clubs specifically tailored for the beat scene were established during Bluesville's lifetime, most notably Sound City and The No. 5 Club. Yet despite the impression that Bluesville left on the nascent pop music scene in Dublin and Ireland, their impact and importance on Irish rock music has been generally overlooked.

IAN WHITCOMB I'm an embarrassment to [music critics and historians], because I don't fit their theories. Here I am, an upper middle class Englishman who was at Trinity College, who does music hall, who plays the ukulele. They think, 'How could this guy be in any way a serious influence on rock n roll?' They just dismiss me completely as a one-hit freak.

IAN McGARRY It's a pity in a way that what we achieved has been airbrushed out because we were the first to break the American Top 10. Even to this day if you pick up books about the Irish rock and rhythm 'n' blues scene you might get a tiny mention, but that's about it.

BP FALLON (radio and club DJ, 60s TV personality and writer): Bluesville were genuinely great, one of the very best groups from Ireland ever. They had balls and roughness and they had intelligence and humour. And they had sex appeal. The girls used get all kinds of feral excitations, including the studenty types from TCD who normally wouldn't embrace such animalistic behaviour in public. Ian Whitcomb was a tremendous front man with an ear for contagious quirky songs and he could holler and poke at the piano with élan, his Jaggered lips sprouting cunning lyrics that the little girls hipped to hotly. [The group] roared and soared like a train almost out of control, the music just making the corners and rampaging on, lifting you with exhilaration and making you hot. Like all great rock'n'roll!

DEKE O BRIEN Without a question it was the biggest, most successful band in Ireland in the rock 'n' roll/beat thing. It was untouchable, there was nothing near.

Part Three

Up until the end of 1964 there were no specific venues in Dublin's city centre to cater for beat groups. There was the odd record hop in small venues, dance studios or community halls, where a DJ would spin records from his collection to crowds of like-minded enthusiasts. The live beat scene developed in local suburbs north and south of the Liffey, thanks to weekly gigs at parish halls, tennis and rugby clubs. The sound systems in these places were rudimentary at best, and the very nature of the venues meant that only the same locals were returning every week. The nationwide popularity of The Greenbeats, the large crowds flocking to hear groups like The Strangers, and the growing success of Bluesville throughout early 1965 soon convinced some wily entrepreneurs that there was a strong demand for this type of new beat music.

One such budding young businessman was Tony Boland, who had returned to his native Ireland at the end of 1963 after three years in London writing a pop column for the *Irish Independent* and scribbling publicity handouts for his friend Andrew Loog Oldham. Tony's first job when he came home was as a showband publicist, a profession he soon realised was financially lucrative but creatively stifling. Still only twenty years old, Tony had seen the kids crammed into Ted Carroll's Rhythm 'n' Blues Club at Longford Tennis Club, and was equally familiar with the numerous clubs sprouting up in London and Liverpool, such as the Marquee, Beat City and The Cavern. Most groups in Dublin were having a very hard time breaking into the potentially well-paid ballroom circuit.

> **TONY BOLAND** None of the showband guys wanted beat groups appearing in ballrooms. They had this notion that a band was a 'dance band'. They felt they could keep an audience entertained all night. There was a whole industry built around the showbands and they understood that. Most of the hall managers managed a band as well so they had it [sewn up] at both ends.

With this in mind Boland purchased the lease for a building on Burgh Quay, centrally located just off O'Connell Street, Dublin's main thoroughfare. The basement, which had formerly housed an old fun palace, stretched underneath the two adjoining buildings, creating a large warren of rooms where raucous beat groups played every Thursday, Friday and Saturday nights. A young BP Fallon, who worked as an office boy for Boland, compered the shows. On the opening night, Dublin's two biggest R&B star attractions were booked into the new club, known simply as Sound City, and the city's teenage beat fans turned up in their droves to see them.

Press ad for Tony Boland's new beat club

> **TONY BOLAND** There was a headline in the *Irish Independent* the following day that the whole of Burgh Quay was jammed. It was a seething black mass and the police went hysterical. They hadn't coped with anything like that, they went absolutely ballistic. On that opening night we had Ian Whitcomb and Bluesville and The Greenbeats, and I think we had BP doing records.

> **KEVIN DUNNE** That was a scary night. The whole of Burgh Quay was jammed with young people trying to get in, the place was stuffed. They were up on the wall of the Liffey, we were [upstairs] looking down on them. I was scared somebody was going to go in [to the water] but nobody did anyway.

The basement was dark, and dilapidated, the other world ambience added to by the presence of old distorting mirrors left over from the fun palace. Young beat fan Muriel Duff, fifteen years old at the time, who had been going to record hops and beat gigs in Ballyfermot, heard about the new clubs opening and decided to take the plunge and see what was going on in the laneways and side streets of Dublin.

> **MURIEL DUFF** We went without telling any parents and ended up in a place called Sound City. When I first went in I was absolutely petrified, because it was really new to Dublin, all that kind of thing, the underground places. Sound City at that time was very much the denim crowd – it was denim skirts, denim shirts, denim jeans. And they sat around on cushions; either that or they held the walls up!

During the summer, when the tide was high, the Liffey's rising waters would come up through the drains and flood the venue causing a potentially lethal situation for musicians and their equipment, not to mention the lingering stench that would take days to clear out. Nevertheless, the popularity of Sound City soon had groups playing there most nights, with the odd jazz band and folk act included for variety. Tony Boland had learnt a trick or two from Andrew Loog Oldham in London when it came to

Sound City hosts Bluesville singer's return from the US, Autumn 1965

publicity stunts and, along with his business partner Rusty Simpson, set about promoting his new club in a variety of unorthodox fashions.

TONY BOLAND There was a newspaper strike on and it was an August bank holiday weekend. We were trying to publicise gigs and we were stuck. So I remember we got five bass amps and we brought them up on the roof of Sound City and it was a glorious summer's day. We linked up a record player to them and we all got arrested! We actually got put in the clink overnight to teach us a lesson for disturbing the peace. I remember at another stage we did fantastic posters, and we used to go out putting up the posters ourselves. We'd put [them] up on the boards right beside the showbands' [ones] and the showband people would come along and cover ours. So we decided how could we best do this? We covered the O'Connell monument with posters and got done again! And we got newspaper headlines for getting done, that was great publicity. We worked out the fine was only a fiver, that was cheap.

In 1965 the showband scene was about to hit its biggest peak in terms of popularity and revenue generation. But there was a huge market of beat-hungry teenagers, in Dublin especially, that showband and ballroom managers didn't understand or didn't wish to understand, content as they were with the crowds flocking to their wholesome nights out. There were no set rules for opening up a new club, putting on a record hop, or forming and promoting your own group. You just went ahead and did it. All you needed was a good idea, some talent and plenty of drive, and then things could open up for you. It was this innovative spirit in the face of an indifferent and sometimes hostile establishment that helped give birth to Ireland's beat scene.

TONY BOLAND I did it on bank borrowings. I remember going into the National Bank on College Green at the time. Somebody told me you had to have a business plan. I didn't know what a business plan was. The guy said, 'I haven't a clue what you're talking about, but you seem so passionate about it I'm going to give you the money and it could be the biggest

> mistake I've ever made in my life.' It was unheard of, I wasn't even twenty-one and in theory not old enough to have an overdraft in those days!

Around the city, others were in similar situations, renting spaces in Georgian houses, getting a basic record player in, sending out a few flyers and gathering friends and music lovers together to experience the new Merseybeat and Motown sounds. Danny Hughes and Stevie Bolger, who would both become fixtures on the beat scene throughout the 60s as DJs and journalists, pasted old album covers to a basement wall in Mount Street in May 1965, and opened Dublin's very own Cavern Club, which ran every Sunday night. On Monday morning Hughes was back at his desk in school. Tony Boland had financed his own move to England from the profits of his Sunday night record hop in a basement on North Frederick Street four years earlier.

> **TONY BOLAND** You could do things. And young people could do things. Most of the people running the showbands and all that really were older guys, in their forties and fifties, so this was an 'our generation' thing.

As Sound City's reputation spread and 1964 turned into 1965 the beat group scene in Ireland really began to take off. There was quite a bit of commotion surrounding the first single release by Bluesville, 'This Sporting Life', and even more excitement when they climbed into the US Top 10 in July 1965. After all they had beaten Ireland's beloved showbands to the title of first ever Irish act to have a smash in America. The momentum of Bluesville was difficult to maintain however, as their lead vocalist was making regular trips out to the United States, leaving the collective somewhat directionless back in Ireland.

> **TONY BOLAND** I always felt Bluesville were the ones who could make it internationally, but I mean the whole band, not just Ian Whitcomb. Ian is very charismatic and quite brilliant musically. The only thing that [stopped them]...they were a funny bunch, they didn't gel very well as people, and Peter Adler and Ian would be very competitive with each other. The egos in the band were unbelievable.

Out of the ashes of the group developed two of the beat scene's most popular acts during its early days. The Mod-sounding 'Action' (not to be confused with the identically named and moderately successful group formed in London around the same time) comprised the trio of Ian McGarry, Peter Adler and Brian Lynch from Bluesville, replaced on bass occasionally by Peter Williams, with Ken Rigley on guitar. Colm Wilkinson, later to experience international fame with starring roles in theatre productions of *Les Miserables* and *The Phantom Of The Opera*, shared vocals with Adler. Although they were nominally an R&B group The Action played a variety of styles, introducing a strong jazz element into their sound, and even venturing, occasionally, into Irish ballad territory. Bob Kelly remembers the group as a more professional unit than Bluesville, and musically more advanced.

> **BOB KELLY** (beat group/showband guitar player): McGarry was a serious drummer, Ken Rigley was a serious jazz guitar player. Colm Wilkinson was doing things like 'I Was Framed' and 'St. James' Infirmary', standard blues things of the day, and doing it with great force and conviction. There were huge crowds there to watch them. Peter Adler was very theatrical. They had all watched [Scottish soul singer] Alex Harvey doing his bit, he used to do a complete mime act.

Although they never got to release any records officially (in the early days there were offers from CBS, Immediate and Tower), a four-track tape of a performance in Mount Merrion's Stella House, where they used to play two band sessions with Belfast's Them, was privately made. This reel-to-reel tape includes the Nina Simone favourite 'Gin House Blues', Muddy Waters' 'The Blind Man' and Irish standard 'Danny Boy', a diverse selection indicative of their range. The group also infamously contributed to a memorable episode of *The Showband Show*, the repercussions of which reverberated around the beat and showband scene for quite some time after, rigorously delineating the split between the two camps.

> **PETER ADLER** We were on as the kind of oddity on *The Showband Show*. We did 'Dinner With Drac' on Telefís Éireann which caused a real scandal. We did it quite deliberately and all the priests started writing into the *Evening Herald* and the *Evening Press* [talking about] these Satans coming out of Trinity College, which of course was just the publicity we wanted. It meant all the teenage girls would then leap to our defence. There were these wonderful letters going back and forth in the press, amongst pro-Action fans which were mostly teenage girls, and the stalwarts of the Catholic Church who were very against us.

Irish TV chat show host Gay Byrne was suitably impressed with The Action's performance, and went into the studio to invite Peter Adler onto *The Late Late Show* that very night to discuss the generational music gap with his renowned father Larry, who happened to be playing in Ireland. Adler Jr. always had a reputation as one of the trendiest hipsters on Dublin's beat scene. Dressed head to toe in sharp threads and permanently wearing shades, he projected a rebellious and aloof beatnik stance. However, the reason he donned the black glasses was not about looking cool.

> **PETER ADLER** I had a major eye problem and still do. Everyone thought I was a drugged out hippie but there was a medical reason for those shades. I suppose it gave me an air of mystery.

It was during his stint with The Action that Peter unexpectedly found himself promoting his *own* single, which resulted from a frivolous brush with some eager bobbies in his native England, during a night out on the tiles with Michael Chaplin, son of silent film star Charlie.

> **PETER ADLER** We'd come back from some party on a Saturday night in London. It was quite a hot night and we were in Marble Arch. People were throwing coins into this fountain. Now I didn't want to get wet but Michael and this other girl leapt in to get the pennies as a sort of joke. And then people gathered and started throwing them coins, me being the coward keeping on the sidelines. These two CID officers arrived eager for promotion and arrested us and charged us with larceny. It was completely hysterical! By the time it got to court on Monday one of the policemen discovered that Michael was Charlie Chaplin's son and that I was Larry Adler's son, so all the newspapers were covering this 'very important' trial. The judge was the son of George Roby (a famous musical comedian) and his court normally had parking fines and prostitutes. It was a very unexciting court. But suddenly he had a hell of a lot of press and he was a star.

The flimsy case was thrown out of court. However, as a result of all the attendant publicity there was a flock of music biz vultures clambering to convince Michael Chaplin to write books, release records or do anything at all possible to earn money exploiting the situation. Larry Page, the well-known impresario who managed The Kinks and The Troggs, signed Michael up to release a pop single, but went about writing the songs in a very unorthodox manner.

> **PETER ADLER** He had a psychiatrist who doubled as a songwriter so he analysed Michael on his couch and then wrote these two songs based upon Michael's character. I was hired to play harmonica, being Larry's son.

The songs were given the revelatory titles of 'I Am What I Am' and

'Restless', Michael Chaplin singing wildly out of tune as Peter Adler wailed away on harmonica in the background. Unworried by the questionable quality Larry Page decided to release another record, this time commissioning Peter to compose both sides, with a full orchestra providing the backing. It was only at this point that Page realized Michael Chaplin couldn't sing a note. He asked Peter to take the lead vocal, and the single, 'Love And Not Hate', a protest song of sorts (and musically a straight rip-off of Sonny and Cher's 'I Got You Babe'), was released in England, Ireland and America in October 1965. It was heavily rotated on Radio Caroline but its chances of success suffered a blow when it became the subject of a BBC ban for the following 'offensive' lines:

To those who are not yet born
Who from the womb are not yet torn
Don't make a move, buddy you wait
Until the world is full of love, not hate

Although a hugely popular draw on the club scene, there were musical differences within the ranks of The Action which resulted in Peter Adler's departure from the group around February 1966.

> **PETER ADLER** There was a philosophical debate going on at the time with Action about the direction the band should take and Ian [McGarry] felt very strongly that we were giving up our musical soul in favour of bigger audiences and I was really the villain of the piece because I was fronting the more commercial music. It became very difficult because Ian was controlling the numbers and the girls wanted to hear more of the stuff I was doing and Ian wanted to keep more of the serious stuff.

Adler decided to throw in his lot with the teen market and got together with a group of musicians who had come over to Ireland from the UK, called The Next In Line. Their big coming out gig was as support to The Hollies at the National Stadium on 3 March 1966 (they also supported The Who at the National Stadium on 7 May where they did a spoof rendition of 'My Generation' in the guise of a drunken showband). This short-lived group, conspicuously fashionable and highly theatrical on stage, was influenced equally by British Mod groups such as The Small Faces and The Who, as well as the fresh young sound of Detroit's Tamla Motown. The players in The Next In Line were not as musically adept as those in The Action, and after one single release in the summer backing Peter Adler ('Gonna Turn My Life Around'), the band called it a day. The Action fizzled out shortly after.

As three members of Bluesville headed down the road of Oscar Brown Jr and Nina Simone covers, the twin guitar axis of Deke O'Brien and Mick Molloy joined the newly birthed Chosen Few, a soul group who were being managed at the time by Pete Selwood, the ex-RAF self-trained engineer who had taped that first session with Ian Whitcomb and his group the previous year in Merrion Square. Deke O'Brien, in particular, had been enthralled by the records of Otis Redding and Marvin Gaye that his friends had brought back from the US, and joined Selwood's group on the premise that his longtime buddy Mick come with him. Fran O'Toole (keyboards and vocals, later of The Miami Showband), Paul Ashford (bass, also later of the Miami), Robbie Brennan (drums) and Donie Ryan (saxophone) made up the sextet. Their main residency was at the Cavalier Club, situated through the archway on Montague Lane just off Harcourt Street, a venue managed by Dermot Latham, who would later open up a string of Cavalier clubs in other Irish towns as the popularity of beat music spread across the country. It was in the Cavalier Club on its opening night, St. Patrick's Day 1966, that Selwood recorded a reportedly blistering live performance of his group supporting British soul sensations The Alex Harvey Band. Unfortunately, like The Action, their music would never see the light of day after the quarter-inch tapes were mislaid, never to be found again. Deke O'Brien and Mick Molloy also re-united with their old pal Peter Adler in The Next In Line on the support bill to The Who, where high profile broadcaster Terry Wogan was compère for the night.

> **PAUL ASHFORD** We were known as The Few, [our fans] had this kind of chant, 'Rave! Rave! Rave! Sex! Sex! Sex!' There was nothing in it; there was no access to alcohol or anything. We had a gang, a busload in the Stadium and they were all shouting at the end, 'We want The Few! We want The Few!' And Terry Wogan says, 'Get off lads, they're shouting for The Who.' No… it's the fucking Few, not The Who!

When not supporting visiting UK groups, a regular spot for The Chosen Few was the Caroline Club in Dún Laoghaire, which had a reputation of being one of the most electrically-charged venues around, with a wild and uninhibited clientele. This distinction earned the club an inquisitive visit by the police, who infiltrated a performance by the group one frenzied night.

> **DEKE O BRIEN** The crowds would go berserk, pulling their T-shirts off, shouting, 'Sex! Sex!' The cops were in miniskirts and wigs, making notes, undercover.

> **MICK MOLLOY** Fucking idiot police. I don't know if they were sent by the local priests or what. It was hot and sweaty in there, everyone was dancing like mad, having a great time. I don't know why the cops felt they had to bust the place but they did. We all ended up in court. The copper who was giving evidence

said about the unruly crowd, 'and they were milling around the place and there wasn't one of them wearing a tie'... What a gobshite.

The Chosen Few, 1965 L-R: Fran O'Toole, Mick Molloy, Deke O'Brien, Alan Hyland, Donie Ryan, Paul Ashford

The Chosen Few members were charged with inciting the crowd to indecency, nudity and obscenity and were fined. Similar to the shocking *exposé* on Ted Carroll's Rhythm 'n' Blues Club, the story was splashed across the front page of the *Evening Press*. Deke's real name, Dermot, was used in the report which only caused further consternation when a high profile accordion player of the same name indignantly contacted the newspaper and insisted they print another story denying that the respectable folk musician had anything to do with such an unpleasant incident.

Although it seems quaint and laughable now, it was not uncommon for rock musicians to fall foul of the fussy authorities, who were genuinely puzzled by and suspicious of the influence that these long hairs had over teenagers. One musician who on occasion found himself the subject of such unwelcome attention was Patrick 'Ditch' Cassidy (born 16 July 1947 in Drogheda). He fronted the widely celebrated R&B group The Kingbees and established a reputation for being one of the most gifted singers in Ireland during the 1960s.

RONAN COLLINS Ditch was a legend; he was like a combination of Muddy Waters and James Brown. Extraordinary.

From an early age Ditch's one true love was singing. A fleeting encounter with The Beatles in the kitchens of the Gresham Hotel convinced him that his future lay in rock 'n' roll. He was working as a commis chef on the night of 7 November 1963 when the Fab Four dashed by him through the maze of pots and pans, pursued by a libidinous group of baying teenage girls. The incident left a lasting impression. The first serious beat group Cassidy fronted was called The Shadracks, who played bottom of the bill at the opening night of Sound City. It didn't take long for the four-piece group to secure more frequent bookings in other city venues, including the No. 5 Club on Harcourt Street (opened on 5 March 1965) where Alan Weinrib, manager of The Kingbees, spotted Ditch's talent and approached him with an offer to join his band that very month. Their original singer was 'a bit straightlaced', according to Kingbees lead guitarist Jaye Malone. 'We wanted something more raunchy.' Initially less than convinced of the group's musical ability, Ditch spent the spring months of 1965 standing in with a variety of other beat groups before finally committing to The Kingbees after Weinrib offered a steady wage of £15 per week.

The Kingbees had taken their name from the classic John Lee Hooker song 'I'm A Kingbee', via the cover version that appeared on The Rolling Stones' influential debut LP. In the early days their repertoire consisted of gutsy R&B peppered with the sweet soul sounds of the American South – tunes like 'Smokestack Lightnin', 'Dimples', 'Hoochie Coochie Man', and songs by Sam and Dave, Otis Redding and Solomon Burke – mixed with some pop hits of the day. The line-up consisted of Jaye Malone on lead guitar, Howard Speir on rhythm guitar, Jim Hudson on bass, Maurice Boland on drums and Ditch, with a belt full of harmonicas hitched to his waist, roaring out the vocals from the front. Between April and June 1965 the band played practically every venue in the rapidly developing club scene in Dublin, occasionally venturing out to the provinces of Munster and Ulster, with little consideration given to practical tour scheduling. Every night after the show, no matter what far flung rural hall they ended up playing in, everyone piled back into the van for the long drive home. An appearance on Telifís Éireann in April dressed in smart suits boosted their profile in the No. 5 club; an audition for Decca Records soon followed but nothing concrete materialised from it.

The Kingbees early publicity shot, 1965

The Kingbees were frequently given appointments few other scruffy beat groups would have dreamt about – posh hunt balls, private garden parties adorned with pristine white marquees, and on one occasion a function for the head of Mattel Toys at his luxurious house in Dalkey (at which, it is reported,

Princess Margaret and Mark Williams made an unannounced appearance by helicopter! Drummer Maurice Boland's wealthy family had connections amongst the upper echelons of Dublin society, a situation he used to the group's considerable advantage. Although The Kingbees were paid handsomely for such engagements, the bread and butter still lay in the small city clubs, playing for anything between £5 and £45, for performances lasting up to three or four hours (Bruce Springsteen would have been very proud of the Dublin boys' commitment to rock 'n' roll redemption!). Their one regular gig was playing to the supportive fan base at Sound City on Wednesday nights, but they also played one-off shows at bigger halls supporting acts like Bluesville and The Kult (featuring the young and not-yet folkie Paul Brady) at The Top Hat in Dún Laoghaire in front of crowds of up to 600 punters.

Although the strident rhythm 'n' blues and passionate soul of The Kingbees was enough to stir up the emotions of the teenage audience, Ditch Cassidy brought an extra dimension to the group's stage performance by adding some outrageous theatrics to the already boiling atmosphere. He had seen Peter Adler of The Action dressed in long black cape, performing John Zacherle's 'Dinner With Drac' at the boisterous Caroline Club in Dún Laoghaire. Carrying on a tradition begun by Ian Whitcomb, Ditch upped the ante a few notches. Hiding a plastic bottle of tomato ketchup (usually lifted from the local Wimpy bar) inside his luxuriant gown, he would crane his neck surreptitiously to ingest a mouthful at the appropriate juncture and spray it generously over the front rows as he delivered the crowning line '...and for dessert, there was bloooooooooood!'

The Kingbees L-R: Ditch Cassidy, Maurice Boland, Jim Hudson, Jaye Malone, Mick Rafferty

When The Kingbees were supporting The Everly Brothers at the National Stadium, their vocalist decided that even this outrageous stunt could be bettered, and arranged to be brought on stage in a coffin. Unfortunately, the two brothers of guitarist Jaye Malone, employed as 'pallbearers' for the evening, found the steep steps down to the stage a little tricky to handle, not to mention having to cope with the weight of a fully grown man and a huge box of solid wood. As they progressed gingerly down the stairs the coffin began to wobble under their arms, the speed of their shuffling feet quickened and Ditch Cassidy found himself tipped face first onto the old boxing ring. The coffin lid and box came crashing down around his head. Unbothered by this he proceeded later in the evening with another bizarre addition to the show – wielding a machete, he leapt into the crowd and chased a group of screaming young girls out of the venue and into the street as the rest of the band carried on playing, oblivious to the whereabouts of their lead singer.

In the summer of 1965 Alan Weinrib departed as manager of The Kingbees (over unresolved money issues) and Howard Speir vacated the rhythm guitar slot around the same time. Tony Boland, who had set up a company called Tempo Productions that March, along with a record label of the same name, took over management of the group. Soon after, The Kingbees appeared in a promotional film miming to a track called 'Sound City Beat'. This inconsequential instrumental, written and performed almost entirely by John Paul Jones (additional guitar flourishes came courtesy of his pal and session stalwart Jimmy Page, and Ian McGarry of The Action played drums), was attributed to a non-existent outfit called The John Paul Jones Orchestra. Jones, who had come over to Ireland at the invitation of Boland, was occasionally spotted in the basement club at Sound City playing the Hammond organ in impromptu jam sessions with temporary amalgams of musicians from popular beat groups. 'Sound City Beat' actually turned up as the B-side to a single release on Tempo from a boy and girl folk duo called Rosemary and Howard.

Various rhythm guitarists stepped in temporarily to play with The Kingbees after Howard Speir's departure until Mick Rafferty joined as a permanent member in July. On Friday 3 September, through their manager's influence, the group got a chance to meet inspirations and idols The Rolling Stones, who were staying in the old Intercontinental Hotel (now Jurys) on their Irish tour. The two lead singers chatted amicably about their blues influences, noting how both groups' names came from lines in blues classics. The Kingbees were also present in the pandemonium backstage at the Adelphi Cinema when all hell broke loose during a mini-riot which saw the Stones almost assaulted on stage by their Dublin fans. The scenes are brilliantly captured in little seen documentary, 'Charlie Is My Darling', shot on the Stones tour of Ireland that brought them to Belfast and Dublin that September (they had also played the Savoy Theatre in Cork the previous January on a short stopover).

> **DITCH CASSIDY** We were right up the front, [it was] just mind-blowing. We were in awe of them. They looked fantastic, everything about them, they just exuded this charisma, this aura.

That October The Kingbees were in even finer company, playing to the invited guests of Lord Mountcharles Senior at a debutantes' ball in Slane Castle. Photographer and friend of the band, Pay Fay, thought it would be an excellent idea to do a photo shoot of the quintet on the recently collapsed main staircase, a grand backdrop of precious oil paintings and majestic statues, emphasising the contrast between the surly working class malcontents and their opulent surrounds. Sensing the ensuing bad publicity if the pictures were to be published (Slane Castle was a functioning tourist draw at the time) Lord Mountcharles ripped the film out of the photographer's Pentax and refused to hand it back. Relations between host and rock 'n' roll band deteriorated further that evening when Ditch, fuelled with complimentary champagne and enervated by a pounding succession of castle-shaking blues belters, jumped up onto the lid of the precious Steinway piano in the drawing room and began to dance passionately with the priceless Venus De Milo sculpture close at hand.

In March 1966, buoyed by their growing popularity amongst the kids in Dublin, The Kingbees decided to release their debut single. The record, 'My Little Red Book' (written by the prolific and gifted team of Burt Bacharach and Hal David) b/w 'I'm A Kingbee' (Hooker), was cut on the soundstage in Ardmore Studios, County Wicklow, with a dapper John Paul Jones on production duties, sporting a Brian Jones style pageboy haircut. 'He was smoking Gauloises at the time,' Ditch recalls. 'We were so naïve we thought he was smoking dope!' The A-side, which was a minor hit for LA folk-rockers Love, in the US in the same month, was a little too complex for The Kingbees to handle, so a coterie of top session players were drafted in to take their place. John Paul Jones played piano.

> **DITCH CASSIDY** I said to [our manager] Tony [Boland], 'This is a great song, I love it, but how are we going to reproduce this? Have you looked at the band recently, have you seen any keyboards?' He was thinking if it hit we'd get a keyboard player in then.

> **JAYE MALONE** (lead guitar, The Kingbees): We said, 'Why "My Little Red Book"? This is not us.' We're trying to be raunchy, get more rock-y. We weren't into the bubblegum stuff like Herman's Hermits. I couldn't figure it out, but we had to run with this.

The regular line-up of the group played on the more straightforward B-side. The Kingbees appeared on Telefís Éireann's pre-recorded *Pickin' The*

Pops show in June, miming their new song to a nationwide viewing audience (it was turned down, two votes to one against). On the night of the programme's transmission the group were doing a gig in Cork where they received a wild welcome from the southern crowd. (In an apocryphal tale Ditch's brand new shirt and suit were ripped from his body before they even began the first number.) Support that evening came from a talented little trio called Taste, featuring Rory Gallagher on guitar.

It was quite a novelty for The Kingbees to be recording their single in the Wicklow film studio, as practically all records cut by beat groups in the mid-60s were done at Eamonn Andrews Studios, whenever they managed to squeeze themselves in amongst the long queue of showbands waiting to do sessions. The Andrews studio set-up was very basic, with eight channels for the instruments going to one track on the mixing desk in the tiny control room. The small cramped space where bands had to wedge themselves and their instruments in, avoiding the baby grand piano tucked into the corner, would be laughed at today. Occasionally, when it was too crowded, a musician would be banished outside to the narrow corridor at the top of the staircase to record his part. The studio was originally used to tape sponsored programmes for Radio Éireann and was not built to record groups. A typical fifteen minute show brought to you by well-known consumer products like Jacobs Biscuits or Andrews Liver Salts would consist of maybe five records, two advertisements and some trivial interjections from a presenter with perfect elocution.

When house engineer Bill Sommerville-Large started work there in 1964, the studio was located above a jewellery shop at 40 Henry Street, across the road from Radio Éireann's broadcasting headquarters. Eamonn Andrews Studios' managing director, Fred O'Donovan, took the decision to branch out from just doing commercial work into the potentially more rewarding field of recorded music. One of the first groups to come through the doors was Bluesville. Although Fred was on the lookout for new talent to include in a variety show he ran at the Gaiety Theatre, he felt the modern blues expounded by Ian Whitcomb and his men was unsuitable for his revue, so he let the Englishman take his tape over to Seattle and Jerry Dennon.

Long before the advent of promotional videos, carefully timed album releases and concurrent nationwide tours, the scene as it developed throughout the period of 1965 to 1967 was an overwhelmingly live one, and few groups had the inclination or financial resources to spend half a day in a studio laying down a track. The situation was certainly not helped by a lack of support from Irish record companies, who were caught up in the more lucrative showband world. The beat groups and their managers found themselves ostracised from the cosy situation the showband fraternity had established, whereby mountains of cash was invested in the production and promotion of records that sold well enough, but were not really demanded, even by showband fans.

JIMMY DUNNE (manager, The Strangers): If you didn't record there [Eamonn Andrews Studios] you didn't get played on the radio. And you paid for your own contracts. We went and paid Pye Records for a contract and they did us a favour. We realised that if we were going in to recording studios and we were going to pay for this recording time we had to be sharp. The showbands would spend fortunes in there, making records which never sold. They'd buy them all themselves. We were innocent of that. We bought some, but nothing like they did to kick-start it.

Press ad for Eamonn Andrews Studios

> **BILL SOMMERVILLE-LARGE** Pye Records were the one company who picked up a lot of this stuff when nobody else would touch them. That was largely due to a man called John Woods. He seemed to have his own autonomy in Ireland for Pye Records, and worked the scene. He understood that if a band wanted a record made it was worth going for it because even though the company didn't make much money it gave good publicity to the band and good turnover for the record label. So he was satisfying the company in the UK by having plenty of product moving off the shelves.

It has been joked that the Bog of Allen in the midlands was raised by ten feet, during the 1960s, from all the showband records dumped by unscrupulous operators, keen to push a fresh single quickly up the charts. One group manager recalls that on the eve of a new release showband managers would go into the offices of promotional agencies and throw down fistfuls of cash which were to be divided out between willing runners who would go to chart return shops and snap up fresh copies. Rumours also abounded of big name showbands tipping boxes of their own records into rivers under the cover of nightfall.

> **LEN GUEST** (The Strangers): They got people, family members and all, to go around the shops and ask for the latest record so it would get into the charts. And if it got into the charts people would come to see you, and you got on television.

> **MAXIE McEVOY** (The Strangers): We know of a showband that had presses full of [singles], but their records were very high in the charts. We didn't have the money to buy them.

With only a handful of chart return shops contributing to the most widely respected chart, broadcast every Monday night on Radio Éireann, it is little wonder that abuse of the system was rife. An editorial in the October 1966 edition of *New Spotlight* magazine draws attention to this increasingly problematic situation:

Doubts were first raised when obviously poor showband discs began to show up around the top spots in the charts. Would even a band's most loyal fans be prepared to spend a hard earned 6/8 on some of the rubbish that was released? So who was buying the discs? Was it the showbands themselves or were they in fact being bought at all? The recent strange case of the record that appeared in the RE chart two days after its official release date and before it was generally available in the shops points a finger of suspicion at the record dealers. We believe that some city shops are prepared to 'fix' their lists in response to certain dubious requests.

> **JOHN KEOGH** (The Greenbeats): What we weren't aware of at the time was that records never sold. Nobody sold records in Ireland, hardly anybody, a handful... Of course we were naïve enough to think if [our record] got the plays [on the radio] it sold. We should have been down taking out bank loans and buying the records in the shops but we never did. We probably sold as many as the [big name showbands] but that means nothing because their record 'sales' did not reflect the actual sales. Even the big ones had an in to the distributors, the stuff didn't even have to go into the record shops. It was only when I got into the showband thing after two years and I looked at myself and thought what an eejit you've been.

Even if a beat group did manage to scrape together the £150 needed to record an A and B side, they still had to pay for the pressing themselves, and then had to face the inadequate and creaking distribution system in place in the mid-60s.

> **SMILEY BOLGER** (DJ): It was really hard to get the records. George Murray [of Murray Records] was getting the stuff in; he might get three copies of it. DJs must have been lending each other records when one of them wasn't working, because you just couldn't get them. You could be waiting weeks for stuff. That's one reason why a lot of things were dancing hits, cult hits. Distribution was bad. Records were probably sold in bookshops a lot of the time, especially down the country. If you were looking for something even like Michael O'Riorda, you'd have to order it, and Dickie Rock [singles] would be going out the door, they probably couldn't get enough copies in! Whatever would be number one would be flying out. Imagine going into some place in Kilkenny and asking for the new record by The Movement or Granny's Intentions and they'd be like, 'The Movement? Eh, never heard of them, what label are they on?'

In spite of all the obstacles strewn in the way of a beat group's path to chart success, highly regarded pop combo The Strangers still managed to hit the Irish Top 10 with their first single, a cover of 'Look Out (Here Comes Tomorrow)', written by Neil Diamond for The Monkees. Photographer and friend of the group, Roy Esmonde, had been on tour in the US with The Johnstons and witnessed the massive impact there on teens and pre-teens of the manufactured enigma that was Mike, Davy, Mickey and Peter. Correctly convinced that The Monkees were going to be the next big thing, Esmonde brought back their debut album to Ireland and strongly suggested to The Strangers that they record a couple of tracks from it. Realising that the aforementioned song would not appear on the syndicated TV show for another few weeks (the series was being broadcast on Telifís Éireann at the time), the Irish foursome quickly thrashed out an arrangement of the number, slowing it down in the process, and headed into Eamonn Andrews Studios where they cut the single with their customary speed and professionalism.

> **JIMMY DUNNE** Bill Sommerville-Large would tell you that [The Strangers] were the most rehearsed band that ever came into his studios to record. He could do a recording with them in an hour and a half, two hours, where it would take most of the others a day or half a day. They were very polished, very focused and dedicated to their music.

The impressive vocal on the A-side was double-tracked for added punch, cutting sweetly through the concise and measured backing. On the B-side was 'Mary, Mary', another perfect pop song from the American prime-time TV stars, written by band member Michael Nesmith. The song allowed The Strangers to cut loose, infusing the track with a muscular feel, with some deft lead playing contributed by Len Guest (sometimes referred to as 'the Hank Marvin of the Irish scene'!). The fan base that the group had slowly accumulated over the previous four years rewarded the north Dublin lads with a seven week run in the Irish charts, hitting a peak position of number six. Its success was no doubt assisted by the eventual appearance of The Monkees' version on the country's television screens, although it was not all plain sailing, as their lead guitarist remembers.

> **LEN GUEST** [Pye] only distributed it. They put no money into it whatsoever. We had to go around and chat up DJs off RTÉ, Larry Gogan and Ken Stewart, and say, 'Is there any chance you'd give it a spin for us?' They liked it; Larry played it a couple of times. He said it was better than The Monkees' version. People were going into record shops, they were asking for it around the country, but it wasn't been distributed. Pye didn't bother until they got orders for it. It sold in the UK even though it wasn't released there; they heard it on Radio Caroline.

Strangers' manager Jimmy Dunne wasn't averse to a little bending of the rules himself when it came to giving his boys a helping hand. Quite innocently he came across a person whose job it was to fill the jukeboxes in cafés full of 7" singles. Not one to miss a trick that the showband managers would have be proud of, Dunne purchased a substantial amount of 7"s and suggested to his new acquaintance that he might like to bring a few of them on his rounds. 'It went into every jukebox in Ireland,' remembers Dunne,

The Strangers lark about for the camera. Len Guest in basket on left, Maxie McEvoy in basket on right

with a hearty laugh, 'but you had to do these things!' The cunning manager also facilitated DJs from floating station Radio Caroline in getting home to England after coming ashore in small boats at Dundalk. He would drive them down to Dublin Airport, press a few singles into their hands, bid them farewell on their Aer Lingus flight and hear the new release plugged eagerly on the high seas a few days later. Radio Caroline was strongly supportive of the Irish beat scene, at a time when there were very limited opportunities to get a pop song by a domestic act broadcast on the airwaves. The station had been established by Irishman Ronan O'Rahilly (who also opened the Caroline Club in Dún Laoghaire) in 1964 and between its two ships, one broadcasting in the Irish Sea, the other in the North Sea, could boast over twenty million listeners by March 1968, after it moved its operations to The Netherlands following a crackdown by the British government which removed all other pirates from the airwaves.

The Strangers' growing commercial appeal throughout the first half of 1967 was reflected in their expanding popularity in towns and cities across the country; their appointment by an advertising agency to supply a jingle and appear in a commercial for a new soft drink called Sinola Cola; and their appearance on the bill supporting The Beach Boys on 3 May at the Adelphi

Cinema, Dublin. At this stage, chief Beach Boys' song composer Brian Wilson was no longer touring with his group, finding the strain of live performance too much for his precarious state of mind, thus his brother Carl was de facto leader. However, Carl had problems of his own to deal with. A few days before the group touched down to an unseasonal cold snap in Ireland on Monday 2 May, he appeared in a New York court charged with evading the US draft for Vietnam. The conscientious objector was unsure whether he would be able to join the rest of the group on their European tour at all, never mind make the first two scheduled shows in Dublin. The group's lawyers eventually arranged bail of $25,000 and Carl was free to dash across the Atlantic in a small charter plane to try to join his band at the Adelphi, on the understanding that he would return for another court hearing on completion of the European tour.

The first Adelphi show at 6.30pm did not go according to plan. Approximately three hundred disappointed fans demanded their money back after large sections of the audience had heckled a sub-standard performance, relatively directionless without Carl Wilson. The all-Irish support bill, featuring popular Dublin beat group The Vampires (with Tony Kenny, later of The Sands Showband, on vocals), The Strangers and 'crossover' showband The Freshmen, outshone the visiting stars. The Beach Boys management delayed the second set for as long as they could, hopeful that Carl would finally turn up and quell the unrest in the crowd. As a result the support acts were encouraged to stretch out their sets. 'The golden rule was that you couldn't sing any Beach Boys' songs,' recalls Jimmy Dunne, 'but what nobody had checked out was that The Vampires would sing Four Seasons' songs, that's what their speciality was.' The Strangers were told to keep playing, elongating their set before The Vampires came on right after them. Tony Kenny and his cohorts were also encouraged to stay on longer as well. Unable to come up with any more suitable material they started to fall back on their store of Four Seasons numbers.

> **JIMMY DUNNE** The Beach Boys' management went spare, because all they could hear was this harmony coming across, stealing their thunder. When The Beach Boys did eventually come on, they were knockout, absolutely knockout.

Carl Wilson finally arrived outside the cinema at 11.20pm and launched into a set that included the smash hits 'Good Vibrations', 'God Only Knows' and new single 'Then I Kissed Her'.

> **MAXIE McEVOY** I was walking by the side of the stage and little Al Jardine said, 'We're gonna do a song this time called, "Then I Kissed Her".' And one of the guys in the gabardine macs, the managers, there was about twelve of them in a line, shouted,

> 'This is your new record'. [Jardine replied] 'They tell me it's our new record.' Capitol had phoned in to say that's their new record, tell the audience!

Vying with The Strangers for the position of Ireland's biggest pop group in the early years of the beat scene were The Creatures. A four-piece from the northside of the city, their casual image was in keeping with the rock 'n' roll ideology of sullen rebellion and anti-authoritarianism, which for many older observers in the 1960s seemed to threaten the very fabric of Western civilisation. The Strangers were well renowned for their professionalism and presentability, which gave them a distinct advantage when it came to attempting to make the leap from beat club regulars to ballroom stalwarts. The Creatures, on the other hand, led by rhythm guitar player Liam McKenna, had classic Byrds-style bowl haircuts, and wore corduroy jackets and black denim trousers rather than pressed shirts, neat waistcoats and skinny ties. They were hardly ever spotted taking the stage in rural dance halls, preferring to build up a feverish following of beat kids through their residency in the underground cellar of the No. 5 Club. Not that their sound was to any large extent grittier than their rivals. The group's big domestic chart success of 1966, 'Turn Out The Light', was a radio-friendly pop number which, apart from some controversial lyrics, was considered highly accessible and commercial – in keeping with the prevailing trends of that year.

The Creatures at the '5' Club, 1965. L-R: Liam McKenna, Brian Harris, Frank Boylan, Ray McDonald

Signed by Columbia Records in the US and promoted heavily in that country, at a time when American kids were besotted by sounds from across the pond, The Creatures were the ones with the caption 'Most Likely To Succeed' printed brightly under their name in the metaphorical Beat Scene Yearbook of 1965/66, out of all the Irish groups in the first wave of the new pop explosion. In 1967, however, the dream of international success quickly soured, and it was left to other groups that came in The Creatures' wake to attempt the escape from Ireland's national boundaries that was so essential for artistic longevity and commercial gain.

The Creatures emerged from the dissolution of the more innocent Hootenanys, an outfit that paved the way for many other beat groups of the mid-60s by recording a single in Eamonn Andrews Studios as early as 1964. Both sides of the record ('Fiona' and '6.10 Special') were reverb-heavy spaghetti western instrumental tracks in the vein of The Shadows and The Ventures. Ray McDonald (drums), Frank Boylan (bass) and Liam McKenna (rhythm guitar) from The Hootenanys were joined by Brian Harris to form the four man Creatures. Harris came from Bray, County Wicklow, and had been spotted by the others in a rock 'n' roll/ beat group called The Tonics in Butlins holiday camp during the summer of 1964. It didn't take long for The Creatures to build up a regular following in the No. 5 club, where they were nominally managed by one of the club's owners, Brendan O'Brien. It was the doorman of the venue Matt Sheffe, however, who got The Creatures most of their other gigs around town – in the tough Club A Go Go on Sackville Place, the Manhattan in Bray and the Caroline Club in Dún Laoghaire to name but a few. In the early days they also trotted around the still thriving tennis club circuit, popping up in the Charleville Tennis Club in Drumcondra and the Templeogue Tennis Club, west Dublin. Some Irish students who were living in France came to see The Creatures in the '5', and suggested that the group go over to play a few dates in Paris (gigs that were warmly reviewed by French pop magazine *Disc Revue*). It was during a break from performing at the Parisian Locomotive Club, in August 1965, that they had a fortuitous encounter with a young American songwriter and band manager called Neil Levenson.

> **BRIAN HARRIS** We just met him on a zebra-crossing one day. Because we had long hair he said, 'Are you guys a singing group?' So he came to see us and liked the band. He came down the next day with a load of demos that he had written.

Levenson was a classically-trained pianist who had gone to school with 1950s teen idol Paul Anka, and shared his love for the simple classic pop song. He had previously written a minor hit for US surf duo Jan and Dean, as well as the uptempo doo-wop classic 'Denise', a Top Ten single for Randy and The Rainbows in 1963, and later a success again when covered by fellow

New Yorkers Blondie (as 'Denis') in 1978. A few weeks after their initial meeting The Creatures and their soon-to-be new manager reconvened in London, at Advision Studios on Bond Street, to do some test recordings, which Levenson then brought back to the US. He hawked them around to various record companies before getting a deal with Columbia Records (more commonly known as CBS in Britain and Ireland). The suits at the well-established label were most impressed with a song called 'Turn Out The Light', written by an Irish songwriter called Derry Lindsay, who is perhaps more famous today for co-writing Dana's middle-of-the-road 1970 Eurovision winner 'All Kinds Of Everything'.

> **BRIAN HARRIS** We did ten numbers in the three hour session, we didn't really work on them, so they agreed to send us back to their studios in Bond Street.

During Christmas week 1965 The Creatures worked on polishing the proposed single and produced what they felt was a far superior take than the earlier rough demo.

> **BRIAN HARRIS** We spent more time tarting it, and I treble tracked the guitar solo and stuff like that, to give it a bit of a lift and polish it off, because the other thing was rough, it was live.

Columbia didn't share the group's opinion and decided to release the first cut, which they felt had an earthier feel. Clocking in at less than two minutes, the song is propelled along by a driving rhythm section and jangly guitar part, with radical time signature changes for verse and chorus. Frank Boylan's airy lead vocal conceals the *risqué* lyrical content beneath (*'Turn out the light dear, let's see what you can do. You say alright dear, I'm gonna take my cue'*). With its uplifting vitality and furtive bite, the song was a deserved triumph when released in Ireland in March 1966 (it slowly made its way up the *Spotlight* chart, stalling at number twelve in June), and a notable airplay hit in some local markets in America when it came out there earlier in the year. It was banned on national station Radio Éireann but received constant plugs on Radio Caroline North.

To capitalise on the promising reaction to this first record The Creatures' manager and record company organised an American trip to push the group. Sadly, many of the TV and radio appearances set up by Columbia Records and Neil Levenson fell through, hampering any future singles' chances of achieving a good chart placement. The reason for the cancellations was down to an ongoing dispute between the union representing American musicians and representatives of overseas touring acts. The natives were fretting about potential income loss due to the huge volume of foreign groups coming over to gig in their country. The Creatures did manage to squeeze in a few TV

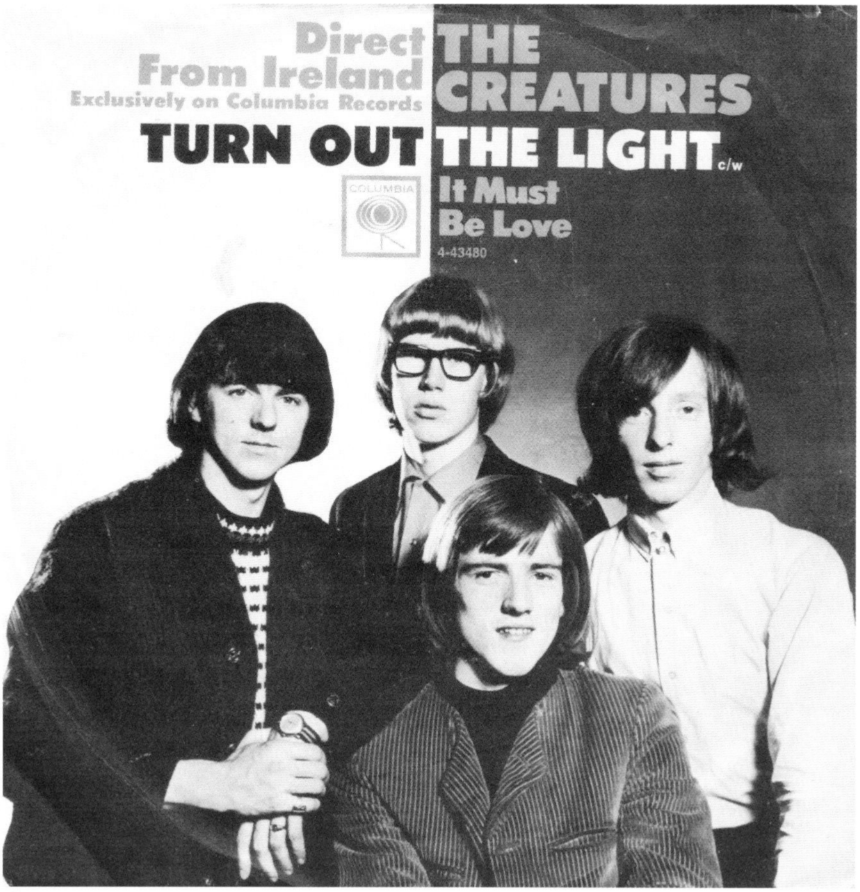

Picture sleeve of The Creatures' first US release

shows, appearing on one Cincinnati programme with Nina Simone, and another with crooner Perry Como in Pittsburgh. In Los Angeles, broadcasts were restricted to a handful of radio spots, so to keep busy The Creatures played some gigs at the Hullabaloo club on Sunset Strip with local garage bands. 'We figured if that was the local standard at the time, the standard [in Ireland] was much much higher,' attests Brian Harris. 'We went a bomb in the place.' Whilst on the West Coast they also recorded a few tracks for a mooted LP, and were assisted on future single release 'Looking For Tomorrow' by Byrds producer Terry Melcher. The Creatures' version of this Barry Mann/Cynthia Weil track featured backing vocals by The Tokens, who had brought the African-tinged song 'The Lion Sleeps Tonight' to number one in 1961. Columbia decided to put their new act on the bill at their annual convention in Las Vegas on 21 July, a huge party for record company reps from across the country. The line up also featured singer-songwriter Tim Rose and folk-pop headliners Chad and Jeremy.

> **BRIAN HARRIS** They had all the record pluggers from all over the States and they'd treat them to a week's gambling, and they'd put on a show at the end of the week. Whoever they thought were

up-and-coming bands that they'd signed [would play]. When [the reps] would go out every week with their half-dozen records to plug they'd remember you. That was the idea.

On the East Coast, The Creatures played some of Greenwich Village's dingy clubs (where a few of them saw the incredible guitar histrionics of Jimmy James one night in a grotty place called the Café Wha; he would soon be re-christened Jimi Hendrix), and through the obstinacy of their manager got on the bill at an open air theatre in Central Park with Mitch Ryder and The Detroit Wheels on 10 August. It was here that some tensions which had been recently fomenting within the group began to manifest themselves more clearly. They had been in the US for over a month at this stage, and despite the excitement of numerous media appearances, not to mention the welcome attention of female admirers, some of the band felt that the record company wasn't acting in the best interests of the group.

BRIAN HARRIS I remember seeing some billboards on the freeways with huge twenty foot high posters for the single. There were magazines like *Billboard* and *Cashbox* with full colour page ads. [Columbia] did plough money in, but it wasn't a really concentrated campaign. They threw something in, see what would happen.

Poster for Creatures' live appearance, New York State

Others were disgruntled about the financial arrangements and were yearning to return to Ireland to build on the experience gained in the US. According to Brian Harris, after completing the soundcheck for the gig in Central Park, drummer Ray McDonald returned to the hotel and was so late in coming back for his group's appearance that the organisers were about to pull the plug on their slot just as he finally showed up. When the group flew back to Ireland, McDonald was fired and replaced by Fran Byrne of Rockhouse. The Creatures' drummer recalls mounting tension amongst his band mates, caused by lack of money and clashes over which direction the group should take.

RAY McDONALD We had no money. We'd have to wait till 11 or 12am every morning for the manager to come around and give us money for our breakfast. Frank and Liam, they didn't want to come back to Ireland. They had gone into a situation here in Ireland that they wouldn't rehearse, they were up all night with women and drink, and as a result that was the lifestyle they wanted. They used to deliberately make noise at night so I wouldn't sleep. When we were rehearsing every day of the week [in Ireland] I'd walk down to McKenna and get him up. I'd walk down to Boylan, [knock for him], then I'd get the bus into the No. 5 Club. I'd be in there by 11am and I'd have all the gear set up by 12am and they'd arrive in at 4-5pm. And that went on day after day, week after week. This is where the hassle started. I didn't blow up after a few days, this was after months. I just got sick of it. Because there was no effort being made. This is what happened in New York – I used to call them and they wouldn't get up. Then Neil Levenson would come in and there'd be war. He'd be giving out and they'd be blaming me. What happened was Frank and Liam wouldn't give me money then to get my meals. There were nights when I had nothing to eat. I decided then that I just wanted out of it.

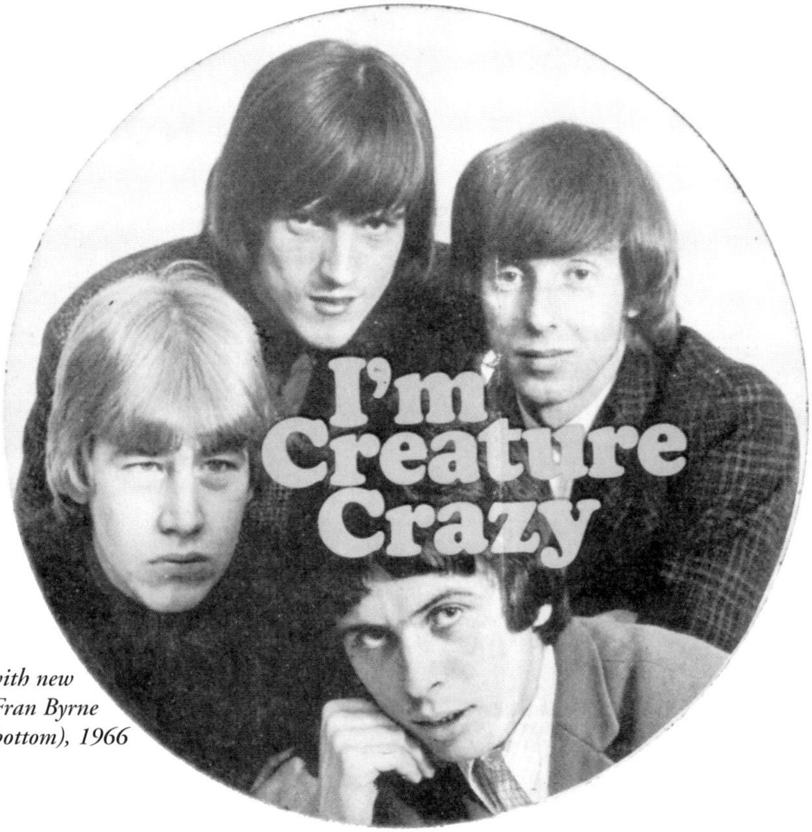

The Creatures with new drummer Fran Byrne (bottom), 1966

A second single, 'Stringalong', had been put out while the group was travelling around the US. It stiffed. In Ireland, the reaction to The Creatures' ambitious trip was frosty. Within the close knit beat group community there was only a smattering of grudging recognition of the group's pioneering attempts to expand beyond the confines of the domestic scene. Many beat groups were understandably jealous of their leap into the big time. 'It had been said in some magazine or paper that we were really in Cork,' recalls Brian Harris incredulously, 'that we hadn't gone to the States at all.' Management relations had soured as well. The O'Brien brothers were seemingly unimpressed with Neil Levenson's admirable efforts to promote The Creatures in America and the erstwhile permanent fixtures on the No. 5 Club's stage no longer felt welcome there. They were also under the impression that they weren't wanted at the O'Briens' other beat venue, the Moulin Rouge on South Great George's Street. As Levenson was still based on America's East Coast he could do little for them, so Greenbeats' manager Kevin Dunne took up administration duties. The new line-up was keen to return to the States, having tasted the fruits of potential stardom. However, at the end of 1966, the one year option that Columbia had signed the group to expired and the company decided not to renew – dashing the talented foursome's hopes of emulating the success of Them and Bluesville, the only Irish pop acts to join illustrious UK neighbours The Beatles and Stones in the US charts. The Creatures released four singles in total during their short tenure with Columbia – predominantly songs in which their manager had a publishing interest in, with one B-side coming from the pen of bassist Frank Boylan's brother. None of the three follow-up releases to 'Turn Out The Light' made any impression at home or abroad.

> **RAY McDONALD** People must remember that a band is a team. You're dealing with individuals, different personalities, different ways of doing things, and sometimes it can be hard to hold [together]. If you get that [right] combination it's good, there's a bit of harmony but if cracks start coming...that's the end of it. The only thing that will keep that going is if you're making good money. I reckon that's the glue to keeping it going, and The Creatures never made any money.

By this time the beat group scene in Ireland had firmly established itself, with numerous clubs joining early trailblazers Sound City and The '5'. (Sound City was under new management in the spring of 1966, and was now called Club Arthur). The main hive of activity was concentrated around the wide boulevard of O'Connell Street and its adjoining arteries. The Flamingo was upstairs over a café at the corner of Abbey Street, where club goers could gaze out over the city's lights whilst listening to the pulsating beat of the capital's top groups. Later the wandering Apartment Club temporarily set up camp in a basement on the opposite side of the street. Further down the road was the slippery metal staircase leading down to the 72 Club. The Scene Club, opened on Friday 14 January 1966 by the in-demand Action, was a short stroll away, on Great Denmark Street just off Parnell Square, close to the less popular Waco. The Jack Of Clubs opened and closed its doors within the space of twelve months during 1966. Club A Go Go, situated east of its competitors on the other side of Abbey Street, down an alley at Sackville Place, had a reputation for housing some of the harder edged groups.

> **SMILEY BOLGER** Probably the best club for the longest period. There was something about the Go Go that was much more earthy, the music was mostly blues, soul, rock 'n' roll.

The O'Brien brothers opened the very popular Moulin Rouge in April 1966 after the phenomenal success of the '5', a mecca for the city's hip beat fans.

> **SHAY HEALY** The most interesting point of conflict was at the bottom of Harcourt Street. There was the 95 Folk Club and across the road was the '5' Club. On a Friday night we'd come out of the 95 Club in our sandals and our tweed trousers and the lads would come out of the '5' Club in their leather jackets and their tight jeans and there'd be this kind of stand off across the street. It never got hostile, but there was a frisson.

At one stage Brendan O'Brien even had plans to install a swimming pool at the upscale Moulin Rouge! The kids usually heard who was playing where through word of mouth, and could flit between clubs any evening of the week, sampling the wide variety of sounds on offer – blues or commercial, pop or psychedelic. The vast majority of groups at this stage were still non-professional – The Creatures being the only Irish outfit before 1967 to leave their day jobs and concentrate on music careers full-time. More typical of many beat groups of the era was a part-time combo going by the deliciously snot-nosed name of The Drags, who had been inspired to form by the first wave of Irish groups like The Action, The Chosen Few and The Vampires. In a conservative world where having a lock or two of your tresses creeping over your ear automatically got you branded

as a degenerate, The Drags had the envious reputation of having *the* longest hair in Ireland. Styling themselves on UK band The Pretty Things (who had a reputation for being even surlier and smellier than the Stones), dismissive of The Beatles as being too clean-cut and poppy, and highly contemptuous of the staid showband scene, this feral four-piece epitomized the experience of being in a young, restless and rebellious pop group in mid-60s Ireland. Self-expression for the young went beyond listening to different types of music – it meant dressing in radically different clothes from your parents, becoming members of such grotty and supposedly immoral institutions as the basement beat clubs and it meant growing your hair into a greasy dishevelled mess.

> **LARRY LYNCH** (bass, The Drags): We ran into a few problems in pubs. Fellas just saying, 'We'll scalp these bastards!' But we were fast on the feet; we had to run a few times!

THE SCENE

OPENING PROGRAMME

FRIDAY, JAN. 14th "The Action"	*ADM. 5/-*	9 — 1
SATURDAY, JAN. 15th The Kingbees	*ADM. 5/-*	9 — 1
SUNDAY, JAN. 16th The Blue Beats	*ADM. 5/-*	8 — 12
MONDAY, JAN. 17th Discs	*ADM. 3/-*	8 — 12
TUESDAY, JAN. 18th Rootes Group and Agents 007	*ADM. 4/-*	8 — 12
WEDNESDAY, JAN. 19th The Coasters and Agents 007	*ADM. 4/-*	8 — 12

Such a booming new entertainment scene (over sixty groups in Dublin alone by mid-1966 according to one estimate) and potentially profitable business environment was bound to attract the attention of concerned society guardians and inquisitive showbiz managers in equal measure. In September 1966 a story was widely circulated in the press that drugs were freely available in these 'seedy' dens of iniquity, following the prosecution of a Dublin beat club for a breach of its public dance licence. Reporting on the contentious matter, *Spotlight* ran a large article in its November issue, restating the impression given by the court trial that the clubs were 'airless, dimly-lit, foul-smelling cellars, where gaudily dressed weirdies [sic] of both sexes misbehaved openly'. But to its credit the publication did come out largely in favour of the beat kids. The youngsters themselves had mobilised their troops the previous month, organising a protest march in the city centre against the spurious allegations. (This wasn't the first time that beat fans had come out in massed ranks. When it was announced that The Greenbeats would not be reappearing on *The Showband Show* after Christmas 1964, a rally was held which ended up outside the gates of Telefís Éireann, demanding the group's re-instatement. One follower even scaled the transmission mast in the grounds of the station to dangle a Greenbeats' banner from it.) Many former beat group musicians recall seeing the odd bit of hash or a handful of pills doing the rounds from time to time ('I won't say it was rampant,' recalls one, 'but it could be easily got'). However the accusation about a pot pourri of freely available substances – including something called 'shot' coffee, which conjures up the bizarre image of hyperactive adolescents knocking back tiny cups of bitter espresso – was certainly far-fetched and may have been concealing a more devious motive.

> **JIMMY DUNNE** There was a smear campaign brought out by the Irish Ballroom Proprietors' Association that, in the beat clubs, drugs were being sold. I got a phone call from *The Late Late Show*. They asked [Club Arthur manager] Michael Ryan and I would we appear. One of the [accusers] got up and waffled on and on. I said [to Gay Byrne], 'You've just been subjected to a load of lies and rubbish that the public of Ireland are expected to swallow.' We went back to Club Arthur afterwards and we were actually carried shoulder high into the place. It was a big coup for all the young crowd. But there were no drugs on sale; drugs were non-existent as such. It was [the ballroom managers'] effort to try and kill off this rising thing.

Feelings ran strongly on each side of the tense showband/beat group divide, which was a constant feature of the musical landscape in 1960s Ireland. Although the scenes did not operate in complete independence from each other – there was the occasional foray from a group into a ballroom but never the other way around – there was no doubting the philosophical, sartorial and musical differences between the two camps.

> **JONATHAN RYAN** (Rootzgroop): We hated [the showbands]. We looked down our noses at them, we thought they were crap. I remember playing once in a big ballroom on Camden Street for an Agricultural Students Ball and there was some big showband headlining, and we went on first and the audience hated us because we were playing rhythm 'n' blues songs. We didn't play country music and the pop music that they wanted to hear. I've never felt so hated in my life. We had long hair, we weren't in uniform and we weren't playing what they wanted to hear. But we felt totally superior, what we were playing was real music and this other thing was old shite, and I think in a way we were right. I still think that!

> **LARRY LYNCH** (The Drags): Fellas like us would never go to see a showband. You'd just have no interest. It would be like saying to kids nowadays, 'Would you go to see Daniel O'Donnell?' The thought would never even enter your head.

> **JAYE MALONE** (The Kingbees): [Showband members would] take fuses out of the amps and doctor the mics so it would really sound crap for your spot. But you could see the talent was there so it was going to surface no matter how hard they tried to keep it down.

> **EILEEN REID** (singer, The Cadets Showband): The groups used to get up my nose. They used to go out and say 'Listen to us; we're great.' They had that thing about them. Their approach was: 'If you don't want to listen to us, then up yours.' They hated the showbands. The bands were making the bread, and yet the groups thought they were better musicians. They weren't showmen. They were very dull." (Vince Power, *Send 'Em Home Sweating*)

> **SMILEY BOLGER** [Beat fans] all had long hair, and the dress to go with it. If you had presented your face at the TV Club [popular city ballroom] on a Friday night you probably would have been refused, because neat dress was essential, a very strict code. Even on Monday night, when there was a concession made [to groups] for the *Spotlight* night out, it got more relaxed, but you still had to have good polished shoes and you might have even had to wear a tie, even if it was a psychedelic tie!

In July 1966 the less-than-formally dressed Kingbees travelled to Germany for the first time, initially for just two weeks to play a few dates in Braunschweig and Hanover. Although they had become a very popular draw on Dublin's beat scene through continuous gigging, a series of TV appearances and a prominent profile in the print media, the group felt this was not reflected in their financial remuneration. Demand for beat/rock 'n' roll/R&B groups in Germany was still very strong in 1966, four years after The Beatles had cut their chops at The Star Club on the infamous Reeperbahn, largely due to the sizeable contingent of American GIs still posted there. Dave Whitren, who put on live gigs at Stella House in Mount Merrion, occasionally sent groups over there to play. Bluesville turned down an invitation to travel overland to entertain the troops and the beat hungry locals in 1965 before their US success. Other Irish beat groups would follow The Kingbees on their travels, most notably the oddly named Gnumps. Ditch Cassidy and his fellow bandmates' reputation in Ireland was considerably enhanced by that short engagement abroad (*Spotlight* described four girls chasing guitarist Jay Malone down Grafton Street in October 1966) and they also managed to secure lucrative support slots with visiting overseas acts on their return. Maurice Boland quit the drummers' stool at this stage; his disapproving parents persuaded him that his future lay outside of a rock 'n' roll band. As the group headed back to Germany in November he was replaced by Dougie McIlwaine from Belfast band The Mad Lads – only seventeen years old but a technically more accomplished sticksman. (His youthful naivety was exposed in the sleazy hotbed of the German club world, where allegedly he scuttled off enthusiastically one night with a stunning looking girl who turned out, on closer inspection, to be a man.)

The Kingbees prepare to leave for Germany

> **DITCH CASSIDY** We went to Hamburg with the intention of going for just one month to play the Star Club, the Top Ten Club, the Hit Club, anywhere The Beatles had been. We ended up the whole year [1967] out there, so we were forgotten about back [in Ireland]. It was the worst mistake we made, staying too long. In the meantime all the other bands came up. We were forgotten, out of sight, out of mind.

According to Cassidy, The Kingbees' German stint sped by in a blurry haze of all night rock 'n' roll rave ups – gatherings of like-minded folk replete with generous amounts of potent weed, brief encounters with red-light prostitutes and local *fräulein*, and hedonistic parties with other expatriate musicians like Richie Blackmore, soon to be lead vocalist with Deep Purple, and Jon Anderson who would latterly become a member of bombastic progressive rock vehicle Yes. After a three month residency in Hamburg's Hit Club they moved south and set up a more permanent base at the Casino Club in Augsburg, where the local 24th Division of the US Army adopted them as their mascot band. In what would become an all too frequent occurrence on the beat group scene, bass guitar player Jim Hudson was persuaded to return to Ireland to join a showband in May 1967 – the lure of a steadier wage proving too difficult to resist. A local German guitarist was invited to join after Mick Rafferty switched over to bass duties but a further blow occurred when Ditch Cassidy split back to Ireland in Hudson's wake. Jaye Malone was forced to put together a trio with two German musicians which allowed the Irish guitarist to earn a few deutschmarks to pay for food and accommodation for himself and the other stranded Kingbees. Although Ditch wrote to Malone shortly after his departure expressing regret at the untimely sojourn, the long term viability of The Kingbees as a group had effectively ended – the slow decline having begun some months earlier, helped on in part by an increasingly prodigious intake of alcohol and drugs.

The Creatures followed The Kingbees' path to Germany, arriving there in April 1967 after hope of returning to America had evaporated. Pat Fay, who had become their de facto manager in Germany, brought the group over to replace Ditch and his group at The Hit Club. The north Dublin lads found themselves in the same unsatisfactory situation as their fellow expatriates – long arduous gigs lasting up to six or seven hours a night with a ten minute break each hour, six nights a week for four weeks in succession; sporadic and unreliable payment by crooked club owners, and a hand to mouth existence which did little to foster harmonious band relationships. After a bumpy ride around some of Germany's bigger beat cities (including Dusseldorf where their equipment was impounded after the club they had been playing in closed down), The Creatures limped home in August, just four months after they set sail from Ireland. They approached a local agent searching for work only to discover that Pat Fay (who had already returned home) was in possession of their work permits, thereby preventing them from completing any more engagements in Germany. On the way home, an incident involving British custom officers in London caused a minor scandal back in Dublin and the group found it difficult to get bookings on their return. Drummer Fran Byrne left the group to join The Sands Showband in September and by October one of Dublin's best loved groups split for good.

> **BRIAN HARRIS** At the end of 1967, blues had become popular. Music had changed a little bit so we would have had to change and adapt even though there was still room for poppy stuff. [The Creatures] had probably run its cycle.

Music, fashion and youth culture were all undergoing rapid transformation at this time and Ireland experienced its own fleeting summer of love during a tumultuous 1967. Although it might be more accurate to describe it as a *weekend* of love, when swarms of nouveau flower children descended on Courtown on the Wexford coast for the August bank holiday weekend and stripped the village bare of its carefully cultivated flora. The hippy movement had its germination in the liberal-minded milieu of San Francisco during 1966 when a concoction of pacifism, hallucinogenic drugs, eastern philosophy, anti-war activism, some more hallucinogenic drugs and a superb psychedelic music backdrop spread optimistic yet naïve idealism amongst America's youth, and latterly the world. Despite Ireland's relative global isolation young Irish hipsters were not immune to the attraction of this new movement. Evidence suggests, however, that far from being a serious life-changing alternative to the grind of an apprenticeship or the monotony of a dreary office job, 'flower power' for the majority in this country was just another fashion trend to be dabbled in frivolously at the weekend. Twenty-year-old electrician/hippy Eamonn Purdy had this to say about flower power when interviewed during the love-in at Courtown Harbour: 'I wear bells and flowers because I enjoy wearing them. I paint my back and chest with flowers and signs of love. I guess I was a mod before the hippie craze started. I know most of what there is to know about the San Francisco flower people. I agree with most of their ideas, except the drug bit.' (*New Spotlight* Vol. 1, No. 15, 25 Aug - 1 Sept 1967)

Unfortunately there was no Wexford equivalent of an Owsley Stanley to spike the Miwadi Orange with acid and send the kids off on a trip of self-discovery but there's little doubt that all involved had a wonderfully carefree time, fuelled by an infectious sense of camaraderie which was common to the beat scene but rarely felt in such concentration.

> **LEN GUEST** Every garden in the village was stripped of flowers on the August bank holiday. All the women had flowers in their hair, their legs were painted with tattoos of flowers. The atmosphere was incredible. I went down on my motorbike, with only a blanket strapped to the back, I had no tent or anything. I slept in a flower sack."

The Strangers, minus drummer Vic McNamara, who was recovering from a recent motorcycle accident, played to the delirious crowds of Irish hippies that weekend.

Flower power at Courtown, Co. Wexford, 1967

JIMMY DUNNE The Strangers had played in the Tara Ballroom and it was jammers. They weren't playing the following night so we thought we'd stay around and have the craic. 'Are You Going To San Francisco?' was the big hit of the day and the crowd picked up on this, [shouting] 'San Francisco! San Francisco!' All you could play was [that song] for the duration of an hour I'd say. Repeat it and repeat it and repeat it! And the following night The Capitol Showband [played]. I wrote out the words of that song for [Paddy Cole] before he went out on stage. He said to me later, 'You wrote the first verse and we sang it amongst ourselves and you told us, which was the most important thing, that they would sing the rest of it. You saved our lives!'

Musically, the impact of psychedelia was noticeable among a few Irish groups, particularly so from 1968 onwards, with the emergence of The Orange Machine as a commercially successful act and the artistic growth of progressive units such as Skid Row. In America, many of the musicians in the so-called psychedelic bands such as Jefferson Airplane and The Grateful Dead had lengthy backgrounds in folk, country and blues music and came to the new sound organically. The social and political situation, combined with the growing availability of LSD, marijuana and other drugs were factors in the emergence of the hippy movement on the West Coast. However, by 1967. many participants in San Francisco were disillusioned with what the scene had become, with busloads of tourists peering out of coach windows at the 'freaks' along the city's alternative thoroughfare, the Haight. In Ireland, the commitment to real social change and the search for an alternative to the accepted middle-of-the-road lifestyle was not top of the agenda.

> **SMILEY BOLGER** I don't think anyone liked The Beach Boys, that was taking things too far, they were a bit naff. So you had The Flower Pot Men, Scott Mackenzie's nice song 'Are You Going To San Francisco?', Woodstock… So there was a spill over, people probably adopted the dress, not completely, just a bit of it. Probably BP Fallon embraced it more than anyone else! A lot of people were going around with beads around their necks, but I don't think it lasted too long. We didn't have the weather anyway!

The Strangers certainly didn't experience any epiphanies that August bank holiday weekend, although they were not immune to the changing musical landscape of the time. Back in Dublin the group began to include more numbers by heavier artistes like The Spencer Davis Group in their repertoire, but found that the material wasn't going down too well with their audience, particularly the young girls. Their chart successes had been based on the crystal clear sparkle of songs by US writers with a keen ear for melody and an understanding of the power of a concise structure. It was unlikely that their fans would want these songs replaced by fifteen minute free-form flute solos.

It is still incredible to consider the pace of change in popular music during the few short years of the mid-60s. In 1963 the Beatles were shaking their mop tops and cooing about girls trying to please, please them. Three years later the backward tape loops and introspective lyrics of 'Tomorrow Never Knows' on the *Rubber Soul* album aptly illustrates their astonishing growth. Of course, not all could scale the artistic heights that the acknowledged kings of pop were capable of. Nevertheless, throughout the pop and rock world this sense of potential and adventure was being refracted. Bob Dylan had single-handedly infused what had been considered disposable teenage garbage with a complex adult sensibility, allowing the rock form to develop and prosper beyond anyone's initial considerations.

THE CHESSMEN

From original screen prints by Robert Ballagh (glasses)

Alan Dee, unique amongst Irish pop musicians of the 1960s for having written and recorded original material with a showband and with beat groups, was one of the first in this country to come under the sway of Bob Dylan and the possibilities unleashed by rock's growth into adulthood. Dee began his colourful career with The Chessmen, a beat group that metamorphosed into a showband at the behest of their manager Noel Pearson. The group started life as a trio, formed at Synge Street school in Dublin city centre, comprising Terry Byrne (piano), Terry Brady (drums) and Willie Halpin (guitar). Their early speciality was American vocal harmony material (the three friends were all talented singers), to which they added British beat songs as that sound began to break big. Dee, who was blowing sax with an outfit called The Belmont Quintet at the time, heard that The Chessmen were looking for a saxophone player and successfully auditioned for the vacant slot. Unfortunately the new member had been experiencing a recurring ailment with his tonsils and was advised by doctors to give up the nightly routine of blowing into a reed for hours on end. His next instrument would be the one for which he is most remembered on the beat scene.

ALAN DEE I bought the first Vox Continental organ in Ireland. It was like a prototype, it was horrendous. The keys were made out

> of plastic over what looked like balsa wood, it was that light. Any moisture getting in there at all and the keyboard would swell.

Afraid of wearing out their welcome in the tennis clubs and beat clubs of Dublin, the group were persuaded by their manager to broaden their horizons and expand with a showband format, which met with some resistance from within the ranks.

> **ALAN DEE** I thought long and hard about it. I was heavily into Ray Charles at the time. I had visions of The Chessmen being like the Ray Charles band and me singing away there but it didn't turn out that way. More and more the showband thing was being pushed.

The Chessmen Showband became very popular in a short space of time, turning professional on Easter Sunday 1965, appearing in a four-page special in *Spotlight* that month, and becoming subjects of a hyped nationwide TV and newspaper publicity campaign orchestrated by their shrewd management. The band's first single, released in April that year, was a recording of the dramatic theme tune from the film *Exodus* which had been going down a storm at live engagements, echoing and booming around the huge ballrooms. On the B-side was an Alan Dee original called 'Fightin', a song built upon a solid Chuck Berry style riff, about a drunken mêlée that the organist had witnessed in the Top Hat ballroom in Dún Laoghaire. Tom Jones' producer, Peter Sullivan, was sent over by Decca Records to set up his high-tech portable studio in a basement in Parnell Square for the recording session and the single was released on one of the British company's dormant subsidiaries, Rex. The judging panel on *Pickin' The Pops* (including BP Fallon and ex-Viscounts leader Paul Russell) slated the A-side when The Chessmen appeared on the show miming to their epic release ('A god-awful piece of crap,' admits drummer Terry Brady today). Undaunted, Noel Pearson persuaded the programme's producer to allow his group to return the following week to perform the B-side, this time dressed up in the latest mod fashions with Alan Dee bashing away at a tambourine in his best Mick Jagger impersonation. The public reaction was in direct contrast to their last appearance, and the single became a huge hit.

> **ALAN DEE** In those days if you went on the TV and farted, you were a STAR! You could open fetes and stuff. Newsreaders were mobbed when they went down the country. Television was brand new to Ireland. We arrived in Cork the next day after that show to do a gig in the Arcadia. We came around the corner and there was a queue a mile long. When we got out of the van it was Beatlesville, it was unbelieveable.

There were more releases to follow as the band toured up and down the country for the next year or so, receiving adulatory receptions in the bigger urban expanses like Derry, Belfast and Cork, but struggling a little to make a strong impression among the more isolated communities in the Midlands. Another Alan Dee original, 'Michael Murphy's Boy', became the band's biggest success, going to number five in the Irish charts in the summer of 1966.

> **TERRY BRADY** That was a condescension to the punters outside of the cities. It was filled with pathos about a young kid who's forced to leave Ireland because there's no work. It seemed to do reasonably well.

The singles were charting well, the crowds were packing the ballrooms, the money was decent, there were prestigious support slots with touring stars (The Searchers, Lulu, Manfred Mann) but artistically and financially Dee wasn't happy.

> **ALAN DEE** The band had a few records out, and I was the front man and I was getting no more money than the rest of them. We were all on £17. 3. 6. a week. There was a band meeting and I went in all fired up. All the managers were there, we had about four managers at this stage. Con Hynes said, 'Right! So you're looking for more money. Is there anyone else in the band that sings?' I said, 'Well, John L. Sullivan sings' so he said, 'Right!

> You're the lead singer, John. And do you know one thing I've noticed in all my time in the band business? The public love an accordion. Now the accordion is the same as an organ, so buy an accordion and you're still in the band!' I think it was about a week later I handed in my notice. Back to the beat scene!

A new group, Alan Dee and The Light appeared on the scene at the end of 1966, an unusual and pioneering trio featuring Derek Boston on drums, Eddie Shaw on bass and Alan on organ, swapping his unreliable Vox Continental for a sleeker Farfisa model. It was initially intended that Chessmen bass-player Robert Ballagh join Dee in his new group. However, when he visited the now famous artist's home and saw his bass guitar laying idle in a corner, surrounded by large canvasses covered with the paintings he was putting his energies into Dee knew he would have to find another accomplice. The Light's sound was heavily influenced by American soul and Tamla Motown, and also by the newly electric Bob Dylan. The leader of the group explains:

> **ALAN DEE** I saw Bob Dylan in the Adelphi [5 May 1966]. I was dragged along by my girlfriend because I didn't dig 'folk' music at the time, and that's what I thought Bob Dylan was. I realise now that the guy, like myself, was steeped in the early rock 'n' roll stuff and really that's what he wanted to do. But I was completely blown away by that concert, it was that particular European tour when he was booed, there was a certain amount of that went on even here. He played for an hour, just himself and the guitar and a stool full of harmonicas. Then, interval time. He never said a word, not 'Hello Dublin', nothing, walked off the stage. Then the curtains went across… 'Like A Rolling Stone'. We weren't told there was going to be a band, no one expected a band, and there were all these tall Canadian guys playing Fenders, Hammond organ on one side and piano on the other side of the stage. Aha! Fabulous! I walked out of there and started to grow my hair as long as I could get it.

No music that The Light recorded was commercially successful and Dee found it difficult to persuade record companies who had known him with The Chessmen that there was merit in his new 'psuedo acid songs', as he now flippantly calls them. Having been back and forward to London a few times, he was aware of the rapidly changing musical landscape. The Light reflected the growing vogue for *outré* stage wear, expanding sonic horizons and psychedelic happenings at live performances. If Dee wasn't firing pellets at dye-filled balloons hung at the back of the stage, he was setting fire to trails of flash powder scattered around the edge of the performing area, while a

Alan Dee (right) and The Light, 1967

plank of wood studded with nails held down a sustained droning wah-wah chord on his organ. Popular soul merchants The Uptown Band, featuring Brush Shiels for a short while on bass, similarly incorporated a strong visual and theatrical element into their live appearances – mostly courtesy of their organ player, a wild looking character known simply as Mojo (it was said he painted his face so often the tint wouldn't come out). Their extravagant stunts led to a ban from the Moulin Rouge club. During a gig one night the group set fire to huge Russian flags and split open fake-blood-filled toy dolls with an axe, splattering the shocked crowd. In a less confrontational manner, having seen the stage antics of Roy Wood of The Move, Mojo decided to copy the British singer by throwing bouquets of gladioli into the arms of his adoring fans at the '5' Club. At other times, in conjunction with Uptown Band's manager Larry Mooney, he would experiment enthusiastically with tins of potentially dangerous flash powder. Many scenesters recall one memorable incident when Mooney's eagerness got a little out of hand.

> **TED CARROLL** [Larry] had the tin in his hand, and went to shake some more onto this metal plate. It was still red hot and the heat just arced up as he poured this aluminium powder in, and the tin turned white hot in his hands. He got second degree burns on his hands and face, his beard was burnt off!

The Uptown Band, 1967. Mojo far left, Brush Shiels far right, Brendan Bonass in noose

BRENDAN BONASS (guitar, The Uptown Band): We were on the stage wearing our capes and everything, our flower power stuff. He threw the match in, he had a big long beard and it caught fire. He was rushed off to the hospital and we went to see him in the Mater the next day. There were burns all over his face and the first thing he said was, 'What did the punters think of it?'

From humble beginnings in suburban tennis clubs throughout Dublin on Saturday nights, the beat group scene in Ireland had come a long way in three years. There was now a thriving club scene in the city; groups were recording and releasing quality singles; musical boundaries were being nudged and breached, and some Irish groups were looking to go abroad to further their careers. The media could no longer dismiss this new music as a fad, and more coverage was given to it in *Spotlight,* as well as in the national dailies. Highly respected DJ and journalist Pat Egan's weekly column in the overwhelmingly showband-oriented *Spotlight* served as a clearing house for all the gossip on the beat scene, as well as giving vital support to emerging groups. Ireland was seen as an important touring destination for many top quality English and American acts, feeding domestic artists with a constant stream of fresh ideas – The Kinks, Herman's Hermits, The Animals, The Walker Brothers, The

Who, The Everly Brothers, The Hollies, The Creation and many others had all played to their devoted fans in this country by the start of 1967.

After a short while the beat bug spread outside the capital, and provincial cities and towns began to produce their own smaller scenes. By mid-1966 two clubs had opened in Cork and were thriving with visits from Dublin groups as well as hosting home-grown talent like The Axills, The Sparks and The Chymes. Kilkenny, Waterford, Carlow and Dundalk became smitten with the beat boom as well, and those town's local groups would impress at regular gigs in the capital (The Word from Carlow were one of the more notable examples, featuring future Tir na nOg founders Sonny Condell and Leo O'Kelly). There was a growing sense of optimism within the scene, with commentators and fans alike speculating on who would be the first Irish group to make it big in the UK and achieve a Top Ten placing in the British charts. Perhaps surprisingly, it would be groups from outside Dublin that made the most impressive forays into the British pop scene in the latter part of the decade, laying the foundation for the continued international success of Irish rock bands and solo artists during the 1970s and beyond.

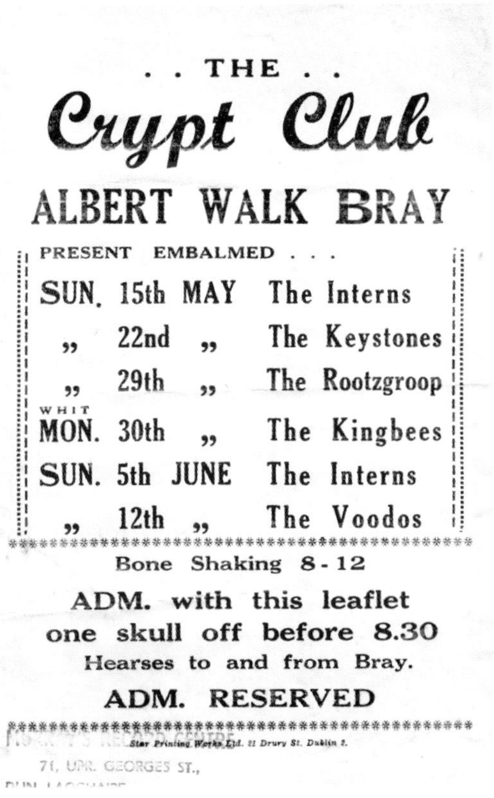

Beat clubs spread outside Dublin city centre

Part Four

During the summer of 1965, Dublin beat fans slowly became accustomed to seeing a new type of beast arriving into town to play in their clubs. With strange accents and a tough, surly demeanour, these hitherto unknown creatures brought with them a gritty, searing rhythm 'n' blues sound that was not particularly common south of the border. Sure, the Republic's capital had seen its fair share of home-grown R&B talent up to then, but there was something about the uncompromising attitude of the new Northern bands that marked them apart. Few of these interlopers deferred to crowds' wishes to churn out anodyne covers of the latest pop smash. Belfast was a blues city, and her beat groups were not about to change their sound to appeal to what they perceived as unsophisticated neophytes in Dublin and other southern outposts. In their home town, loud, wild uninhibited R&B was positively encouraged and indeed demanded by young music fans, and during the mid-60s the industrial urban heartland of Ulster fashioned a scene to rival any in the whole of the UK. Indeed, it could be said that Belfast produced the very finest exponents of pure, unadulterated foot-stomping rhythm 'n' blues in the whole of the British Isles – that spirited group with the constantly changing line-up of obdurate young men known as Them. Tragically, the onset of the 'Troubles' at the end of the 60s would kill off Northern Ireland's music scene almost overnight, but not before it had produced some of the best sounds this island has ever heard, and served as a launch pad for two of Ireland's most successful artists of the 70s, 80s and beyond, Rory Gallagher and Van Morrison.

> **SMILEY BOLGER** There were great bands from Northern Ireland. They kick started the Dublin scene. The Few, Sam Mahood and The Soul Foundation, The Method. The guys down in Dublin might have thought they were good until they heard these kids, who were really serious. They were probably the ones who influenced Granny's Intentions, and The Movement and The Uptown Band and people like that. The southern scene seemed to have a lot of MOR – The Bye Laws, Some People, The Vampires. Boy meets girl situation, lots of young ones screaming.

The Interns, 1965. Singer Paul Divito is second from the right

Although the showband phenomenon was born in County Tyrone with the emergence of The Clipper Carlton, by the mid-60s beat groups and R&B outfits in the North didn't have to play second fiddle to the big names as much as their counterparts did down south. A beat scene of sorts had developed in Belfast in the early 1960s, with nightly gigs centred around dance halls like Betty Staff's and Sammy Houston's, and ballrooms such as Romanos. The infrastructure was well enough established to support the emergence of Them in April 1964, months before Dublin's first clubs began to open their doors. The Interns, one of the longest running combos from Northern Ireland during the 60s, were gigging consistently by 1962, and made their first trip to the Republic a couple of years later.

PAUL DIVITO (lead singer, The Interns): We went to Limerick and we were billed as the Belfast Beatles or some stupid thing like that. It was so crazy, they mobbed us on the stage. They hadn't seen anything like us, with the long hair and all. And you'd be walking down O'Connell Street in Limerick and they'd be all running over to you asking for autographs.

As in Dublin, The Beatles caused consternation when they appeared at the Ritz in Belfast on 8 November 1963, the night after they played the Adelphi Cinema. The city's constabulary were on hand to restrain an estimated crowd of 8,000 hysterical youths. 'I only went along to scream but as soon as they came on stage I fainted and was lifted out to the foyer by two policemen. I ran back into the hall and fainted again when I saw Ringo in the spotlight,' recalled fifteen-year-old disciple Robin Dynes in an interview with *City Week* magazine sixteen months later. 'I was almost as bad – I cried all the time they played,' added her friend Penny Kirkwood.

Belfast's beat scene coalesced and solidified around the Maritime Hotel, near Queen's University, where Them became resident band at a new Rhythm 'n' Blues Club opened by three forward looking entrepreneurs responding to local students' and school kids' demand for top quality live music. Originally built as a recreational club for the seamen housed at next door's mission, the Maritime was a basic structure which had previously hosted variety shows and dances, and was home to a trad jazz club when the young promoters first brought in their radical new group.

> **PAUL DIVITO** The Maritime was just a big hall with a big stage. It was like a smaller ballroom with a very high stage and maybe two sixty watt bulbs lighting the place.

A teaser ad campaign ran in the *Belfast Telegraph* to announce the arrival of Them, who had emerged out of local rock 'n' roll group The Gamblers with the addition of ex-Monarchs showband saxophonist Van Morrison. Morrison had recently returned from a gruelling baptism of fire in Germany where he played marathon seven hour sessions with The Monarchs, developing his stagecraft and showmanship to an extraordinary degree. A moment of epiphany had occurred in Soho when the East Belfast native witnessed a bruising performance by The Downliners Sect, early purveyors of the new R&B sound on the London club scene. Van had been exposed to a wide range of musical styles during his childhood, including the blues, via his father's remarkable record collection which had been built up from a period working in America and numerous trips to Atlantic Records on High Street in Belfast.

> **VAN MORRISON** When the blues started getting noticed, I could hardly believe it. It was like all my Christmases at once. Because this stuff wasn't new to me at all. I'd been listening to it most of my life. By the time that stuff started to be popular, it was in my bones. It was like breathing by then. Blues was my calling card.(Interview with Jon Wilde, *Uncut*, Issue 98, July 2005)

Drawing on a deep well of classic American influences all delivered with an arrogant strut and a brusque sneer, Them stood apart from the rest of the groups on the Belfast scene and helped foment the fervent rhythm 'n' blues mania in the city over the next few years.

> **SAM SMYTH** (band manager, club promoter): The live shows were great. It was all to do with the people who were there, and Van jumping up and down, going mad. It wasn't very sophisticated. Their gigs just pulled together all these streams – the young people wanted their own identity, they wanted their own bands. Van was also a mysterious figure. He was a laconic figure, didn't say much.

> **ROD DEMICK** (guitar, The Wheels): There wasn't a gig like [the Maritime]. It was the first of its kind. In a way it was like what the Crawdaddy was in London. It was a place for the new music. It was a great time; there was so much optimism about. The sectarian side of things didn't matter. It was just the music, everybody loved this music. [Them on stage were] drunk most of the time on scrumpy! I've seen Van lying on the stage singing 'Stormy Monday' and telling the audience he was Eartha Kitt! There were no drugs or anything around then. There was a place up the Falls Road called the Spanish Rooms which was a really rough pub where you could go and buy a barrel of scrumpy cider. That's what everyone was into.

After a few more months, Them built up a reputation as the wildest and most obstinate act playing in the province, much to the annoyance of other groups whose thunder was being unceremoniously stolen. In Cookstown, County Tyrone, well-dressed four-piece The Stratatones witnessed the group's dogged character first hand when Them refused to play popular songs demanded by an expectant crowd. Belfast's *City Week* newspaper reported the incident: 'When the audience became restive and started slow hand clapping, one of Them used what Stratatones' manager Eric Crymble described as "somewhat ungentlemanly language" and a minor riot broke out. "We were caught in the middle of it all," laughs Jackie Middleton (lead guitar), "but when the crowd saw we were The Stratatones they gave us a free passage, but our minibus was tampered with in the confusion; one thing is for certain – we won't ever play alongside Them again if we can help it."'

A lucky break arrived for Morrison and his cohorts when they were invited down to British Peter Lloyd's studio to record a short demo tape in early summer 1964. Twenty-four-year-old Lloyd was a local electronics expert. He had previously worked as an engineer with Decca in London and also ran a business manufacturing and selling amplifiers and sound systems in Belfast. Like Eamonn Andrews Studio in Dublin, Lloyd's on Cromac Street (later

Van Morrison fronts one of the many line-ups of Them. Guitarist Billy Harrison is on the right

housed in a more modern set-up on Bank Street) was the only recording facility in town, and all manner of showbands, jazz types and pop groups had availed of his services in the short space of time that his studio had been open. Lloyd was also responsible for alerting Phil Solomon to the obvious potential of Them, which quickly led to a deal with Decca Records in London.

The Solomon family played a significant role in the development and nurturing of Irish pop music talent during the 1950s and 60s. Patriarch Maurice ran a record distribution company called Solomon & Peres and was well connected to Dick Rowe, head of A&R at Decca Records in London, due to a substantial shareholding in that company. Maurice's son Philip was an artiste manager based in London, who in conjunction with his wife ran Dorothy Solomon Associated Artistes from a busy office in the heart of the city. Most musicians remember Phil as a tough, no-nonsense old school operator who had already proven his managerial worth with the success of easy-listening pop trio The Bachelors.

SAM SMYTH He wasn't quite Don Arden. [But] he was exotic, noisy and bombastic. He annoyed everybody he did business with. He took the lion's share of every deal and dressed like a millionaire.

Phil Solomon would later help propel The Dubliners on to *Top Of The Pops* after signing them to his own record label Major Minor, which was set up in December 1966. Brother Mervyn was a more quiet and reserved character. Based in Belfast, he busied himself checking out the dynamic local scene, evaluating the competitors and trying to spot the winners from the also-rans. He set up his own company, Emerald Records, in 1965 with the idea of releasing compilations by unsigned showbands.

Them's first single, a cover of Slim Harpo's 'Don't Start Crying Now' (a hyperkinetic run through by the band with a strangulated vocal performance by Van) b/w 'One, Two Brown Eyes', came out in September 1964 with a follow-up emerging just two months later. Produced by American song-writing and production veteran Bert Burns, the second 45 coupled two of Morrison's most famous compositions, 'Baby Please Don't Go' and 'Gloria', and provided Them with their first monster hit, landing on the edge of the British Top Ten. The A-side was also chosen as the theme music for ITV's prime time pop programme *Ready Steady Go*. Although relegated to the flip side, 'Gloria' became a substantial airplay hit on the West Coast of America, in the process influencing an entire generation of US garage punks, who were unable to resist its simple insistent riff and seemingly sexually charged lyrics. Hundreds of American bands covered it, including Chicago rockers Shadows of Knight who brought the song into Billboard's Top 10 in January 1966. Van's namesake in The Doors sang the song regularly at live concerts, and it was also radically re-invented by punk high priestess Patti Smith on her influential debut LP *Horses* in 1975. Following their UK chart success, towards the end of 1964 the Belfast band journeyed to Dublin's leafy Mount Merrion suburb to expose beat fans in the Stella House to their rough and tumble sound. *Spotlight*'s beat scene columnist Pat Egan witnessed the performance.

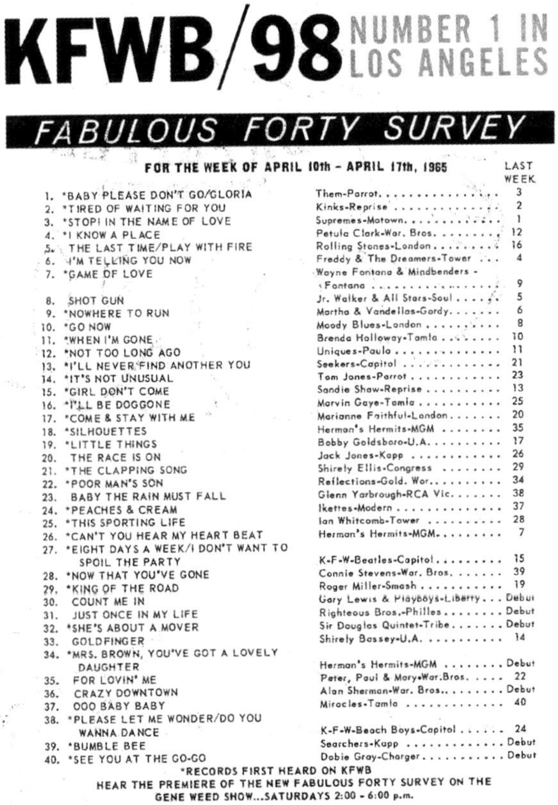
KFWB/98 NUMBER 1 IN LOS ANGELES

FABULOUS FORTY SURVEY

FOR THE WEEK OF APRIL 10th – APRIL 17th, 1965

			LAST WEEK
1.	*BABY PLEASE DON'T GO/GLORIA	Them-Parrot	3
2.	*TIRED OF WAITING FOR YOU	Kinks-Reprise	2
3.	*STOP! IN THE NAME OF LOVE	Supremes-Motown	1
4.	*I KNOW A PLACE	Petula Clark-War. Bros.	12
5.	THE LAST TIME/PLAY WITH FIRE	Rolling Stones-London	16
6.	I'M TELLING YOU NOW	Freddy & The Dreamers-Tower	4
7.	*GAME OF LOVE	Wayne Fontana & Mindbenders - Fontana	9
8.	SHOT GUN	Jr. Walker & All Stars-Soul	5
9.	*NOWHERE TO RUN	Martha & Vandellas-Gordy	6
10.	*GO NOW	Moody Blues-London	8
11.	*WHEN I'M GONE	Brenda Holloway-Tamla	10
12.	*NOT TOO LONG AGO	Uniques-Paula	11
13.	*I'LL NEVER FIND ANOTHER YOU	Seekers-Capitol	21
14.	*IT'S NOT UNUSUAL	Tom Jones-Parrot	23
15.	*GIRL DON'T COME	Sandie Shaw-Reprise	13
16.	*I'LL BE DOGGONE	Marvin Gaye-Tamla	25
17.	*COME & STAY WITH ME	Marianne Faithful-London	20
18.	*SILHOUETTES	Herman's Hermits-MGM	35
19.	*LITTLE THINGS	Bobby Goldsboro-U.A.	17
20.	THE RACE IS ON	Jack Jones-Kapp	26
21.	*THE CLAPPING SONG	Shirely Ellis-Congress	29
22.	*POOR MAN'S SON	Reflections-Gold. War	34
23.	BABY THE RAIN MUST FALL	Glenn Yarbrough-RCA Vic.	38
24.	*PEACHES & CREAM	Ikettes-Modern	37
25.	*THIS SPORTING LIFE	Ian Whitcomb-Tower	28
26.	*CAN'T YOU HEAR MY HEART BEAT	Herman's Hermits-MGM	7
27.	*EIGHT DAYS A WEEK/I DON'T WANT TO SPOIL THE PARTY	K-F-W-Beatles-Capitol	15
28.	*NOW THAT YOU'VE GONE	Connie Stevens-War. Bros.	39
29.	*KING OF THE ROAD	Roger Miller-Smash	19
30.	COUNT ME IN	Gary Lewis & Playboys-Liberty	Debut
31.	JUST ONCE IN MY LIFE	Righteous Bros.-Philles	Debut
32.	*SHE'S ABOUT A MOVER	Sir Douglas Quintet-Tribe	Debut
33.	GOLDFINGER	Shirely Bassey-U.A.	14
34.	*MRS. BROWN, YOU'VE GOT A LOVELY DAUGHTER	Herman's Hermits-MGM	Debut
35.	FOR LOVIN' ME	Peter, Paul & Mary-War.Bros.	22
36.	CRAZY DOWNTOWN	Alan Sherman-War. Bros.	Debut
37.	OOO BABY BABY	Miracles-Tamla	40
38.	*PLEASE LET ME WONDER/DO YOU WANNA DANCE	K-F-W-Beach Boys-Capitol	24
39.	*BUMBLE BEE	Searchers-Kapp	Debut
40.	*SEE YOU AT THE GO-GO	Dobie Gray-Charger	Debut

*RECORDS FIRST HEARD ON KFWB

HEAR THE PREMIERE OF THE NEW FABULOUS FORTY SURVEY ON THE GENE WEED SHOW...SATURDAYS 2:00 - 6:00 p.m.

Them make waves in LA. Look who's not too far behind at No.25

PAT EGAN I got in eventually, they wouldn't let me in at first, the guy said I was too young. 'Baby Please Don't Go' had just gone into the charts in England, it was a big hit. I just saw two, maybe three numbers at the end of their set. I went around the side of the place, there was a guy letting people out because there was no proper toilet in the place and I got in there. It was amazing. Before that I thought Cliff Richard was brilliant.

BP FALLON Van was the blues-soaked pugilistic punk in this tough band, all 'Gloria' and 'Mystic Eyes' and 'Baby Please Don't Go' flirting with the ghosts of Rimbaud and Mez Mezzrow, fierce, ferocious and fantastic in its take-no-prisoners power. Fuck, yeah.

Initiated by groups like Them, The Interns and The Misfits, the trickle of Belfast bands going south gradually became a deluge and many found themselves playing the '5', the Go Go and Club Arthur as regular as or even more often than venues in their native city.

PAUL DIVITO I must say it was one of our best gigs, doing Dublin, the scene was loads better at that time. You used to go down and get a fabulous reception and the clubs were mighty. The clubs in Belfast were halls as such, not like the 5 Club which was a cellar basically.

Not everyone had such favourable experiences, particularly when it came to the financial side of things. An anonymous member of Belfast's Spectres was none too pleased about their trip south, as he recounted to *City Week*: 'We played a date at a Dublin beat club recently and collected a cheque for £30. A week after I'd cashed it I had a letter from the bank saying it was a "bouncer", so we lost our fee and £10 travelling expenses into the bargain. At least one beat club there is blacklisted. The great majority are OK, but the club owner who tricked us has been booking Belfast groups because he's known in Dublin as a bankrupt. Those German clubs might be bad but here's the same thing on our own doorstep.' Johnny Rob, a journalist for the same publication, was sceptical of beat groups from the South, sniffily dismissing The Greenbeats as the 'best of a bad lot', after their Belfast debut at the Boom Boom Room in March 1965. He certainly had plenty to be proud of in his hometown by this stage. Because Them bestride the Belfast scene like a colossus, it is easy to forget that a lot of other bands of note emerged at the time. Although Van Morrison's singular talent and driving ambition has ensured a long career dotted with many musical highpoints, Northern Ireland's incredibly fertile and well-organised music scene of the 1960s produced many other great groups whose notable achievements have been pushed further to the peripheries as the lights of that decade have dimmed.

Perhaps the best of these groups were The Wheels, fronted by charismatic singer Brian Rossi, who had been a fixture on the city's entertainment bills since the late 1950s fronting local skiffle groups and big bands. Previously a waiter, farmhand, bread server, and building labourer, Rossi was a huge fan of James Brown and PJ Proby, and was conscious of always delivering a captivating show for his devout audiences. When he DJ'ed at the Plaza Ballroom 'there were literally hundreds of dancers who went just because he was different' (*City Week*, 1 Jan 1965), according to another local singing star, Tony G. Ford of The Seekers. Ever the enigmatic individualist, Rossi (more prosaically known to his family as Brian Rosbotham) shaved his head completely bald at a time when all the other beat musicians were growing their hair long. Putting together The Wheels in the summer of 1964 from the remnants of The Golden Eagles (house band at the Plaza, who were dismissed for playing Chuck Berry numbers at the over-21 dances), he brought the group straight over to Warrington, Lancashire, to try their luck on the northern soul and blues circuit. Initially struggling to get work, the band members were forced to pick potatoes to earn some extra cash, before finally establishing themselves in Blackpool with a residency at a local ballroom. They were soon in high demand around the north west, playing numbers by Bobby 'Blue' Bland, Elmore James and Sonny Boy Williamson during support slots to The Drifters, Little Eva and Tommy Roe. Victor Catling played the drums, Tito Tinsely was on bass and vocals, Herbie Armstrong was one of two guitarists along with Rod Demick (who also did a lot of the singing), and Rossi played keyboards whenever he wasn't shaking the maracas or bashing a tambourine.

The Wheels. L-R: Victor Catling, Rod Demick, Brian Rossi, Tito Tinsley, Herbie Armstrong

By the following year The Wheels were comfortable enough to turn down a slot at Liverpool's Cavern Club because the proffered fee was too low. Noticing the success of fellow countrymen Them, Rossi's group borrowed a cheap tape recorder, stuck a microphone in front of a PA column at one of their gigs in Wigan and sent off the resulting lo-fi 'demo' to Phil Solomon in London. Increasingly frustrated at Them's reluctance to comply with the level of professionalism demanded of his pop stars, Solomon saw in The Wheels an opportunity to groom another hip R&B group for stardom and quickly arranged for them to go into Regent Sounds studio in May 1965 to cut three tracks – Van Morrison's 'Gloria', Bo Diddley's 'Mona' and a composition by Tommy Scott, a young songwriter in Phil Solomon's stable who had been penning songs for Them.

> **ROD DEMICK** Them cultivated this sort of rebel image where they didn't want to talk to people. Whereas we would talk to anybody, we wanted to make it! I think [Solomon] probably did see us as doing what he couldn't get Them to do. He came from the old school where he didn't understand this new attitude. But we were all naïve. Even Van and the lads were naïve at that time. You just wanted to get a record out. We didn't think about contracts, that was the last thing on your mind.

Despite support from The Rolling Stones' Brian Jones, who was reported to have said that The Wheels' version of Gloria was one of the three greatest R&B numbers around at the time, their first single could only boast the status of regional hit in their north-west stronghold, after picking up solid airplay on Radio Caroline. It failed to make much impression elsewhere.

By the time Them released their debut album in June 1965 (preceded by 'Here Comes The Night' which sold 16,000 copies on its first day of release in the UK), kids in Belfast and other parts of the province couldn't get enough of the sizzling rhythm 'n' blues and beat sounds. They were understandably proud of a home-grown group making it big 'on the mainland', and were still very well served by scores of top class acts doing the rounds of ballrooms and clubs, despite seeing less of Van Morrison and associates on the domestic front. Popular Dublin DJ Danny Hughes recalls the special atmosphere in Northern Ireland venues where he was regularly hired to spin discs during the mid-60s.

> **DANNY HUGHES** The young kids up there were more switched on. There was no scene [in the South] that would [attract] 600 or 700 people, except the showband scene. I would get all the latest releases from England for free. If I saw a Tamla Motown label coming in, demonstration copy, bang! You'd stick it on. The kids would be up in their plastic redcoats making new steps to it. They were very trendy and the mod scene was definitely heavy in Belfast. And where people couldn't afford the clothes, they went out and bought second hand granddaddy clothes.

> Stuff from the twenties or thirties, the wide lapels and all that, [they] got them altered. While the kids down in Dublin didn't care about that scene, Belfast's young kids tried to be trendy.

DJ Danny Hughes

Stephen Lennon, drummer with Bangor outfit The Hoods, received ample confirmation of the beat fans' devotion when his group played a gig in the Co-Op Hall at the seaside town. 'The other night a girl came to the club and asked to get in for free because she was our biggest fan,' he recounted. 'I laughingly asked her for proof and she immediately rolled up her sleeve and showed me something that staggered me. She had "The Hoods" scratched on her forearm with a needle. Needless to say she got in for free.' (*City Week*, 30 July, 1965)

City Week succinctly reviewed Them's first album, *The Angry Young Them*, in their issue of 2 July: 'There is no British made long-player presently available which can touch it for sheer dynamism. For real blues feeling, Van Morrison is equalled only by Animal Eric Burdon at his very best. As a composer, he has no one to touch him for contemporary British blues.' Despite the record's raw vitality and obvious brilliance, the group's lead singer, for one, was not happy with forces that were influencing the direction that the group were taking.

> **VAN MORRISON** What happened with Them is that they tried to manipulate us, turn us into a pop group. Suddenly it seemed like we were working to someone else's agenda. They expected us to be slick and showbizzy. Well, I was neither of those things. For me, that was going nowhere. I couldn't pull that off. It was an alien thing to me. Them started out as something straightforward and it got twisted into something else. We became fodder, that's all. (Interview with Jon Wilde, *Uncut*, Issue 98, July 2005)

Them's success brought A&R men to Belfast in their droves, eager to snap up any other budding R&B groups that were being bred in the city. The Mad

Lads, who had started off supporting Them at the Maritime, were signed by their seniors' own label, Decca.

> **KENNY McDOWELL** (lead singer, The Mad Lads): We played a mixture of R&B, like Don Covay, and blues, like Howlin' Wolf and Muddy Waters, and I even remember doing a few of Otis Redding's early things and the more middle-of-the-road Chuck Berry sort of thing. And the guys who ran the Maritime were these blues enthusiasts and so you were always being fed this music in the interval on the old reel-to-reel tape recorder. (Colin Harper and Trevor Hodgett, *Irish Trad, Folk And Blues*, pp95-96)

The Mad Lads, 1966

Betraying the group's more down-at-heel blues roots, management shaped The Mad Lads into a commercial pop outfit for their one and only single, 'Out With My Baby Tonight' in October 1965, changing their name to Moses K and The Prophets just prior to release (Stax Records signings, The Mad Lads, were due to tour the UK at the time). The single did well at home, debuting at number eight in *City Week*'s chart, which was compiled from five leading central and suburban retailers. The Prophets were unhappy with the new direction though and exercised their divine will by leaving Moses K (aka Kenny McDowell) in January the following year. Three months later they were back with a new lead singer, Billy Williamson, but they were unable to recapture past glories and disappeared from live venues by the end of 1966.

Strong political and economic ties to Great Britain meant that the passage to the 'mainland' was considerably smoother for Northern Ireland groups compared to their Southern counterparts. It helped that the shrewd Solomon family had a tight structure in place to spot and nurture home-grown talent, and plenty of bands wishing to break away from the Belfast circuit signed up with the respected showbusiness agents. Others did it the hard way, none more so than The Bats who left for London in July 1964, the same month as Them, with just five pounds between them tucked away in their drainpipe trousers. After spending the first few nights dossing in Euston Station they found a more permanent home in a beat-up old post office van beside the river at Kingston-on-Thames. Gigs were hard to come by and money was scarce. On one stomach-rumbling occasion the group's guitar player had to scrounge some stale bread from a local bakery. He duly handed over the precious bounty to the group's manager who carefully divided it up with a ruler. With patience and cash at an all-time low, A&R man Mickie Most (The Animals, Herman's Hermits) recorded Burt Bacharach's 'Accept It' with The Bats in December. A session for Radio London was arranged, but the single itself only got a few plays on Radio Caroline. After labouring on a London building site The Bats returned to Belfast with tails firmly between legs. Proficient songwriters (the B-side of their debut 45 was self-penned), the group managed to get one of their originals onto a compilation album released in February 1966, just as they metamorphosed into a country duo called The O'Brien Brothers (they supported Eddie Arnold at the Ulster Hall on 7 February).

The various artists' record in question was confidently titled *Ireland's Greatest Sounds: Five Top Groups From Belfast's Maritime Club*, and was put out by Mervyn Solomon's Emerald Records. 'The musical range takes in all the major developments on the local scene from far-out soul, R&B through pop-folk protest to country-tinged beat,' gushed a writer in *City Week*. Blues was supplied by The Alleykatz and The Luvin' Kind, who performed spirited versions of 'Chicago Calling' and 'It's A Cruel World' respectively. The latter were also responsible for the sprightly anti-nuclear ditty 'Answers Please'. The People, who developed out of early 60s beat group The Telstars, were represented by two fine commercial numbers, one of which was Buddy Holly's 'Well Alright'. Within two years they would find themselves on a radically different musical trip under the name The Eire Apparent. The quintet of 'top groups' was rounded out by Just Five, featuring legendary Belfast soul man Sam Mahood on lead vocals.

Mahood's fame across Ireland was steadfastly established after he joined The Soul Foundation in October 1967, a roaring soul monster comprising three tenor saxophones, bass, drums, guitar, and the closest thing Ireland's group scene ever had to a sex symbol, Karen Byrne on co-vocals. The wild-man leader of this feisty soul revue was the most impressive singer seen in Belfast since the heyday of Van Morrison. He captivated crowds with his caveman-like long hair and beard, stomping around stages from Cork to Derry in bright orange corduroy jacket and black knee-length boots. Mahood lived for live performance, and his raw energy was never likely to be captured on record. After more than a year with The Soul Foundation he put together The Big Soul Band, expanding the line-up to ten people. 'My eventual aim,

Wild man Sam Mahood, 1968

of course, is to have a touring pop orchestra with about thirty-eight pieces, including strings,' joked Mahood in an interview (*City Week*, 3 Oct 1968). Comparisons with the showbands were strictly numerical however – no pop was allowed, and sweaty punters feverishly lapped up the Wilson Pickett and Otis Redding numbers when they weren't dragging Sam off the parapet of the stage and onto the drink-sodden floor.

Just as Emerald Records were flooding the stores with their affordable beat group compilation, The Wheels were preparing to issue their next 7" single. If Brian Jones had still been listening he would have heard one of the finest singles released by an Irish band during the 1960s. Rod Demick snorts and snarls his way through the ambivalently misogynistic lyrics on 'Bad Little Woman' as the band attack their instruments with a ferocity that must have been extraordinary in a live setting. 'Road Block' is as scintillating as the A-side – a menacing amphetamine-fuelled one chord romp, the tribal drumming and chugging guitars building up a jittery tension that is never fully relieved. In America, a tamer demo version of 'Bad Little Woman' was released under the name 'The Wheel-A-Ways' to avoid (seemingly non-existent) confusion with Mitch Ryder and The Detroit Wheels. Coincidentally, this song too was covered by The Shadows of Knight, who were unable to do for The Wheels what they had done for Them. The Illinois five-piece received confirmation of their status as one-hit wonders when their version of 'Bad Little Woman' barely crept into the Billboard Top 100.

When The Wheels weren't tottering down the motorway to London to pop into Regent Sounds studios for recording sessions, they were busy enjoying a hedonistic lifestyle at their base in Blackpool. The Belfast group shared a rambling farmhouse with The Rockin' Vickers, a wild mod combo featuring future Motorhead leader Lemmy on guitar, and would happily invite touring musicians out to party and jam with them into the early hours.

ROD DEMICK All the bands used to come through Blackpool – The Walker Brothers, PJ Proby, Lulu and The Luvvers. They'd come out after their gigs and we'd all have big parties out at the farm. The farmer had moved to a bungalow next door and just rented out this big farmhouse. We used to run a power line out and just play in the yard. Them came up and they had a jam with us and the farmer came and said we were frightening the cows!

The Wheels on their farm, 1966

Brian Rossi, perhaps always more at home in a mixed cabaret-type band than an earthy R&B group of wild teenagers, quit The Wheels just as 'Bad Little Woman' was released. He was also becoming sidelined as key vocalist and was content to take up a solo slot at the Oyster Bar in Blackpool, adopting a Frank Sinatra persona during renditions of smooth jazz standards. Eric Wrixon from The People filled the vacant keyboard slot in the group. Rossi did rejoin his erstwhile colleagues for one last triumphant show at the Plaza Ballroom back in their home town that August. Ever willing to make a dramatic impression, Rossi burst onto the stage in a furry Mongolian waistcoat and gold medallion, multi-coloured spotlights bouncing off his bald plate. It wasn't long before both items were torn from his body. Swept along by the celebratory orgy of rhythm 'n' blues, the kids soon had the rest of the group swept off stage and mobbed in the crush of their sweaty ranks.

Belfast beat fans were delighted to see the prodigal sons returning, as previous heroes Them were stuttering and stumbling their way to an ignominious end. Van Morrison had grown more distant from and antagonistic towards the other group members over time, eventually precipitating the departure of original member and important driving force Billy Harrison. New members were joining and leaving with frightening regularity, and the group had seen a string of singles flop miserably, their efforts superseded by the emerging clarion call of folk rock and protest music. Them's second album, *Them Again*, was released amid a heavy fug of apathy in January 1966, and with a completely reconstituted line-up compared to the debut (excepting Van Morrison). The liner notes of the record were partly correct when they stated that the group 'are not content to stand still musically and rest on the laurels of three big hit records, and are moving towards a sound very close to the jazz idiom. This is an album to enjoy! To dance to! But it is also an album for connoisseurs.' True, the scope of material contained on the sixteen-song LP was wider than the first, incorporating pop, folk rock, jazz and soul as well as R&B, but creatively Morrison had withdrawn a great deal and the majority of the tracks were covers or songs written by producer Tommy Scott. That's not to say the record did not have its highlights – that powerfully loud, almost-live feel evident on the first record is present throughout again, lending drama and emotion to crowd favourite 'Turn On Your Lovelight', and to a commendable adaptation of Bob Dylan's 'It's All Over Now Baby Blue'. The most impressive offering is the stunning punk stomper 'I Can Only Give You Everything', which is nothing less than the sonic equivalent of a group of violent street urchins beating a randomly chosen victim to a pulp in a rain-sodden underpass. If any journalists had felt that Them's conduct, in some interviews, was a pose then this song was a serious rejoinder.

It was a shame that such energy could not be harnessed for the good of the group however. Motivation was flagging even as Them flew off to the West Coast of America in May for a fruitless tour of Californian clubs and stadia. By the time they returned a couple of months later, their relationship with manager Phil Solomon was in tatters, and all they had from their trip were hazy memories of wild drunken nights out with rock stars such as Jim Morrison and Frank Zappa. Van Morrison hung around Belfast for the remainder of 1966, unsure of his direction and unable to pull together a suitable grouping of musicians to satisfy his needs. The Wheels had stopped rolling by the end of the year as well. Their third and last single, a version of the Paul Revere and The Raiders hit 'Kicks' had stiffed on its August release and the group dissolved shortly after. Herbie Armstrong and Rod Demick fell into conversation with Van Morrison one night when all three were searching for a new direction.

> **ROD DEMICK** [Van] was actually interested in joining the band, but he was waiting for a call from Bert Berns. I had a chat with Van about four years ago at Bishopstock Festival and he was saying that he wanted The Wheels as his band, he would have loved to have The Wheels as Them…the rest is history, as they say.

The call from Berns came and in January 1967 Van Morrison embarked on his solo career that persists to this day. Herbie and Rod went to London, got a publishing deal and put out a couple of singles as The James' Brothers, before joining eccentric schlock-horror rock 'n' roller Lord Sutch in his touring band.

Less than three years had elapsed since Them debuted at the Maritime Hotel, and the music scene in Northern Ireland was changing rapidly. There was still room for more commercial pop acts in amongst all the snarling blues for those punters that preferred a dash of pop fizz with their sounds.

Dave Davies of The Kinks joins The Stellas on stage in Germany

Although early groups like The Telstars, Vibratones and Twilights, who took their cue from Johnny Kidd and The Pirates and Eddie Cochran, had in many cases evolved into meatier R&B groups, a versatile outfit like The Seekers could still boast substantial support on the domestic scene even while their counterparts were sticking rigidly to traditional blues templates. Hailing from Newcastle, County Down, Tony G. Ford and The Seekers were re-christened The Stellas when Dave Whitren of Stella House in Mount Merrion offered them a contract to tour Germany in early 1965 (he had previously sent out a showband to the German clubs under the same name). Absent from Belfast for large chunks of time, their reputation was upheld by favourable notices in the local press when they released their first record on the continent, 'Wooly Bully', and also when Tony G. Ford was hospitalised after being mobbed by crazed fans. Bangor's coastal venues played host to a thriving scene as well, particularly throughout the summer months. Not only did regional acts such as The Carpetbaggers, Continentals and A-sides enjoy the patronage of local and visiting teenagers, but touring UK artistes like The Kinks and The Searchers also included the County Down coast on their itinerary, assured of an enthusiastic reception.

By early 1967 the original promoters of the Rhythm 'n' Blues Club at the Maritime Hotel had moved on, bringing to an end an important chapter in the birth of R&B in Northern Ireland. Their place was taken by local ballroom dancer Eddie Kennedy, who started up his own weekly happening, Club Rado, at the old seaman's mission. Soon, a guitar wonder from the South, with unruly long hair and an ability unrivalled by anyone else in the country, was drawing crowds of blues enthusiasts to the new club in University Square with his ground-breaking three-piece powerhouse, Taste. Living eight miles up the road in Bangor, Rory Gallagher arrived on Belfast's music scene via Dublin's basement clubs, where he had already stunned the capital's beat aficionados.

SMILEY BOLGER Rory Gallagher in the Scene Club on a Sunday afternoon. Absolutely fucking unreal. I was DJing there. The Movement, I think, were playing the same day and Rory came on to do a short set, half an hour during the intermission. The whole place was just 'Wha?' People had heard of him, but no one had seen him. 'Blister On The Moon' hadn't come out, but he played it that day. He was probably the most humble of all the stars that have come out of Ireland, all the time. He was on

> a mission from God and he just stuck to it. There was something about that sound, that three piece. I was so sad when the Taste broke up, that combination was really electric. You know the way some bands have it and some bands don't…they definitely had it.

Gallagher was born in Ballyshannon, County Donegal, in 1948 but moved to Cork with his family when he was eight years old. The typical roll call of influences that the first wave of beat musicians always acknowledge were shared enthusiastically by Rory as well – Chuck Berry, Elvis Presley, Eddie Cochran, Lonnie Donegan and old-time blues. In 1964 the self-taught guitarist answered an ad in the *Cork Examiner* placed by a local seven-piece seeking a new member and quickly found himself touring on the demanding country ballroom circuit with The Fontana Showband. Updating their name to the more hip-sounding Impact, the band was causing quite a stir by the summer of 1965, and not just with their music. Image-wise, this young showband (average age nineteen years) dressed more like their contemporaries on the British pop scene, markedly at odds with the older be-suited colleagues. Dressed head-to-toe in tight black trousers and black polo necks, The Impact shocked viewers when they appeared on RTE's *Pickin' The Pops*, who were particularly disapproving of their unkempt hair styles. The Impact's

Rory Gallagher (centre) with The Impact, 1965

manager at the time was unperturbed by the consternation: 'Some of the boys wear their hair short, some long, according to their own individual taste. Rory, who has really long hair, is just seventeen. At the moment he is studying for his Leaving Cert exam in June. He sings four nights a week with the band and rehearses for two. He has also found time in the past month to compose nine songs. He doesn't smoke or drink, and as far as I'm concerned he is quite welcome to grow his hair any length he likes – provided he keeps it clean and well groomed as at present. Anyway, when would he find time to get a haircut?' (*Spotlight*, June 1965)

When Rory's educational commitments had been fulfilled, the band took off to Spain for a two-month stint playing in American army bases, followed by engagements in the UK. This led on to the rites-of-passage tour of the German nightclub circuit, at the end of which the ambitious Donegal man parted company with his less committed band members. Gallagher had always been more interested in stretching himself musically rather than churning out country and pop covers to waltzing couples. Having supported touring groups such as The Animals in Ireland, and having witnessed gigs by The Byrds and Rolling Stones in England, the teenager pressed for change within The Impact, encouraging his colleagues to adopt the sounds and styles of a beat group. Not everyone in the band shared his vision, and the six-piece unit split at the end of 1965 just as they were preparing to go to Germany for a few shows which an agent had arranged for them. To honour the outstanding commitment some of the last gigs that Rory Gallagher played in Hamburg, under the name The Impact, were in a three-piece set-up of guitar, bass and drums. He found the structure suited him quite nicely.

It would be a little while before Gallagher pursued his vision of a rock trio on a more even footing. Few beat groups of the time made a decent living out of the German club circuit and The Impact were no different. A gruelling schedule, lack of money and the reluctance of promoters and punters to embrace the radical concept of just three musicians on stage meant the experiment came to an end in early 1966. Rory returned home to find a lively group scene developing in Cork, where local boys The Yaks and The Axills ruled the roost. The Axills were a promising four-piece outfit that were the first group from the banks of the river Lee to appear in Dublin's clubland. At the time that Rory met them, an American tour was being planned, with the group's first record due to appear in October that year. Neither event happened. After stepping in with The Axills for a couple of gigs, Rory took Eric D'Amery (drums) and Norman Kitteringham (bass) away from the others and formed The Taste. If music fans on the Continent were unwilling to accept a three-man group it was unlikely that the new band would fare any better in their home town. Out of necessity, The Taste would often employ non-musician friends to stand idly behind unplugged instruments on ballroom stages to counteract the Federation of Musicians of Ireland's restrictive policy of insisting on a minimum of seven members in any one line-up. Dublin was more receptive to the novel concept, and the Scene Club on Parnell Square became a regular haunt for Eric, Norman and Rory. It was in Belfast, however, that they found their true spiritual home.

In late 1966, ex-Yardbird and Bluesbreaker Eric Clapton, along with Ginger Baker and Jack Bruce (both of whom served time in The Graham Bond Organisation), came to the attention of music lovers under the guise of Cream, who turned out to be one of the most influential groups to emerge in 1960s Britain. Through their devotion to hard urban blues and the deification of the guitar hero via the persona of Clapton, Cream were at the vanguard of psychedelia-tinged blues rock, and along with groups such as Led Zeppelin and Deep Purple paved the way for the subsequent development of hard rock in the 1970s. Rory Gallagher's Taste were fashioned along similar lines – a loud forceful three-man blues juggernaut, centred on the technical brilliance of their lead player, with a disdain for conventional pop mores and a dedication to the earthy sounds of Muddy Waters, Howlin' Wolf *et al.* Rory was keen to play down comparisons with Cream however, and that other three-piece outfit to whom they were commonly compared, The Jimi Hendrix Experience: 'They're both great groups. But we're not trying to copy either of them. We just want to play our own type of music…we just want to be The Taste from Cork.' (*Spotlight*, Volume 1, No. 35, 8 Jan 1968)

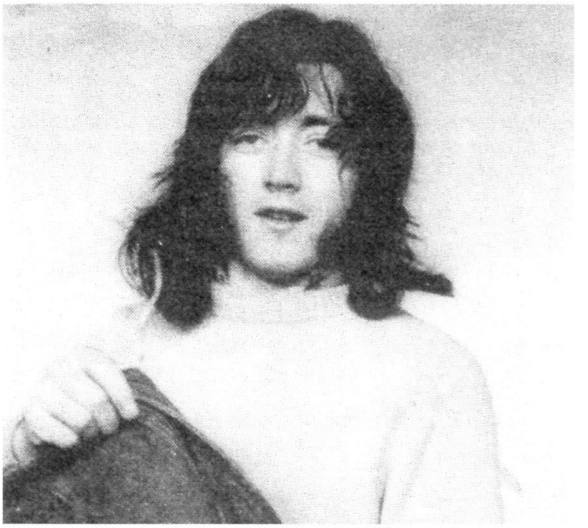

Rory Gallagher, 1968

So well received were they in Belfast that the group became inextricably linked to the scene in that city, particularly in the minds of fans in Great Britain, where they toured with increasing regularity as 1968 progressed. In an interview for TV documentary *Rock 'n' the North*, taped shortly before his death in 1995, Gallagher spoke fondly of the early days in Ulster.

> **RORY GALLAGHER** My times in Belfast are ultra clear to me. I made so many friends and had a great time. We did the whole thing – the Maritime, called the Rado, Cecil Clarks, Betty Staffs, Cloud 9 in Bangor. We did Ballymena; we did Derry, the whole shebang. And I miss those days to be honest with you.

The group's first single, the riff-heavy 'Blister On The Moon', was released on Major Minor Records in May. Written by Rory, it was one of a handful of songs recorded in Emerald Records' new studios in Belfast under the supervision of Mervyn Solomon, who recognised huge potential in the young guitar ace. The by now prolific songsmith had penned so many tunes that the group had gone to England in February to lay down tracks for what their manager Eddie Kennedy hoped would be their first album. Playing in between sessions, The Taste's reputation grew rapidly, and they were talked up by none other than highly-respected outfit Bluesbrakers, led by John Mayall. Their rivals in Cream came to see them play at the Marquee. After being released from their short-term contract with Major Minor, top producers Jimmy Miller (who had worked with The Rolling Stones and Traffic) and Kit Lambert (involved with The Who) bid for the recording rights of the Irish trio. *Melody Maker* praised them as the finest three piece blues sound in the world.

While The Taste were making headway in the London rock underground another Irish trio were on a similar trip, having outgrown their beginnings in the clubs of Belfast and Dublin over the previous few months. When they played the famous Marquee club just three days after Taste – 6 June 1968 – supporting Keith Emerson's The Nice, they were strangely (albeit temporarily) known as Red Light District. Their fans back home in Belfast knew them as The Method, a thundering blues-rock outfit led by sixteen-year-old Dave Lewis, who in a rapid rise to prominence amongst progressive psychedelic types found himself swapping the short pants of his school uniform for the flowing hippy kaftans and colourful beads of the counterculture set in London within the space of eighteen months. Inevitably their three man set-up (Wilgar Campbell on drums and Nigel Smith on bass accompanied Lewis, who played guitar and sang) drew comparisons with Cream, not without some justification.

> **DAVE LEWIS** Here I was playing a Gibson Les Paul like Eric Clapton. Wilgar had two bass drums and was hitting them like Ginger Baker, doing fifteen minute drum solos and the bass player was really good. We could really play. It wasn't like someone pretending, we were totally absorbed in it all the time, all day and all night. Rory and The Taste were more Hendrix. We were more Cream, but we were actually doing our own stuff way back then too. Wilgar wrote a couple of songs and I seemed to be writing all the time. We would rehearse a lot, maybe three times a week, knocking out new songs.

Lewis had joined the group in Northern Ireland when they were a five-piece soul band, their manager George Mechan spotting an obvious talent that the youngster was hardly aware of himself. Largely oblivious to the geyser of R&B groups that Belfast had spewed forth since 1964, the schoolboy spent his time mimicking the vocal tics of Elvis Presley and Roy Orbison, encouraged by a Welsh father who in his own day was blessed with a great tenor voice, and a mother who entered her son into talent contests from the age of nine. The moment of revelation for Lewis came about not from the music in his own locale, but from the product of a white English boy's fascination with the American blues.

The Method, 1967. L-R: Paul Hannah, Dave Lewis, Wilgar Campbell

> **DAVE LEWIS** My life changed around the age of fifteen, when someone gave me a copy of John Mayall's Bluesbreakers' album. When I heard Eric Clapton play, it really got under my skin. For about six months, even before I came into contact with The Method, I'd been practicing and starting to go that way.

The five-piece soul band soon trimmed down to a blues three-piece, and with original bass player Paul Hannah, The Method built up a name for themselves in venues north and south of the border, with an ear-splitting sound delivered through hand-made fuzz tone boxes and huge stacks of Marshall amps. In late 1967, just as the group were making Dublin their permanent home, Hannah fell out with George Mechan and was replaced by Nottingham-born Nigel Smith, a veteran of soul revues on the German army bases during his time with UK soul-rockers The In-Crowd. Living away from his parents for the first time in Sandymount, Dave Lewis found life in the Republic's capital exhilarating. Their purposeful and industrious manager was keen to push his boys and organised arduous boat trips to England where they would drive all the way to London's West End in their Ford Transit for one-off appearances. A car accident in June 1968 momentarily derailed the group's momentum, with lead guitarist and bass player both suffering serious injuries, necessitating a three week stay in hospital for the former. An old school chum of Dave Lewis, who used to come around and practice in his friend's attic whilst listening attentively to Jeff Beck records, stepped in to fulfil outstanding engagements. His name was Gary Moore.

It became increasingly impractical to undertake marathon sea and road journeys over to Great Britain just to play one or two gigs, a situation that irked Method members just as they were securing more dates at the Marquee and Eel Pie Island, playing support to emerging rock groups like Spooky Tooth and Free.

> **DAVE LEWIS** I was hungry to go on. We were getting fed up going backwards and forwards, going through all the hassle, the driving. I thought, 'I really want to stay in London; I want to make the break.' So we were standing looking in a music shop on Shaftsbury Avenue, thinking how can we work it so we don't have to go back [to Ireland]. This guy taps Wilgar Campbell on

> the shoulder and says, 'Are you guys a band?' [Wilgar] looked around and there's this little guy, dark skin, in a bomber jacket. He said, 'It sounds ridiculous but my band just walked out on me and I've got a summer season in Jersey starting at the weekend.' We were pretty crazy, we just said, 'Yeah we'll do it', and sent the road manager back to Ireland to face [George Mechan].

Rocky Shahan was a Pakistan-born musical entertainer who had a residency at the West Park Pavilion on Jersey, singing chart covers to the islanders, dressed in exotic bull fighter's garb. Dave, Nigel and Wilgar backed him for two hours on their first night in Saint Helier before Shahan sheepishly recognised how good his discoveries actually were. He immediately ditched his aspirations to be a pop star and changed his focus to managing the band, taping a live performance by his new discoveries before scurrying off back to London in search of a record deal. 'We completely took over this island,' declares Lewis. 'They had never seen the like of us. Hair down over our shoulders, walking around in robes!'

Meanwhile, fellow Irish trio Taste came to a grinding halt when Rory decided to let Eric D'Amery and Norman Ketteringham go, and reform his band. They played their last gig at Belfast's Tiffany Club on Wednesday 21 August 1968. Their leader made light of the situation in a contemporary interview.

> **RORY GALLAGHER** It was a difficult decision. We took the group to its peak and The Taste didn't get stale but it would have. Time musn't be wasted, so I'm restarting immediately, taking John [Wilson] and Richie [McCracken] to London just to see how it works out. I've been listening to Coltrane, Ornette Coleman, Charles Lloyd – the '*avant garde*'. If you trace back, all these players were once with blues bands, so it's an interesting parallel to see how they came from blues to jazz, and it'll be interesting to see how it'll influence me. But blues will always be the main theme. (*Spotlight*, Vol. 2, No. 15, 7 Sept 1968)

In the dirt that caked the group's van outside Tiffany's fans had scribbled 'Norman and Eric must stay', but it was to be the last involvement of both musicians in Irish rock groups of any note. Kitteringham played for a short while with The Martell's Showband before pursuing a career in printing. Interviewed in March 1970 by Pat Egan, the bass player had no regrets about his sacking.

> **ERIC KITTERINGHAM** It happened because Rory was advancing too fast for us. We just couldn't keep up with him. He is, I feel,

> still improving and will soon be huge all over the world. I had been finding things hard with Taste. Actually I had wanted for some time to leave. When the break came I was glad to come home. (*Spotlight*, Vol. 3, No. 41, 20 March 1970)

Richie McCracken, who took over bass duties from Kitteringham in Taste Mark II, and John Wilson, who became the drummer, were previously members of another Irish power blues trio from Northern Ireland, Cheese, who, as their name suggests, were also fascinated by the possibilities inherent in Cream's set-up. The path was cleared for the new Taste to become the pre-eminent group of their type when the weight of egos in Cream proved too heavy to handle and they went their separate ways at the end of 1968. In a metaphorical passing of the baton ceremony, Rory and his new cohorts played support to Cream at their farewell concert at the Albert Hall on 28 December.

Taste's self-titled debut LP was released by Polydor in March 1969, its nine tracks mostly written by Gallagher with a few traditional blues tunes thrown in. This was the material that both line-ups of the group had been playing in their live shows for the best part of two years. The technical ability of Gallagher evidenced throughout the album is not in doubt, but depending on your penchant for blues improvisation, the abundance of solos and preponderance of driving riffs can become a little tedious. Some lukewarm reviews at the time lamented the fact that the record didn't reflect the incredible energy of Taste's live shows. It was upon these live appearances that Taste continued to enhance their standing in Europe, building up loyal followings in Denmark, Holland and Germany. Later that year the group were invited to support Blind Faith (now home to Eric Clapton and Ginger Baker) on a tour of North America, which helped spread their name on the other side of the Atlantic. Rory Gallagher spoke with Royston Eldridge of the *Melody Maker* about the group's ongoing development.

> **RORY GALLAGHER** The effect of touring with Blind Faith was that we tightened up the act. Basically we were playing massive stadiums in front of a lot more people but we didn't arrange the numbers to suit the bigger crowds, we just tried to let the music happen naturally. We've matured a little and tried to give our music a little bit more taste [pun intended?]. On the new album for which we're just doing the final reductions, we've included all original material as compared to the last album which had about six or seven originals. It is an abstract goal that we are aiming for; we just want to play what is natural to us regardless of what it is. The 'underground' as most people call it has done a lot of good. Musically the whole scene is improving although sometimes people seem to forget the

> enjoyment thing. If you intellectualise a thing too much, it loses its freedom. (*Spotlight*, Vol. 3, No. 21, 24 Oct 1969 in association with *Melody Maker*)

Taste in London, 1969

The new album, *On The Boards*, hit the shops in February 1970, incorporating some of those jazz elements that Taste's lead guitarist was so keen to discuss in contemporary interviews (he even plays alto sax on the title track). It sold better than its predecessor, entering the UK Top 20, but it would be their final release. Hitting a commercial peak by appearing at the legendary Isle of Wight Festival that year, Taste's demise coincided with the death of the group scene in Belfast brought on by the beginnings of the Troubles. The precise reason for the termination of a group on such an upward musical trajectory is difficult to ascertain. To this day participants are sketchy on the actual details, but a combination of personal and managerial problems seems to have contributed to the break.

> **JOHN WILSON** No band splitting is a nice amicable affair. It's always very mucky. Between Rory, [Richie] and myself it should never have been allowed get to that because we shared a magical thing that most musicians never get a chance to experience in their lives. (*Rock 'n' The North*, TV documentary)

A few months before Taste put out their second and final record, Dave Lewis managed to write, record and release the debut long player for Andwella's Dream – yet another new name for The Method that neatly reflected the ephemerally idealistic era in which that LP *Love & Poetry* was created. Rocky Shahan made contact with Andrew Miller of Reflection

Records in London, who encouraged the prolific Lewis to record his compositions at any available opportunity, keeping the group on a retainer and putting them up in a flat in Bayswater. Andwella's Dream's front man was like a lightning rod conductor for his songs, channelling the notes, chords and words down onto paper in a feverish burst of creativity.

> **DAVE LEWIS** I dreamt a lot of the songs I was writing. It was all a bit dream-like back then, the 60s! I was writing songs every day. Very quickly [Miller] was on to me about my song-writing and he had me in the studio as much as possible, rather than [playing] live gigs. They just came through me. I'd be on a bus or I'd wake up…I never actually sit down [to write]. I mean I sat down to develop things. My apartment was always full of paper. I'd have my little machine to record onto, that was it. I was knocking out a song a day.

A lot of the material on *Love & Poetry* had featured at the odd live gig that Andwella's Dream were doing at the time, a fact evidenced from the compact and confident nature of the delivery on the record. This assurance was in spite of a last minute disruption in the ranks, which threatened to scupper the group's plans.

> **DAVE LEWIS** Just before we started to do the album, Wilgar pulled out. He's actually only on one track, 'Felix', which is the best drumming on the album. That's when the bottom fell out of it for me. Wilgar had a wife and two young kids back in Belfast. It was difficult for him; he wasn't in the same situation as myself and Nigel Smith.

Lewis was unsure of the suitability of the replacement candidate, Gordon Barton:

> **DAVE LEWIS** He was like Keith Moon. I thought this is never going to work. But the studio was booked. We were slung in the studio and I thought this guy was always too busy on his drums, but anyway we did it. He was only with us about three weeks before that album.

Invariably tagged as a progressive rock record, *Love & Poetry* thankfully shies away from the overblown excesses that came to characterise the worst of that genre's output. In fact, scattered throughout the LP are a number of concise psyche-rock gems that would not have been out of place on radio playlists of the day – from the fatalistic folk-rock strains of 'Man Without A Name' to the delicate Beatles pastiche 'Midday Sun'. Elsewhere, there is a beautifully nostalgic feel to the record, the tone deftly set by wistful opener 'The Days Grew Longer For Love'.

Think about the times when we sat on the grass by that river
When words that I'd learned made you laugh
And your mind grasped the meaning
And the days grew longer for love

Days turned to years and the tears
Caused life's pipe to stop burning
Together we would stand, hand in hand,
Bound to the cause of each other

Andwella's Dream, 1969. L-R: Dave Lewis, Nigel Smith, Gordon Barton

The basic three-piece sound of Andwella's Dream on the album is occasionally supplemented by the restrained inclusion of strings, courtesy of the group's arranger.

> **DAVE LEWIS** All of a sudden John Hawkins would put an orchestra on something like 'Take My Road'. We thought 'oh, this is quite nice' but it wasn't the plan. We just went in as a three piece and laid down the tracks. Although we did rehearse a lot in the flat with Bob Downes, the flute player who was amazing. He did the intro to 'Lost A Number, Found A King'. I loved that. This guy was walking across the studio on dry leaves and that was all being recorded. And he was playing wooden flutes and finger bells. We were in our element then!

The record positively shimmers in the hazy golden sunlight of the late 60s; an elegy to that era's fading hopes and dreams, recounted personally through the pen of seventeen year old Lewis. The best Irish rock album of the 1960s? Quite possibly.

After the record's release there was hardly time to take stock of what was happening. Lewis continued to churn out the songs, and Andrew Miller struggled to keep up, neglecting to formulate a coherent plan for the group's development. A single called 'Mrs. Man' was casually issued in September 1969. Andwella's Dream's lead singer was hardly aware of its existence.

> **DAVE LEWIS** As I was writing the songs there seemed to be a studio available. I think it was a built-in clause in the publishing deal that they would supply a studio to put the songs down in as they were written. So the guys and I would go into the studios and record songs as I wrote them. It surprised me that it came out as a single.

The Reflection Records' boss was shrewdly aware of the potential returns from publishing royalties, and encouraged his young dependant to keep writing, passing on the compositions to anyone who would have them – bizarrely including daytime soap actor Stuart Damon who at the time was starring in English TV series *The Champions*. Andrew Miller also inadvertently came up with the genesis for Andwella's second album.

> **DAVE LEWIS** *Love & Poetry* was well received to such an extent that they stuck up a lot of money to do another album. Andrew Miller originally asked me to write something about [what was called] the Rape of Chelsea at the time. The council were redeveloping the World's End area at the top of the King's Road. Of course I couldn't write anything about that, so I started

> thinking about the end of the world and I was off on that one! The songs I felt were stronger, they were more interesting melodically. We went into a bigger studio and John Hawkins stuck more brass on it and more strings and all his musicians got fed. It was over-produced. I was green and didn't know anything. I just got up, ate cornflakes and wrote songs.

From his own point of view, one satisfying aspect of the recording sessions for the *World's End* LP (1970) was that Lewis got to work with jazz veteran Bobby Scott, an established figure who had played keyboards for Aretha Franklin. When long player number three, *People's People*, came out a year later, Andwella (the 'Dream' part now officially dropped) was about to wake from its reverie. 'By that time [Reflection Records] weren't interested in the other guys [in the band] at all,' laments Lewis. 'We had lost what we had set out to do when we left Ireland. But my song-writing was getting better and better.' Indeed, his song-writing skills were justly recognised when the darling of the 1970s middle-class dinner-party set, Greek singer Demis Roussos, had a breakthrough hit with one of Lewis' creations, 'Happy To Be An Island In The Sun'. 'I didn't even know who Demis Roussos was at that time!' confesses Lewis.

Andwella came to an end in 1972. By then, the music scene back in Dave Lewis' hometown was also truly finished. Political and religious tensions had been simmering throughout 1969, and by the end of the summer British Army troops were on the streets of Derry and Belfast, deployed to keep the peace in the face of escalating riots. It would be the beginning of an unforeseeably lengthy period of turmoil and tragedy. A by-product of the Troubles was the decimation of the live music scene in the province.

> **SAM SMYTH** You couldn't go out at night. People who went out at night were taking their lives in their hands. There were random killings. Whatever about music, it dramatically changed Belfast for the poorer, because people stuck very closely to their own areas. No one knew the Troubles were going to last thirty years, everybody thought it would be over in a few months.

With people fearful and suspicious, club dance floors emptied – fewer groups were coming through and many promoters were forced to shut their doors. Some commentators had already bemoaned the state of Belfast's beat scene a full two years before the Troubles began. Desi Duke, DJ at the Plaza ballroom, was unequivocal in his denunciation of what he saw as a staid musical environment: 'The Belfast scene is really dead, and as far as I am concerned, and most of the other beat addicts in town, it will probably stay that way. The groups are disillusioned, the promoters are working like milkmen, and the fans are fed up. The promoters are to blame. They do not give the fans what they want. Promoters in Dublin do and the scene is not dead there. All they are interested in is raking in the money from the dances they run. The only decent clubs that are still trying to cater for fans are the Maritime and the Jazz Club. The rest of the clubs have gone to pieces.' (*City Week*, 3 Aug 1967)

In truth, the scene was still relatively healthy at that stage. The Bats, Alleykatz, Wheels and other originators of the R&B boom were perhaps no more, but there were plenty of eager youngsters willing to take their place. The Electric Honeypot opened in Bangor and put on psychedelic happenings featuring newcomers The Set and The Few, as well as hosting The Crazy World of Arthur Brown from England. The Marquee Club celebrated its launch at the Astor Ballroom in October 1967, entertaining fans with far-out slide shows and movie projections. The Creative Mind, The Gentry and Sunshine (who had evolved out of The Interns) were just a few of the names now regularly featured in the pop columns of the *Belfast Telegraph* and *City Week*, whereas before it was Them, The Luvin' Kind and The People. But optimism would be short-lived. The initial burst of creativity that had produced the first R&B groups could only last a finite amount of time. A lot of groups looked to the Dublin club world for steady work, whereas others decamped abroad to pursue their careers. In an atmosphere of tension and violence the freewheeling, all-encompassing non-sectarian attitude of just a few years previous began to dissolve. It wouldn't be until the late 1970s that heirs to Them's throne, like The Undertones and Stiff Little Fingers, came along to re-invigorate a waning industry.

Part Five

Initially America was quite taken aback by the deluge of British beat musicians (The Beatles, Herman's Hermits, Dave Clarke Five, etc.) that invaded their country in the early months of 1964, and the harder edged R&B kings (The Rolling Stones, Animals, Yardbirds, etc.) that followed soon after. The very idea of British rock 'n' roll seemed a puzzling oxymoron – rock music was American through and through, while the Brits were a quaint homely race with crooked teeth and an outdated monarchy, so what were these Limeys doing stepping off transatlantic flights and sending the nation's youth into hysterics? The response from rock's birthplace was not too long in coming, and took the form of what is now universally referred to as 'garage rock'.

All across the fifty states, in mostly middle-class suburban homes, young kids (almost always boys, nearly all still in school) convinced their post-war wealthy parents to buy a guitar or a set of drums, and quickly cobbled together groups to try and emulate the music played by their British R&B/beat heroes. A lot of these new regional garage bands (the Pacific Northwest, California and Texas had particularly lively scenes) mastered only a very basic command of their instruments. Some achieved an acceptable level of dexterity and contented themselves with playing local frat houses and teenage dance parties. A few talented ones managed to write their own songs and get them played alongside big stars on their local radio station. And a handful achieved that lucky smash hit record out of the blue, momentarily breaking out of their local market and going nationwide before quickly returning to relative obscurity again due to bad luck, bad management, bad judgement or simply the inability to come up with another decent song. Few of these groups were taken seriously, and were largely dismissed or forgotten about when rock matured into its psychedelic, progressive and culturally 'important' phase in the late 1960s. Many of the musicians involved with the original garage bands found themselves either in a Vietnamese jungle by this time, or on college campuses trying to avoid that fate. Their legacy however was much more far reaching than they ever could have anticipated – their drive, exuberance and passion were recognised by musicians in the nascent punk rock scenes, both in the US and England in the mid-70s, who were appalled at the complacency of the West Coast singer/songwriters and the over-indulgence of the serious progressive rockers. The 60s garage rock bands were belatedly acknowledged as torch bearers of the true rock 'n' roll spirit of the 1950s.

It is a little known fact that two Irish expatriate musicians were major participants in this first wave of garage bands to emerge in the wake of the 'British Invasion', and although their success was fleeting at the time, their groups – The Beau Brummels and The Count Five – have firmly secured their place in 1960s rock history, one as the very first band to fire a return volley at the marauding Brit armies (anticipating the birth of folk rock in the process) and the other as the creator of a classic 45rpm that encapsulated all that was and is exciting, brilliant, timeless and true about rock 'n' roll.

The Count Five

While his fellow musicians were rocking, hopping and thrashing their way around the burgeoning beat group scene in Dublin in 1964, one particular Irishman, John Byrne (aka Sean Byrne), reluctantly found himself on an aeroplane travelling across the ocean, bound for California. Over in the sprawling suburbs of San Jose, he was soon fronting a snot-nosed rock band that would release one of the greatest garage punk singles of them all, 'Psychotic Reaction'. Just like Ian Whitcomb and Bluesville and hundreds of other bands at the time, The Count Five were dismissed as flash-in-the-pan purveyors of derivative throwaway nonsense, having just that one hit single to their name. Indeed, nothing they released after this debut 7" ever had the same impact – but that's beside the point. Listening to it today it's patently clear the song's power and impact has not diminished over time – a simple fuzz guitar riff, a persistent thudding back beat, John Byrne's casual delivery of those universal lyrics about frustrated unrequited love and the *psychotic reaction* of the song title expressed in frenetic breaks of frustrated noise – the song is three minutes of rock 'n' roll perfection. Re-assessed by infamous rock scribe Lester Bangs* in 1971, five years after its release, and re-issued alongside other garage greats on the era-defining *Nuggets* compilation in 1972 (and again on the *Nuggets* CD box set in 1998), 'Psychotic Reaction' can rightly take its place amongst the classics, thrilling new generations of listeners with each passing decade.

John Byrne, the youngest of eleven children, from the working-class suburb of Drimnagh, west Dublin, was initially smitten by Elvis Presley and the rockabilly explosion of the late 50s and later obsessed, like so many

* Lester Bangs wrote about rock music for such magazines as *Creem*, *The Village Voice* and *Penthouse* from the late 1960s until his death in 1982. Famed for his passionate diatribes and often confrontational interviews, he was highly influenced by the 'gonzo' writer Hunter S. Thompson. His reputation as a maverick 'punk' journalist has grown over the years as his work has reached an ever-expanding circle of devotees through its publication in anthology form.

others, with The Beatles. He ran into some like-minded individuals whilst attending the College of Commerce in Rathmines and formed a short-lived beat group called The Scorpions (named after his star sign). The group, with Brendan Walsh on vocals (John played rhythm guitar), never became truly established. Their live appearances were limited to a few gigs at local halls and a couple of support slots to the main feature film playing at movie theatres like the long-gone Leinster in Dolphin's Barn. When John's mother died he moved to the United States with his father to join an older brother Leo already living there, arriving in the sun-soaked Golden State in July 1964. His bandmates in The Scorpions begged John's father not to leave, seeing the talent in their guitarist and the unrealised potential in their group. Mr. Byrne left the difficult decision up to his son.

Across the street from his new house in San Jose, John could hear a local band practising. They were called, with typical Brit overtones, The Squires. The group had been formed by friends Ron Chaney, John 'Mouse' Michalski and Kenn Ellner, who spent their early days in the group bashing out surf and R&B covers to college fraternity and sorority parties. As Merseybeat acts such as The Searchers and Beatles began to make an impact in the US their songs were incorporated into the band's repertoire as well. Fortuitously for The Squires, Beatles fanatic John Byrne happened to turn up at just the right time, crossing the street to Ken's house to see what all the racket was about. Soon enough he was invited to join.

> **JOHN BYRNE** I was kinda confined when I came over [to San Jose] and I had no way to get around and they were the closest thing to me. I walked over one night and I said, 'Can I sit in?' and they said sure and then they said, 'Okay, you're hired!'

The instrumental numbers were dropped and in time the set developed into one full of all things British – The Kinks, The Yardbirds, The Rolling Stones and other more obscure fare such as The Mojos and The Merseybeats – as well as John's fellow Irishmen, Them. Soon enough, when the group had gained some confidence, John began to impress on them the need to incorporate original material into their set, offering a recently written song called 'Move It Up Closer' (not officially released until 2003 when it came out on the Big Beat Records' definitive compilation *Psychotic Revelation*). Dedication to his beloved beat music and the flourishing US garage rock scene compelled John to be fashionably dressed and suitably hirsute.

> **JOHN BYRNE** My father was very Irish, he believed in short, back and sides. We were sitting at the table in my brother's house one night, I was growing my hair long because I was trying to get into that 60s thing. My father looked at me and he says, 'You have to have your hair cut, John', and I said, 'No, I'm not doing

it.' My brother then joined in and so I walked out of the house and I never went back.

John Byrne (left) with his father, California, 1965

In late 1965 the band changed their name to The Count Five (drummer Skip Cordell made up the numbers, soon to be replaced by permanent member Craig 'Butch' Atkinson). A gimmick was needed to differentiate the group in the cluttered local scene. Ken came up with idea of wearing vampire capes (a classic promotional photograph of the time show the group in their Dracula outfits outside a suitably eerie-looking house, Ken Ellner sporting a fetching Brian Jones-style wig!) It also helped that John was from the 'British Isles', which was a great selling point that the group worked to their advantage in those days of Beatlemania. Initially the band developed a strong following in the locality, playing teen clubs and universities, mixing the lesser known album cuts of the Brit groups with some fledgling originals. John was an avid record collector and would travel up to San Francisco with the other guys from the group, trawling the record stores for new British imports. It was around this time that he came up with the music for 'Psychotic Reaction' – a spontaneous creation about a broken love affair that had echoes of a recent radio airplay hit by The Yardbirds called 'I'm A Man'. Ken Ellner, speaking to archivist Alec

Palao for the *Psychotic Revelation* liner notes, remembers that the structure of the tune was worked up between the other Counts at a practise session.

> **KEN ELLNER** It was one of those nights where we weren't really rehearsing, people just sorta floated in, it was weird. And so John started playing chords along to the harp [harmonica], and then Butch came in the room and did a drum beat to it, and then Mouse and Roy kinda added a whole thing, and the next thing you know we had this song.

The song certainly made an impression on Ken's father Sol Ellner, who witnessed the hysterical reaction to its performance at one of their shows and decided to become the band's manager in the spring of 1966. Sol was a tenacious operator and got to work lining up auditions with prospective record labels, insisting they play their new composition to the suits each time. No one was biting. As the group trudged through one audition after the next the song began to evolve, little bits being added or changed, until that distinctive thrilling intro was created. Finally, after being turned down by seven different labels, including Capitol Records twice, in June 1966 a newly established LA company by the name of Double Shot Records took the leap of faith and offered The Count Five a contract (realising their mistake, Capitol would try to buy out the group's contract from Double Shot a short time later). Rushed into a recording studio in Hollywood the group laid down the basic track for the song, but when the completed mix was sent to them a couple of weeks later they hardly recognised it. Producer Hal Winn of Double Shot had spliced the 'rave-up' section in the middle of the song on to the end (originally the song came to an abrupt stop after a clumsy key change) and also altered the overall sound using studio equalisation techniques, emphasising the pounding rhythm section to the detriment of the chiming guitar. The single was released to the market only a few weeks after that session (marketing campaign? what marketing campaign?), backed with another John Byrne original 'They're Gonna Get You', a tale of paranoia featuring an odd falsetto turn by the lead singer.

Initially 'Psychotic Reaction' received minimal play across California (there were accusations that the song was a drug ode simply because of the word 'psychotic') but after hitting big in a few out-of-state locations momentum began to gather. Climbing up the airplay lists of various key radio stations, by October 1966 The Count Five had managed to reach number five in Billboard's Top 100 nationwide singles (it hit the number one spot in many local markets and also in Canada), which was a remarkable and confounding achievement for a young band hardly prepared for this sort of success. John remembers that radio stations which had previously fobbed the group off during initial rounds of promotion were a lot more accommodating as the record became a fixture on their playlists.

> **JOHN BYRNE** We went to this radio station, KLRA in Los Angeles, and they picked us up in a limousine and I'm thinking, 'Something's going on here!' There was this huge mob outside, and all the girls were jumping on the car – it was a lot of fun.

The success of the single propelled them from the carousel of the local garage band circuit into a string of juicy support slots for some of their British Invasion heroes like The Yardbirds. One particularly memorable night was at the Warren County Showgrounds in Santa Barbara, on the same bill as Them.

> **JOHN BYRNE** We were doing a show, sandwiched between two Morrisons – Jim Morrison of The Doors and Van Morrison of Them. Van wanted to meet me, because he heard I was from Dublin. He was backstage having his hair teased, and he was drinking from a bottle of Bushmills. He told me that Dublin was his favourite city in the whole world... Underneath [the venue] was a restaurant, so we went down and Jim Morrison was in his typical stance, leaning against the bar. He said, 'I wanna know who sings "Psychotic Reaction"' and they all pointed at me. So he came over and shook my hand and he said, 'I love your voice and I love that song.'

The cordial atmosphere between the new friends did not last the whole night. The Count Five noticed later on that their snare drum was missing and their suspicions fell on the Lizard King and his entourage – after a quick pow-wow The Counts swiped Jim's precious leather jacket to even things up.

The group were soon whisked into LA's Nashville West recording studios by Double Shot Records to work on tracks for a full-length album.

> **JOHN BYRNE** They needed an album *right now* and they were pressurising me to write songs. I was writing songs on the way down to LA in the aeroplane. I had to come up with a lot of stuff immediately.

'Psychotic Reaction's' shadow loomed large over the sessions, and a few of the tracks sound as if they have been hewn from the same rock as the demented single – notably 'Double Decker Bus' and 'Peace Of Mind'. Given more time the group may have been able to create something more personal and expansive, rather than having to rely on a repetitive formula and the two Who covers (admittedly well executed) that fill out the record. Despite this, the album (also called *Psychotic Reaction*) has an appealing sound that is full and strong on the low end and over the course of its brief thirty minute duration is infused with teenage effervescence, unbridled angst and, most

John Byrne on stage, 1966

importantly, mischievous fun – not least the playful misogyny and snaky groove of third track 'Pretty Big Mouth'.

The LP, with its timeless cover of the group staring malevolently down into what seems to be an open grave (but is in fact part of a derelict building site) fared poorly on release in November 1966, with the record company failing to put much financial clout behind it. All of the members were still in college at this juncture and not yet out of their teens, so time had to be made for gigs and recording sessions in between their studies. Spotting an opportunity for some good old-fashioned hucksterism, manager Sol Ellner circulated the story that the boys had turned down a $1m offer from a New York promoter for a nationwide tour. The explanation given at the time seemed too sensible and logical to come from the mouth of a nineteen-year-old who just had a massive coast-to-coast hit record – 'officially' the boys felt that the music business was fickle and they were concerned about finding themselves sidelined and rejected a few months down the line with nothing to show for their success. Apart from $200,000 each, one presumes. The group also declined an offer to appear on the nationally syndicated *Milton Berle Show* because they couldn't get the time off school, exposure on which might well have propelled them onto a higher level of stardom. However, there may have been a more pressing issue that convinced The Count Five to keep their noses in their textbooks rather than jet around the US being serviced by willing groupies – Vietnam and the spectre of the dreaded draft.

Although 'Psychotic Reaction' was still causing a stir across the country, Double Shot Records released its inferior sound-alike 'Peace Of Mind' the same month as the album came out. The single bombed. Tensions between band and producer were beginning to show, with Hal Winn taking a more domineering role much to the chagrin of John, Kenn, Mouse, Butch and Roy. Like many other music men of the time, the group's producer was fixated on capturing a 'British' sound, to the extent that he even had them record that excruciating seaside novelty 'I've Got A Lovely Bunch Of Coconuts'.

Notwithstanding the lack of success in the recording studio, touring continued when time permitted (usually only at weekends) and the group found themselves backing some big stars such as The Beach Boys (who once demonstrated their new toy, the Theremin, to the group backstage, soon to be employed to stunning effect on 'Good Vibrations'), The Young Rascals, The Hollies and even 'Irishman' Ian Whitcomb. The rewards were handsome: Roy claims that three shows totalling sixty minutes netted the group members $6,000 each per night (interview with Alec Palao for *Psychotic Revelation* line notes). In March 1967 another single was released, a cover of Curtis Mayfield and The Impressions' 'You Must Believe Me' (after 'Psychotic Reaction', probably their most radio-friendly single and another crowd favourite), but by this time Double Shot Records had managed to expand their artists roster and subsequently invested less time and money into The Count Five. Still, three months later *another* 7" came out ('Contrast' b/w 'Merry Go Round'), again a non-album cut written by John, and this time closer to what the group felt was their true live sound. It's a wonder that a third single was put out that year at all, what with the band/label relationship hitting a negative low. Unsurprisingly, the wah-wah laden 'Revelation In Slow Motion' went the same way as the other records. It might have been more appropriate to release the B-side, 'Declaration of Independence', a much stronger tune altogether, but at this stage the fate of the group seemed sealed, destined for a slow obsolescence. These later song-writing efforts, incorporating self-consciously trippy lyrics and daring arrangements certainly reflected the growing influence of psychedelia and the acid rock scene that was exploding up the coast in San Francisco. John Byrne claims never to have been too impressed with the bands that came out of that milieu, apart from the excellent and similarly overlooked Moby Grape. Relationships within the band were also faltering as well, the stress of failed releases and a diminishing number of live appearances taking its toll. In June 1968 the two founding members, Roy Chaney and John 'Mouse' Michalski, were dismissed by management. A letter was sent to both explaining that their sacking was a result of their 'refusal to attend practice sessions, [and] refusal to maintain the required conduct and appearance necessary to promote the purposes of The

Count Five group' (Alec Palao, *Psychotic Revelation* liner notes). John recalls that they were declining to play 'Psychotic Reaction', it had become disliked so much.

There would be no coming back from this loss of the group's core element. Draft problems, commitments to college and day jobs, and a jaded lack of enthusiasm all round conspired to close the lid on The Count Five by the end of 1968.

> **JOHN BYRNE** I went into an induction centre in Oakland [for the draft] and I passed all of the tests. At the end they give you an interview and ask, 'Is there something we might have missed?' I had this eye that I had an operation on and it was half closed.

The board sent John straight down to see a specialist and he was soon back in line, clutching a sealed envelope given to him by the doctor.

> **JOHN BYRNE** I hand the envelope to the guy and say, 'If I go back to college, can I get a deferment?' and he opens it up and says, 'Shut up. You're not being drafted. The doctor gave you an excuse.' You should have heard the crowd cheering behind me.

Double Shot Records made one last attempt to flog the dying horse, bringing John Byrne into the studio on his own to record the unimpressive Hal Winn-penned 'Mailman'. In infamous rock journalist Lester Bangs' fantasy world (published in rambling freeform style in underground magazine *Creem* in 1971), the San Jose garage rockers went on to record four more albums, amongst them the imaginatively titled *Cartesian Jetstream*, *Ancient Lace & Wrought Iron Railings* and *Snowflakes Falling On The International Dateline*. According to Bang's fertile imagination the latter featured 'the unparalleled "Schizophrenic Rainbows: A Raga Concerto", which no one who's sat through its entire twenty-seven minutes will ever be able to forget, especially the thunderous impact of the abrupt and full-volumed entry of George Szell and the Cleveland Orchestra in the eighteenth minute'. (Lester Bangs, *Psychotic Reactions And Carburetor Dung,* p16)

Fanciful and totally constructed from the frazzled cells of the gonzo journalist's mind though it may have been, it was not entirely uncommon for naïve, pliable garage bands of the mid-60s to be co-opted by ambitious producers with their own grand designs in mind. The Electric Prunes, another one-hit wonder psyche-pop band from the same era, released an album in 1968 of organ driven church songs with a space rock twist – a pity that hardly any of the Prunes played on it, the record being the idea of classical composer David Axlerod and backed almost entirely by session guys. Bangs' piece, however, was certainly never meant to be derogatory to The Count Five, and in fact probably helped to keep the legacy of the group alive.

Surrounded by the confessional soft rock mush of James Taylor *et al* and the self-important cock rock of super groups like Led Zeppelin, the writer was celebrating the deliciously crass and immediate appeal of John Byrne and his fellow Counts – the true purveyors of rock 'n' roll's stomach-churning, knee-trembling thrill. (Steve Tyler of Aerosmith once told John Byrne he used to play the single at deafening volume whilst blow-drying his hair back in '66!) Anyone who has become addicted to the sound of that arrogant kick drum, the wailing harmonica and the cacophonous middle eight will nod in agreement with Bangs when he says, 'I'm gonna rock it up and kick out the jams with "Psychotic Reaction" forever.'

Despite some tenuous evidence to the contrary, John Byrne did not become a member of minor British progressive rockers Public Foot The Roman in 1973, nor did he join the sleazily titled 'Legover' in 1978. Apart from a brief trip back to Ireland in 1970 he has remained in the United States, writing proficiently (by his estimation his canon now composes around three hundred songs) and recording occasionally. The Count Five have reformed to play live on a few occasions, firstly in 1987 and more recently for some benefit shows at their old school, Pioneer High. A new aggregation of the original group, The Count, featuring John and Roy Chaney, was formed in 1994 and released an album called *Can't Sleep* in 2002, containing new John Byrne compositions.

The Beau Brummels

A US teenager, flicking through the racks at their local record store in January 1965, on the lookout for some hot new sounds from the UK, would have come across a very English-sounding group called The Beau Brummels, right after scouring the overflowing section dedicated to kings of pop, The Beatles. Assuming they were from the same exotic part of the world, the young beat enthusiast may have been tempted to fish out a few cents from her pocket to purchase the group's brand new single, 'Laugh Laugh'. As she dropped the needle of her record player onto the grooves she would have heard a clean, catchy pop tune with a distinctive twist. Not quite derivative of the Brit sound clogging the country's airwaves, yet atypical of the standard American fare of the time – whitebread folk, surf, goofy novelty songs, Motown – that the British Invasion had been doing its best to sweep away. Neither a folk tune nor a rock tune, but a smooth hybrid of the two, a golden pop single characterised by a smooth mixture of acoustic and electric guitars riding on an infectious bouncing rhythm, topped off with the silky soulful vocals of Sal Valentino, the impressive lead vocalist with the teen idol name. The Beau Brummels from San Francisco were the first to successfully defend the battlements against the Brit Invaders, hitting the US Top 20 with their first two singles in the early months of 1965, paving the way for the belated American response to the shaggy haired strangers from Great Britain. They also presaged the full flowering of the San Francisco acid rock scene, appearing over a year before more internationally famous bands from the area like Jefferson Airplane and The Grateful Dead. The Beau Brummels' fanciful name was deliberately opportunistic – the closest thing to a Brit that the group had was rhythm guitarist Declan Mulligan, a twenty-six-year-old former insurance clerk from Clonmel, County Tipperary.

Declan came from a family steeped in musical and theatrical tradition. His uncle had gone to California to work for the Walt Disney Company and in 1952 brought back an acoustic guitar for his young nephew. On frequent visits to the US he also purchased the latest popular records by emerging talents, who were mixing hillbilly styles with gutsy rhythm 'n' blues. Like much of his generation Declan was also exposed to early rock 'n' roll sounds on Radio Luxembourg and the US Armed Forces Network. His first experiences playing with groups were in short-lived skiffle combos, graduating to second tier showbands when he was studying at University College Dublin in the late 50s.

> **DECLAN MULLIGAN** I was on guitar and I was feeble because I was playing rhythm and also trying to play some of the leads. Ireland had a lot of natural talent but musical education was very much according to the nuns! Wind instruments and piano dominated the musical scene, not the guitars. (Marti Smiley-Childs and Jeff March, *Echoes Of The Sixties*, p146)

In 1960, he emigrated to Canada, hoping to learn the insurance underwriting trade and see the world a little before returning to his father's life insurance business in Clonmel. He kept up his interest in music, playing a mixture of pop and folk songs in a duo around the bars of Toronto, at the same time maintaining an early morning stint on a local radio station spinning rock 'n' roll records. Impressed with San Francisco after visiting the city with a touring soccer team, Mulligan moved there in the summer of 1962, and soon bumped into three younger musicians who would end for him any notion of pursuing a career in the strait-laced business world. They would instead help to propel him to the top of the US pop charts.

> **DECLAN MULLIGAN** One night in early 1963 I went to an Irish dance at this place on Clement Street called Richmond Hall. And Ron Elliot, Sal [Valentino] and John Petersen were there, just like that, playing as a trio. They had no name back then, just playing. And they were refreshing to me, because it wasn't the same old 'heedly, heedly, ha', which was what most of the people there wanted to hear. Most of the bands at Richmond Hall did that 'skeedly-aye-oodley-aye' stuff, but I wanted to hear rock 'n' roll. And these guys were more, excuse the word, 'hep'. (Interview with Jud Cost, www.sundazed.com)

Sal Valentino, who previously sang with his own vocal group The Valentines, and Ron Elliot, a lover of musicals, opera, country music and show tunes, were both from the North Beach area of San Francisco, famous as a hangout for the literary beatniks in the 1950s. Performing as a duo at local weddings and social functions, they soon hooked up with drummer John Petersen who had been bashing the skins for a local group called The Sparklers. Ron Meagher, a university student in Oakland, was introduced to talented songwriter Elliot by the girl he was dating at the time, and with the addition of his bass guitar the five-piece became The Beau Brummels.

The group soon established a name for themselves as the house band at a club called the Morocco Room in San Mateo during the summer of 1964, playing a mixture of Ron Elliot originals and the usual covers from Liverpool, Manchester and London. Two big name DJs on local station KYA in the Bay Area, Bob Mitchell and Tom Donahue, were invited down to the club to hear the new combo. The well-known local personalities had recently set up their own label, Autumn Records, and having tasted success with a novelty hit for Bobby Freeman, were keen on getting some of the new sounding bands onto their roster. One night Tom and Bob waltzed in – two big shot record executives accompanied by their in-house producer, Sylvester Stewart, who would later enjoy great acclaim with his groundbreaking multi-racial funk-rock band Sly & The Family Stone. Impressed with what they saw, the DJs began dropping The Beau Brummels' name regularly on their radio shows, creating a huge buzz around the San Francisco Bay area. They also asked the quintet into their studio to record some demos. The Brummels had made one previous unsuccessful attempt at cutting a few tracks, when the Morocco Room's owner dragged the group down to Gold Star Studios in LA late one night after a tiring club performance. The sessions with Autumn proved to be much more fruitful.

The Beau Brummels, 1965. Declan Mulligan, back row left

> **DECLAN MULLIGAN** Sly was like I wished all producers would be. Maybe it was because it was a new thing for him, but he was alive, very alive. He was very effusive behind the glass. When you're in the studio and you see blank faces staring out at you when you think you're playing something really great, it takes all the steam out of you. Sly would dance around and give us energy. (Interview with Jud Cost, www.sundazed.com)

That energy transferred itself readily to the groups first few singles. As well as scoring a Top Twenty hit with their debut 'Laugh, Laugh', the follow-up 'Just A Little' climbed into the Top Ten, sticking at number eight in May 1965. The group did not see any royalties from record sales but when they were put out on the road following their chart success the dollar bills began to roll in. The stellar acts they appeared with reads like a who's who of the pop universe's biggest names – The Byrds, The Rolling Stones, Marvin Gaye, The Lovin' Spoonful, Stevie Wonder, Sonny & Cher and The Beach Boys. TV appearances were thick on the ground, and the group also featured in teen schlock horror movie *Village Of The Giants*. They even got themselves drawn into an episode of prehistoric cartoon caper *The Flintstones*! As The Beau Brummels were propelled from local attraction to national superstar status, a gruelling touring schedule and the pressure to follow up success with success took its toll on relationships within the group. Mulligan developed a reputation for being a fiery and confrontational character, personality traits that were exacerbated by the band's hectic environment.

> **DECLAN MULLIGAN** I was unhappy on the road. But my departure was partly my fault. I thought things would come easier than they did. I thought if I had talent, I didn't have to work at it. When we came back off the road in the summer of '65, Donahue called me and said, 'Hey, the boys don't want to play with you anymore.' In every band some personalities don't fit. (Marti Smiley-Childs and Jeff March, *Echoes Of The Sixties*, p147)

The group had just released their debut LP, *Introducing The Beau Brummels*, but commercially they would not hit the heights of early 1965 again. A series of disappointing single placements and a poor selling second LP helped contribute to the financial collapse of Autumn Records and their contract was sold to Warners in 1966. Inexplicably, instead of capitalising on the obvious writing talents of chief composer Ron Elliot, the group's new label decided their next album should be composed entirely of cover versions of hits made famous by various groups – The Mamas and the Papas' 'Monday, Monday', The McCoys' 'Hang On Sloopy', even Nancy Sinatra's 'These Boots Were Made For Walking'! A later incarnation of The Beau

The Californians, late 1966. Declan Mulligan, far left

Brummels would be instrumental in defining country-rock with their 1968 release 'Bradley's Barn', recorded in Nashville. Meanwhile, Declan Mulligan put together a group with three fellow expatriate Irishmen and two natives and began to play at the Carousel Ballroom in San Francisco, a popular venue which would later become the famous Fillmore West (where the cream of San Francisco's acid rock stars got their start, including The Grateful Dead, Quicksilver Messenger Service and Janis Joplin). This new collective, christened Samuel Pepys by the group members, was a lot closer to the Irish showband format than Mulligan's previous group. Indeed they were brought over to Ireland in November 1966 and hailed in a half-page ad in *Spotlight* as 'Ireland's First American Showgroup'. The venture never lived up to its amplified billing however, and after The Californians (as the group were more commonly known) fizzled out Declan returned to San Francisco, forming Mulligan Stew who were the resident band at the Carousel Ballroom for almost three years. Ex-Brummel Ron Meagher joined Declan in his next project, The Black Velvet Band, which lasted until an ill-advised reunion of the original Beau Brummels in 1975. Old tensions quickly resurfaced between the erstwhile colleagues and within a matter of months the musicians went their separate ways once again.

David McWilliams

£20,000 to make a Pop Star

Can money make a star and build him into an image? How much would it cost then? And how do you go about it?

Under this sceptical headline appeared a full page article in *Spotlight* in October 1967, one of many across Ireland and the UK during September and October of that year – introducing not only the delicate talents of a shy singer/songwriter from the Cregagh area of Belfast called David McWilliams, but also announcing an unprecedented hyperbole-fuelled publicity campaign orchestrated by notorious Irish impresario/agent Phil Solomon. The song that McWilliams is most remembered for today, the baroque folk pop classic 'Days Of Pearly Spencer', never made it into the higher reaches of the charts in the UK or Ireland despite heavy rotation on Radio Caroline and a steady flow of plaudits from some of England's most prominent and influential entertainment personalities (it did hit big in overseas markets, notably France, Holland and Japan). David McWilliams, a self-effacing character who was always uncomfortable with the cut-throat commercial aspects of the record business, was never able to live up to the unmanageable expectation placed on his broad shoulders. After the distinctly unwise decision of his record label Major Minor to release three full albums of original material within the space of twelve months, the six foot tall bushy-haired Northern Ireland man retreated from the pop world in 1969, to re-emerge in the early 1970s free of his former manager and exploitative label. Approaching the art of creating music in a more cautious manner, McWilliams was finally able to find solace in recording and distributing his songs at his own sporadic pace up until his untimely death in 2002, belatedly receiving widespread recognition when 'Days of Pearly Spencer' became a UK Top 10 hit for Marc Almond in 1992.

Local record label boss Mervyn Solomon was hanging around Peter Lloyd's recording facility in Belfast in mid-1966 when a young man shuffled unobtrusively into the studios and asked the engineer on duty if he could record a few songs that he had recently finished writing. This tall, rugged character had already been involved in a minor scuffle with the music industry earlier that year – a 7" single 'God And My Country' had been released on the CBS label, which was well received by elements of the anti-Vietnam war crowd but made no impression on record buyers at large, exposure limited as it was by a pressing of just 500 copies. Out of curiosity Solomon delayed his next appointment to listen to the twenty-year-old local folk singer and was reputedly floored by what he heard. He immediately alerted his brother Phil in London and encouraged him to sign up the young singer-songwriter on the spot. David McWilliams had been born into a modest working-class area of west Belfast, and after an academically undistinguished time at school in Ballymena (where he moved when he was three), was in the process of completing an apprenticeship at a local torpedo manufacturing plant when the fortuitous recording session at Lloyds took place.

Over the next eighteen months, a disciplined regime was put in place by McWilliams' management team at Phil Solomon's newly established Major Minor Records, diligently grooming their young protégé for the demands of imminent stardom. The level of detail attended to would not be out of place in the life of a manufactured TV talent-show of the twenty-first century. 'We have had a comprehensive study of stage technique and presentation,' enthused Mervyn Solomon in a *Spotlight* article in October 1967, quietly confident of the impact his introspective discovery

David McWilliams, c.1967

would soon have. Limiting his live exposure in order to stoke up anticipation (McWilliams had previously played in The Coral Showband and subsequently worked the folk club circuit in Northern Ireland), Solomon got his artist together with producer/arranger Mike Leander (whose CV included sessions with Marianne Faithfull, The Rolling Stones and The Beatles) and within weeks Major Minor could release David McWilliams' first album, in January 1967.

Lyrically, the songs on *David McWilliams Sings David McWilliams* predominantly dealt with simple observations on life that the Belfast born musician/poet saw around him, as well as more delicate reflections of a deeper personal nature. The doleful lament of the working man's existence on 'Redundancy Blues' and the politicised 'Hiroshima' are typical examples of his empathetic character; the more intimate and brooding tone of 'In The Early Hours Of The Morning' brings us closer to his innermost concerns. The style was reminiscent of Bob Dylan (an early influence, along with Buddy Holly) and English troubadour Donovan, but McWilliams' voice was noticeably smoother than the former and not as overtly foppish as the latter. Musically, his producer employed subtle arrangements of delicate percussion, evocative woodwind instruments and deftly deployed electric guitars which enhanced the music's blend of Irish and American folk traditions, and placed McWilliams' debut in similar territory to Tim Buckley or Tim Hardin's early efforts. In a publicity release, Mike Leander spoke about his work with the gifted songsmith.

> **MIKE LEANDER** He comes to me with raw songs, which reflect his thoughts about life and people, and I orchestrate these thoughts instrumentally. I try to keep the arrangements of his songs as uncomplicated as possible because I want to be faithful to David. He is making a simple statement and I try to enhance it without distorting it. (*Spotlight*, Vol. 2, No. 15, 7 Sept 1968)

To plug the release of the LP Major Minor arranged for a tour of the UK by The David McWilliams Band, featuring future Moot The Hoople front man Ian Hunter on bass guitar. The record was certainly popular with the folk crowd, reaching number four in the UK folk charts and climbing to an impressive number thirty-eight on the national pop charts, all without the assistance of a 7" release. It wasn't until the second record was ready for release that the promotional machine truly kicked into top gear, and the unprecedented advertising blitz was launched.

At midnight on 14 August 1967 the British government's 'Marine Broadcasting Offences Act' became law, shutting down overnight a plethora of pirate radio stations which had been broadcasting pop music not only to Britain's teenagers, but to Irish and continental European youngsters as well throughout the 60s. Radio Caroline, however, refused to close, moving its operation out of British waters. Devoid of revenue from advertisers who were now under threat of prosecution if they placed commercials with illegal operators, the station started to push new releases on the label owned by one of its directors and major stakeholders, Phil Solomon's Major Minor Records. David McWilliams would suffer the consequences of such an arrangement. He was sent back into the studio by Solomon where he laid down twenty-four tracks during the spring and summer, enough to fill his next two long playing releases. Mike Leander was on hand to produce again, overlaying McWilliams' simple demos with heavy orchestration. The suitably autumnal 'Days of Pearly Spencer' was originally released as the B-side to 'Harlem Lady', a track which did not appear on long-playing format until McWilliams' third record. Rotation of both sides of the single on Radio Caroline was excessive, and a huge advertising campaign hit the streets of London. But it seemed that the people to whom McWilliams' management were trying to appeal quickly became jaded and cynical with this calculated ploy.

> **GIL McWILLIAMS** (David's first wife): [There was] too much publicity in England. It was everywhere, even on the buses. Photos and words – *'Are you ready for the sound of David McWilliams?'* It was totally over the top and killed any chance [the single] ever had in England before its release.

The BBC set up Radio One as the UK's only official pop station after the crackdown on the pirates. However, the establishment's brand new addition to the airwaves didn't pick up on McWilliams' single and it failed to chart despite, to this day, being one of the most instantly recognisable tunes of the poptastic 60s, with its swirling strings and distinctive megaphone-style vocals on the chorus. McWilliams, more used to the slow paced life of the countryside rather than frenetic crowded cities, was struggling to adapt to life in London and the demands placed on him, not to mention the lack of remuneration coming his way. In an interview given to *Melody Maker* in the late 1970s, he recalls playing his first gig in the English capital at the Royal Albert Hall.

> **DAVID McWILLIAMS** I came here with about two pence halfpenny in my pocket and was getting on buses with my face stuck on the side of them, buses that I had to jump off between stops because I didn't have the fare in my pocket.

Lyrically *David McWilliams Vol. 2* focused on more personal and romantic concerns – the political commentary of earlier song-writing notably downplayed. Leander had given the record a highly commercial sheen, careful at the same time not to obstruct the plaintive vocals of the Belfast singer. Overplay of the single notwithstanding, it may be that the politely inoffensive

David McWilliams, c.1968
Sjef Kolen

sound (this was late 1967 when psychedelia was in full swing and the heavy guitar sound of Jimi Hendrix was beginning to infiltrate the rock scene) juxtaposed with the wordy imagery failed to convince either mainstream or alternative record buyers to part with their cash. One can only speculate on what might have been if McWilliams had been allowed space to develop organically and showcase his sound in a less deliberately constructed manner. Nevertheless, the LP did make it to a respectable number twenty-three in the UK Top 30, hanging around for six weeks on the national charts. After the blow-out of the ridiculously exaggerated ad campaign it would have been beneficial for all to retreat, regroup and re-plan a suitable way forward for artist and label alike. Instead, Major Minor went beyond overkill and released *David McWilliams Vol. 3* in January 1968. Unsurprisingly the public didn't take to this record any more than they did its predecessor, cut from the same sessions and issued just a matter of months apart. Always a reluctant performer, McWilliams did little to promote the release, by this stage too overwhelmed and jaded by the mercenary pop business.

He remained with Major Minor for another three single releases before the label went bankrupt at the end of the decade. It was probably a relief to the songwriter, who saw very little money from his association with manager Phil Solomon. The fact that his manager also doubled as head of his record company was an alarming situation unimaginable for any recording artist today. McWilliams was a humble man, who cared little for the complexities of music business contracts, royalty payments, advances and publishing rights. It is thought that he may have missed out on up to £2m throughout his life from over a hundred different cover versions made of his most famous song.

> **DAVID McWILLIAMS** I got burned, badly burned, but who didn't? When I think now how much I could have had and how much I didn't see. And I'm not talking in terms of small sums of money. In those days to have £10 in your pocket was to be rich. Yes, you could say I had contractual problems. (interview with Jim Evans, *Record Mirror*)

After unsuccessfully running a small farm in Northern Ireland he made a tentative return to the music world in the early 1970s and continued to record and release records occasionally throughout the next three decades (there are over ten solo albums to his name), but rarely appeared in public. Once a promising goalkeeper who looked set for a career with Linfield FC before injury diverted him into pursuing music on a full-time basis, McWilliams' timeless legacy to the world is his beautifully nostalgic song about a homeless man he once befriended, 'Days Of Pearly Spencer', included on countless 60s compilations and irrevocably associated by thousands of music lovers with that fondly remembered golden era of pop. He died in Ballycastle, County Antrim on 8 January 2002.

Nirvana

Which band is responsible for releasing the very first rock concept album? The casual music fan would probably nominate The Who for their LP about the life of that mean pinball-playing hoodlum Tommy, lapped up by a large established fan base in April 1969. But surly R&B bad boys The Pretty Things had preceded their countrymen by five months when they boarded the psychedelic spaceship and produced their own mini opera entitled *SF Sorrow*. Plenty of groups sped along quickly in their smoke trails, not least The Kinks with their weighty effort concerning *The Decline and Fall of the British Empire* told through the story of common everyday Englishman 'Arthur'. But one forgotten pop group beats them all. In October 1967, emboldened by the devil-may-care atmosphere of the time and drawing deep on a concoction of novel musical influences, Nirvana released the groundbreaking baroque chamber-pop concept LP *The Story of Simon Simopath* on Island Records.

This was the *original* Nirvana which Kurt Cobain's lawyers claimed their client was unfamiliar with growing up in rain-soaked Seattle in the late 1980s. Nirvana (UK), as they are sometimes labelled to avoid queues of grumpy skate kids in oversized hoodies returning CDs to their local record store, was the psyche-lite product of a meeting between Greek national, Alex Spyropolous and County Waterford man, Patrick Campbell-Lyons. Born and reared in the small town of Lismore in Ireland's south east corner, Campbell-Lyons' early exposure to music was minimal – he occasionally witnessed the odd trad session when visiting an uncle's house and briefly joined a ramshackle skiffle group while still a teenager at school in Tipperary. Trips to see The Dixielanders and The Royal Showband were inspired more by the prospect of tasting forbidden female fruit than an overwhelming desire to study chord progressions and vocal technique. Enrolled in the Catholic University School in Dublin, Patrick travelled to London in 1963 to work his summer break at an ice-cream factory in the city's western suburbs. Attracted by the bohemian lifestyle he encountered at lunchtime music sessions around the Ealing School of Art, the Irishman abandoned his studies and moved to England permanently the following year. Already adept on piano and bass guitar, he put together a five-piece R&B group called Second Thoughts, made up from various hepcats hanging out in the fertile breeding ground of the art school. A solid if unspectacular outfit, the combo earned some pocket money supporting bigger names at the Ealing Jazz Club (Manfred Mann and The Rolling Stones were two of the headliners), or occasionally playing in Soho with pioneering rhythm 'n' blues merchants The Downliner's Sect.

An opportunistic promoter packed the group off to Germany where Second Thoughts slogged through marathon late-night gigs in Hamburg and Frankfurt, appearing with The Chris Barber Jazz Band, Bo Diddley and Rory Storm and The Hurricanes. As happened to scores of young innocent groups at the time, the promoter hightailed it with their hard won earnings and left the boys to hobble home with empty pockets as Christmas 1965 approached. Second Thoughts' optimistic return to Germany early the following year was short lived, when Campbell-Lyons moved to Sweden, following a female journalist he had met after arriving in Hamburg. The next few months were spent as singer and bass player with domestically famous pop band The Merrymen from Stockholm, with whom Patrick toured the Scandinavian clubs. Falling into a pot-smoking counter-cultural milieu made up of arty dropouts and Vietnam AWOLS the Waterford native developed an illness which forced him back to England to recuperate. After a lengthy stay in hospital he hooked up with one of his previous colleagues from Second Thoughts, Chris Thomas, and together they formed a song-writing partnership. Their promising compositions found a home with Ed Kassner Publishing, whose offices were located on Denmark Street in London's bustling Tin Pan Alley. It was in a nearby café, close to St. Martin's School of Art, that Patrick Campbell-Lyons bumped into George Alex Spyropolous.

Spyropolous, enrolled in a film making course at St. Martin's, was himself a budding songwriter and had come to England from his home city of Athens, via Paris. A few of his early efforts had been accepted by the same publisher that had the ex-Second Thoughts duo on his books. Campbell-Lyons' recording career got off to an inauspicious start when Ed Kassner decided to release some demos that the Waterford man had recorded with Chris Thomas*. Christening (or rather damning) the duo with the ridiculously bland sobriquet 'Hat & Tie', the publisher saw their two singles vanish swiftly after minimal sales. One of their songs, 'I'm Finding It Rough', did achieve a modicum of success when The Everly Brothers included it on their album *The Everly Brothers Sing* later that year.

> **PATRICK CAMPBELL-LYONS** I thought, 'Wow! I should stop now really.' Who writes their first song and gets it cut by The Everly Brothers? That was the first group I ever heard in music. I though either you're a very lucky person or your life is going to be made up of omens like that. I thought we might get some money but in fact I have never seen one penny in royalties from that song.

* Chris Thomas' extraordinary career as producer has brought him into contact with some of the biggest names in pop, and seen him at the controls during the recording and mixing of some of the most famous albums in rock history. A quick glance at his CV reveals the names of John Cale, Badfinger, Pink Floyd, Roxy Music, The Pretenders, INXS, Elton John and Paul McCartney. Not only was he co-producer of one of the seminal releases of British popular music, The Sex Pistols' *Never Mind The Bollocks*, he also helped craft one of the defining statements of Britpop in the mid-90s, Pulp's *Different Class*. Thomas was involved in the creation of U2's *How To Dismantle An Atomic Bomb* in 2004 and Dave Gilmour's solo LP *On An Island* in 2006.

Fed up with the failed attempts to groom him as a disposable pop star, Chris Thomas fulfilled a long-held ambition by accepting an offer of employment at Abbey Road Studios, leaving Campbell-Lyons free to pursue other projects. Alex Spyropolous, who was unimpressed with churning out songs for others to perform, was keen to form a new group with the Irishman, and at the beginning of 1967 Nirvana was born.

Alex's own song-writing partner, Ray Singer, was initially brought into the group on lead guitar. This trio was responsible for creating the group's first song, 'Tiny Goddess'. The Greek-Irish partnership begat a further three tunes.

> **PATRICK CAMPBELL-LYONS** We had a very strong feeling that we had four good songs and we said we'd do the round of producers. Mickie Most was top of our list. A chap called Ron Richards, who produced The Hollies at the time [was next], [then] John Burgess who was producing Manfred Mann. We just picked them from NME, [saw] who was in the charts. Our fourth one was Muff Winwood. We got turned down by the first three. Then we went to Oxford Street where Island Records had a little office and asked to see Muff. He wasn't there but he had arranged for us to meet Chris Blackwell.

Performing two of the songs live with a couple of guitars in the label's offices obviously impressed Blackwell, who snapped up the group straight away. He impressed on them the need to round out the group with additional members (a few classically trained musicians were accosted at the gates of the local school of music) and sent them into the small studio at the Marquee Club to record some demos. The two sides of Nirvana's first single were cut at the more impressive Olympic Studios, augmented this time by professional session musicians. Blackwell's vision for the group was a pure pop entity, releasing singles with lush baroque overtones. These were the days of Procul Harum and 'Whiter Shade of Pale'. Patrick and Alex had other ideas, imagining the group as a vehicle for serious artistic expression, a conviction borne out by the high concept theme of their first album. At this early stage, however, everyone was positive and buoyant, and the group were unveiled to the public at an outlandish gig at London's Saville Theatre, decked out in their finest flower power frippery on a stage mocked up to resemble an Edwardian drawing room. 'Tiny Goddess', chosen as the first single, contained all the elements of their trademark sound – tender piano based melodies, opulent orchestration and light, almost childlike vocals – that varied little throughout their career. Nirvana was never a true psychedelic band per se, but they did share some elements of their sound with contemporary groups who dabbled in the dreamlike version of English acid-inspired whimsy. John Peel certainly liked what he heard and spun the 7" regularly on his much-listened-to show, *Perfumed Garden*, on Radio London. Unfortunately Nirvana would fall foul of the draconian measures instigated by the British government to shut down pirate stations in much the same way that David McWilliams did. The capital's illegal radio station was outlawed along with other unauthorized broadcasters and after only four weeks 'Tiny Goddess' all but disappeared from the airwaves.

Sessions for Nirvana's debut album had begun around the same time as the first single came out. One of the stronger cuts from those recordings, 'Pentecost Hotel', was released as Nirvana's second 45, with the full length LP *The Story of Simon Simopath* arriving in a vibrant technicolour sleeve in February 1968. An album firmly moored in the experimental and idealistic era of the late 1960s, the cover artwork gives a good indication of what to expect from the 'science fiction pantomime' contained within the grooves – a winged boy with golden hair hovers above a mythological centaur who gazes upon what appears to be an enchanted arabesque castle. Expanding on the concept, the sleeve notes do an admirable job of trying to link the songs into a coherent narrative. According to the explanation, Simon escapes from his unhappy existence in 'a six-dimensional city', receives permission to become a space traveller from 'the Ministry of Dreams', encounters a half-man, half-

Cover of Nirvana's debut LP

horse who guides him to an utopian paradise, and meets a beautiful woman with whom he lives happily ever after! Despite its solemn pretence, underneath the fairytale trappings the album also reveals itself as a poignant tale about that most universal of themes, love.

> **PATRICK CAMPBELL-LYONS** A lot of people took our stuff too seriously. We were always laughing a little bit at ourselves as well. There's an element of giggling through the whole thing, but there are some serious songs in there [too]. I think our secret was variety. Because on that first album there's a trad jazz song as well called '1999', which was covered by Kenny Ball at that time. We weren't adverse to just throwing something in. It may have been a mistake in the end because maybe those were the kind of things that might have upset Chris Blackwell, but we didn't know at the time.

Failing to find much favour with the record buying kids in the UK, Nirvana toured continental Europe on the back of better sales there. Herman's Hermits and Francoise Hardy were just two of many acts that released cover versions of songs plucked from the first LP.

Work began in earnest on the second album in June 1968. Four months before, Nirvana had been approached by film producers who were working on a 'summer of love' exploitation piece called *The Touchables*. Patrick and Alex were commissioned to write the title theme for the movie, a song called 'All Of Us', which also gave its name to their sophomore LP. Unencumbered by the weight of a high-minded concept to drag it down, 'All Of Us' is for the most part a more satisfying and coherent affair. The group were still dealing with serious issues in their song-writing and approach. The cover of the album is a chilling black and white still taken from a Nazi propaganda film depicting legendary figures of warfare proceeding on horseback through a sea of naked carcasses. The full loquacious title of the album, printed in banner form across the top of the sleeve, reinforces the mood of pessimism and dread: 'The existence of chance is everything and nothing while the greatest achievement is the living of life, and so say ALL OF US'. The group were invited to perform on French television, in a bizarre experiment where surrealist artist Salvador Dali splashed them with globs of paint while the musicians improvised a drawn-out free-form jam. Incorporated into the beginning of this extended piece of music was Nirvana's only UK chart hit (number thirty-four in May 1968), the grandiose 'Rainbow Chaser' which featured liberal washes of phasing, an accidentally discovered studio trick which would swiftly become *de rigueur* for any psychedelically-inclined band looking to add some exotic ornamentation to their songs.

Patrick's old pal from his song-writing days, Chris Thomas, having gained invaluable experience working with George Martin at Abbey Road Studios, was invited to sit in the producer's seat for Nirvana's third album. Members of rock band Spooky Tooth were also on hand to beef up the increasingly lavish sound sculptures. On completion Spyropolous and Campbell-Lyons were invited to the head of Island Records' house.

> **PATRICK CAMPBELL-LYONS** There's a song on there called 'Christopher Lucifer'. Maybe Chris Blackwell thought it was about him. That was our kind of humour, and he had a sense of humour but maybe we pushed it too far. He gave you all the freedom to do what you wanted but then at a certain point he'd say, 'That's it, now let's hear it.' When he heard [the album] he said it sounded like *A Man And A Woman* by [French film composer] Michel Legrand. He said it's time you went your way because I don't think the sound of this album is the sound I hear for Island Records anymore. He said Chris Thomas made us too lush. He found the arrangements lush, sweet and saccharine.

A mutual agreement was reached between label boss and group whereby the duo was free to take the master tapes to another label at no additional cost. Without a record company to pick up the bill extra money was required to re-record some songs and remix the final version. A wealthy cousin of Alex Spyropolous stepped in with the necessary funds; a dedication to his son on the back cover of the record ultimately resulted in the LP being re-released on CD as *To Markos III* and not *Black Flower* as was originally intended. In fact, the album never made it out of the warehouses in 1969 when the American label that Nirvana signed to, Macromedia, went bust shortly after the masters were delivered. Nirvana's signature sound is again evident on *To Markos III*, a mixture of highly-produced chamber pop incorporating a ragbag of European chanson, light jazz and film soundtrack influences. Spyropolous and Campbell-Lyons went their separate ways soon after. 'We'd been in each others pockets for the best part of four and a half years, every day,' remembers Patrick, 'it was time to breath different air. [The split] was very amicable.'

Patrick Campbell-Lyons made two more albums for Phonogram under the Nirvana guise, eventually drifting into film and TV soundtrack composition. The group's existence was revealed to a new generation as a result of the court case involving the American Nirvana. More positively, DJ Shadow used a section of 'Love Suite' from *To Markos III* to construct 'Stem', the centrepiece on his groundbreaking 1996 hip-hop opus *Entroducing*. Fans of Campbell-Lyons and Spyropolous' work abound in the music world. Now defunct 1990s trip hop/soul band Morcheeba invited the duo to play support at some gigs in London's Shepherd's Bush Empire. Emboldened by a loyal fanbase across Europe Alex and Patrick have periodically written together since the late 1980s but nothing has been officially released and there are no current plans to put out any new songs under the Nirvana name.

Part Six

The smartly dressed followers of Ireland's showbands may have snorted derisorily at the unkempt beat groups with their page-boy haircuts and wild jungle music at the beginning of 1965, when the new sound appeared to them as a frivolous adolescent novelty and one without much staying power. Two years later the cosy hegemony of the showband scene had been interrupted. A sizeable number of underground beat clubs were now firmly established in the major cities, pulling in big crowds week in week out, and supplying a growing audience with a type of music, style and attitude that the showbands couldn't hope to emulate. Bluesville had shown that international success was not an unattainable pipe dream. In different circumstances Ian Whitcomb and his group may have found themselves as crucial contributors to the emergence of the American rock vocabulary as other British Invaders like The Yardbirds and Animals did. The Creatures were poised for success as well, only to see their dreams broken by inter-band squabbling, union problems outside their control, and a record company with a too-full roster. On the domestic front The Chosen Few, The Action and The Strangers were just a few of the early Irish beat groups that built up considerable reputations without turning into successes abroad. As the beat scene expanded exponentially and the confidence of everyone involved grew, there was a dawning realisation that Irish acts could compete with those international artists played on Radio Caroline and Radio Luxembourg, but not within the confines of the tight-knit home-grown music community. Hopping from club to club and playing to the same few hundred people each week was all very well for a part-time covers act, but for anyone with serious artistic ambitions and long-term financial considerations, finding new audiences and a sympathetic creative environment was essential.

A daring trip up to the big smoke to see The Rolling Stones at the Adelphi Cinema in October 1965 was to prove pivotal in the lives of a group of young lads from the small provincial city of Limerick. It would also turn out to be crucial for the expansion of Irish rock music outside of its restrictive borders, as the group in question mapped out a route for other musicians to pursue in the years to come. As is usually the case, those followers enjoyed a level of success far beyond that experienced by the pioneers. Granny's Intentions, a name that whiffs heavily of incense, Victorian hippy garb and whimsical psychedelia, were the first Irish group to base themselves in the dynamic environs of the London music scene to further their careers; they were also the first Irish act to get signed by highly regarded progressive UK label Deram; and their album *Honest Injun* (recorded during 1969) was one of the first examples of a cohesive full-length Irish rock LP to come from the Republic of Ireland (Bluesville had technically proceeded them by four years, but that record was rush released to capitalise on the surprise success of 'You Turn Me On', and contained more than its fair share of filler). Over the decades Granny's Intentions' memory and legacy has dissolved as ephemerally as a puff of marijuana smoke. Their early singles are rarely heard outside of collectors' circles and a CD re-issue of their only album appeared for the first time as late as 2004. Blighted by inter-group conflict, poor management, record company disinterest, disruptive drug use and the myopic frivolity of youth, Granny's Intentions never quite made it as big as their champions and fans in Ireland so dearly wished they would. They were definitely not lacking in talented songwriters and gifted players however, and the music they released in a short three year period between 1967 and 1970 stands up impressively in comparison to many British and American contemporaries of the time.

After seeing the mayhem caused by The Stones at the Adelphi that infamous autumn night, Johnny Duhan and two of his friends decided to form their own group. They originally christened the band The Intentions, hoping it would sound similar to The Temptations and The Impressions, two of their formative vocal R&B influences. A singer called Cha Harren from another Limerick group, The Fifth Edition, soon joined the new band. Granny's Intentions (the prefix was later added to modernise the group's image) would gain a reputation in the clubs of Dublin as the best soul band in Ireland, particularly of the Motown variety, Johnny and Cha sharing vocal duties, fashionably dressed in the Detroit style of double breasted suits and trilby hats. Their tastes were quite catholic for a young inexperienced group. An early member of the band, Ger Tuohy, introduced the others to his sizeable collection of blues records by the likes of Leadbelly, Howlin' Wolf and Brownie McGhee. The twin vocalists were also big fans of Del Shannon, Buddy Holly and Chuck Berry, with Duhan in particular, who had been singing from an early age, enamoured with the music of Ray Charles.

> **JOHNNY DUHAN** I loved Ray Charles, for he was coming from gospel music, and church music was the first major influence on me – the lovely choirs I heard in the many chapels that surrounded us on Wolfe Tone Street in Limerick.

The group began playing their mix of soul, blues and pop in the ballrooms of Limerick and Cork as support to touring showbands.

CHA HARREN What work you were getting was relief work, as it was known in the day. You'd travel to Mallow to play in front of Joe Dolan; you'd play in Macroom in front of Dickie Rock. Any of the old showbands at the time, you'd get a half an hour in front of them, that was it. Fifty per cent of the showband crowd were into the music we were doing, and fifty per cent were looking at us with their mouths open. Because we dressed completely different – the showbands would come out and they'd have five heads on the stage with suits on them. We had a pair of jeans and a kaftan on us!

The beat scene in the south west was fairly under-developed as the Intentions were finding their feet. They regularly travelled to Club A Go Go in Cork and then up to its sister venue in Dublin to play for more receptive audiences. On one trip to the capital the group were due to do some recording in Pete Selwood's basement studio and realised they would need a keyboard player to fill out the sound. Cha Harren head-hunted John Ryan, a talented songwriter and pianist who was playing in a Dublin beat group called The Circle. Visually, the look of the group was of key concern to Cha. The co-vocalist, from a family steeped in the military tradition, had quickly assumed the role of de facto leader, charged with dictating the musical direction of the group and also maintaining the correct symmetrically aligned stage presence.

JOHN RYAN The Small Faces were out in England at the time. [The Intentions] were into that whole mod [thing]. Johnny Duhan, when I met him first, had a little mod haircut, the long locks. I was the right size, but what Cha didn't realise...everyone was so young, we only stayed the same size for about a month! I went down to Limerick to meet them and it turned out they weren't doing any Tamla Motown at all, that's what they wanted to do. I knew about that kind of music so we went down to George Murray on the quays and we bought all this Motown stuff and we just started from scratch.

After rehearsing diligently in Limerick, perfecting their image and working hard on the visual aspects of their live show, the group decided to move to Dublin, somewhere they needed to base themselves if they were to stand any chance of furthering their career. Some of the early Intentions had moved on by this point, so the new line-up of the band, which would always be subject to unexpected arrivals and departures, comprised: Johnny Duhan and Cha Harren (both vocals), Johnny Hockedy (guitar), Jack Costello (bass), John Ryan (piano and keyboards) and Italian-Irishman Guido DiVito on drums. They were firmly established as a major draw on the Dublin beat

Early shot of Granny's Intentions, c.1966. L-R: Guido DiVito, Johnny Hockedy, Johnny Duhan, Jack Costello, Cha Harren, John Ryan

scene by the second half of 1966, although life was a struggle as they sought to carve out a niche for the group.

> **JOHNNY DUHAN** After a German tour fell through we spent a month or so living in a squat in Baggot Street, living on our nerves and a hooker who generously provided us with fish and chips at our lowest ebb. On the music scene, there were tons of competing beat groups all vying for gigs in a handful of beat clubs. Cha was a great gig hustler and we were musically ahead of many of the other bands. Most of all though, we were hungry, literally starving at times.

> **JOHN RYAN** We did two weeks on porridge, we had nothing else. When you're doing that you don't know how long it's going to go on for.

The Scene Club on Parnell Square became a regular haunt for Granny's where they would play two sets a night, totalling four hours with a twenty minute break. A stunt which went horribly wrong one night helped spread the word about this hot new band from Limerick making a name for themselves in the Dublin beat world. At this particular gig, Duhan and Harren wanted to release live doves into the audience as a symbolic gesture of hope, peace, love and various other ideals held dear to the hippy throngs. Unable to find a rich supply of pure white birds in the city they had to settle for second best – pigeons.

> **JOHN RYAN** It was supposed to be like white doves flying up, a big effect. But they wouldn't even get out of the box, so we fucked them out. Of course they hit the ceiling, and the next

thing they're on the ground getting walked on. The pigeons all died anyway, but the story kind of grew…it was a bit like Ozzy Osbourne, people tearing the heads off pigeons and putting blood all over their T-shirts. I didn't see that but that was the story that went around. It was only done once.

Pat Egan had been talking up the group in *Spotlight* magazine since Granny's arrived from Limerick and their reputation was really taking off.

CHA HARREN They were expecting culchies at the gigs when we started off in Dublin, and we used to start off with the first few chords of a Larry Cunningham number, and we'd say, 'Good evening, we're up from Limerick', and we'd see the faces drop. [Then] there would be a drumbeat and we'd go straight into James Brown and they were gob smacked!

Things began to develope further when the group replaced their original manager with Brian Tuite, an ex-musician with a playboy image. Tuite had been part of The Stellas, a showband/jazz combo not unlike The Viscounts, that toured Germany in the early 1960s. A suave and wealthy character, who had a reputation for dressing in smart crombies and driving fast cars around the Phoenix Park, the new manager had serious ambitions for the group and soon arranged for a small tour of Scotland, England and Germany. The soul music that Granny's specialised in went down a storm with the enlisted officers in the clubs in Germany, where they played support to Philadelphia girl group The Orlons (proud owners of three US top ten hits during 1962 and 1963). On their return, the Limerick group and their manager decided that bypassing the over-crowded Irish scene was the smart option for success and they decamped to London in June 1967. Even at this early stage, before any record deals had been inked or before any original material had been written, Johnny Duhan was uneasy about relationships within the group, the straining of which led to the departure of their original drummer.

JOHNNY DUHAN The change that had the biggest impact on the morale of the band was the sacking of Guido DiVito. The conspiracy that got rid of Guido, and I have to admit that I went along with the move, was the beginning of the end for the band, even before we got into our stride. There's such a thing as a band's spirit. With the sacking of Guido we inflicted a mortal wound on ourselves, even though it took a long time for Granny to finally croak it.

The group were overawed by their surroundings in the English capital. Low funds meant they all had to bundle into just two rooms at the Madison

Granny's get into the swing of London, 1967. L-R: Johnny Hockedy, Jack Costello, Martin Brannigan (temporary drummer), John Ryan, Johnny Duhan, Cha Harren (front)

Hotel near Paddington Station, where they rubbed shoulders with The Yardbirds and Taste, along with dozens of other up-and-coming bands as well as plenty who were down at heel and going nowhere. They kept themselves occupied playing venues like the Speakeasy and the Bag O' Nails as Jimi Hendrix and members of The Rolling Stones drifted around holding court. The summer of love was in full swing, and Granny's were invited to play at a big outdoor celebration for the Duke of Bedford featuring Jeff Beck, The Small Faces and a pre-disco Bee Gees. Quite a few record labels became interested in picking up the Irish lads based on their fearsome live renown, which was spreading by word of mouth amongst the rock elite. Deram, a subsidiary of Decca Records, was well known as a forward-looking imprint with serious potential that already had The Move and Procol Harum on its books. Manager Brian Tuite had a contact there in the shape of Frank Rodgers, A&R man, whom he met on tour in Germany a few years previously. After signing the group Deram wasted no time in sending Granny's Intentions into the studio with Moody Blues' producer Tony Clarke, who emphasised the need to write some original material. When not partying with the rock 'n' roll aristocracy, John Ryan had been doing the rounds of music publishers in London looking for demos that his group could record. Amongst the many acetates that Granny's passed on was a lo-fi recording of a song called 'I Think It's Going To Rain Today' by young unknown songwriter Randy Newman, which the group felt unsuitable for their sound and image. Instead, they focussed their collective energies and came up with the A-side of their first record, a veiled rumination on the struggles and tribulations of a young rock band witnessed by the group up to that point, told through the story of a fictional character called David Millar.

> **JOHNNY DUHAN** I went off to Hyde Park and came up with the chorus: 'If you're stuck you'd better give up and go back to work', which was based on a character from a band I ran into who was quitting the music scene after failing to get the big break which we were enjoying. Then Johnny Hockedy and John Ryan came on board and added the many other musical variations that the song took on, including the idea of making Mr. Millar a failed poet rather than a failed musician. It's quite a convoluted mix of styles.

Many bands' first efforts at writing and recording are often their best, when the lifetime of experiences and the bristling energies of youth converge to create something spontaneous and fresh (although some of this group's lifetimes had not yet stretched beyond twenty years). A case can be made that Granny's Intentions never bettered 'The Story Of David', their first single, which was released in Britain and Ireland on 10 November 1967. A sumptuous organ-driven psychedelic nugget, it showcased for the first time on vinyl the vocal prowess of Johnny Duhan, incredibly resonant and soulful for someone who had yet to celebrate his eighteenth birthday. The lyrics of the chorus would prove eerily prophetic. The B-side, 'Sandy's On The Phone Again', was of equal quality, about a girl's prayers going unanswered, which was inspired by John Ryan's religious background. Once more the song was perfectly redolent of the times, its sadder edge tempered by the inclusion of swirling keyboards and sweet backing vocals. The group should have returned to Ireland in December dressed in their finest Carnaby Street gear with a chart hit under their belts, but Deram failed to promote the single adequately. There was an ad taken out in *NME*, reviews were favourable, some radio play was secured, but that extra effort required to turn the single into a success was lacking. At home there was a lot of good feeling towards the returning *émigrés*, and their domestic popularity was recognised with an appearance on national institution *The Late Late Show*, and a cover feature in the best-selling TV listings magazine, the *RTÉ Guide*. Irish fans voted them the second best beat group of 1967 in *Spotlight*'s annual poll, just behind home-based favourites The Strangers.

The top placing in that poll was to be the peak of Balbriggan boys The Strangers' popularity, helped no doubt by their impressive support slot with The Beach Boys at the Adelphi the same year. As other bands experimented with contemporary styles, The Strangers consolidated their reputation by sticking to what they knew best. Following Top 20 success with The

The Strangers' second single

Monkees' 'Look Out (Here Comes Tomorrow)', they turned to another popular American song craftsman, John Sebastian of The Lovin' Spoonful, for their next record. Their rendition of 'You Didn't Have To Be So Nice' had all the recognisable Strangers' traits in place – sharp playing, flawless singing and crisp guitar riffing. Times were changing however, and the group were criticised in some quarters for not writing their own material (although the B-side *was* composed by drummer Vic McNamara and rhythm guitarist Maxie McEvoy). The Strangers were quite keen to release their own songs on the top sides of their singles, but it was an ill-advised decision by management to cover yet another track for the group's third and final record. To compound the problem, the session for 'I'm On An Island' (written by Ray Davies of The Kinks) was a rushed affair, the group entering the studio at 11am for a two hour stint after spending half the previous night driving back from an arduous gig in Limerick. 'You'll hear me banging the guitar in frustration at one point,' says lead player Len Guest. 'I hated the song. It's garbage.' Evidently Vic McNamara felt the same; he left the group in early 1968 to play with Northern Ireland showband Derrick and The Sounds. Later that year Len took his leave as well and The Strangers as beat group came to an end. In 1969, the group's new line-up turned showband, prompted by financial necessity, as lead singer Jimmy Fanning revealed in a *Spotlight* interview: 'We had gone as far as we could on the group scene. We played clubs where eight to nine hundred people each paid 10/- admission. But we got a tiny, fixed fee. We worked very hard for very little reward.' (*Spotlight,* Vol. 3, No. 16, 19 Sept 1969)

By the time Granny's Intentions first 7" came out, original member Cha Harren had left. The singer was the only one of the five with a wife and child, and the attendant responsibilities, coupled with a realisation that the presence of two vocalists was hindering the band's development, sadly forced him to quit the group he had helped establish. After a two week stint in Germany at the start of 1968 Deram rushed the group back into the studio to record a follow-up to 'The Story Of David'. A new producer was drafted in, the more avuncular and approachable Wayne Bickerton who had played bass in The Pete Best Four, the unlucky ex-Beatle's short lived post-Fabs project. Bickerton handed Granny's Intentions a song that he had co-written with Tony Waddington, fellow member of Pete Best's band. 'Julie Don't Love Me Anymore', a song firmly in Procol Harum territory, was weak in comparison to Granny's self-written debut, and many in the group were distinctly unhappy with it. In an interview given to BP Fallon in *Spotlight* that July, a couple of months after it was clear that the single had been a flop, John Ryan confirmed that dissatisfaction: 'Half of us didn't want [it] released. When we were recording the B-side, we thought it was just a preliminary take and 'Hoddy' [Hockedy, lead guitarist] and I were having a giggle and weren't taking it seriously at all!' (*Spotlight*, Vol. 2, No. 9, 27 July 1968). After two failed single releases, the relationship between band and record label was starting to strain. The kinship within the group was also coming under increasing pressure. Johnny Hockedy and Johnny Duhan were sharing a dingy flat in London away from their band mates, and without the glue of Cha Harren to hold things together the affinity between the two primary songwriters, Duhan and Ryan, had worn somewhat. Granny's continued to maintain a high profile by playing support to The Nice, Marmalade, Family, and Skip Bifferty at the Marquee Club, but the free availability of chemical substances on the London rock scene was not conducive to patching up petty rifts caused by personality clashes.

14 March 1968 National Stadium gig

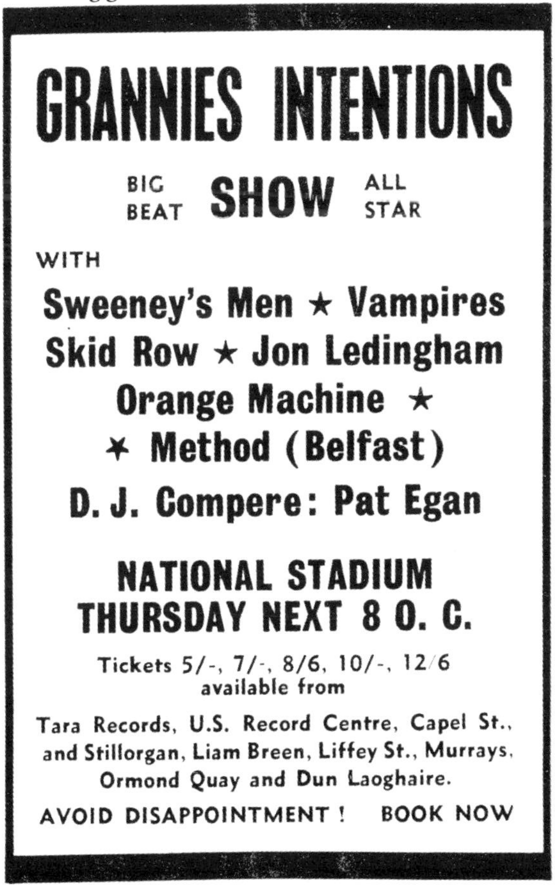

> **JOHNNY DUHAN** A lot of drugs were being consumed and confusion was rife. The writing was on the wall, but it was melting in a hallucinogenic haze. I was lost. I later developed a real hatred of hash and drugs in general. One of my favourite lines by the poet Robert Lowell is 'Every drug that numbs alerts another nerve to pain.'

Regular trips back to Ireland continued throughout 1968, where Granny's Intentions could always be sure of a hero's welcome. On 14 March they headlined a stellar show at the National Stadium, which brought together the cream of the Irish beat and folk worlds under one roof. On the bill were Belfast blues power trio The Method; ex-beat group musician and rising folk-pop star Jon Ledingham; progressive psych bands The Orange Machine and Skid Row; perennial pop favourites The Vampires and celebrated folk trio Sweeney's Men who were a couple of months away from recording their debut album.

> **SHAY HEALY** The Granny's were extraordinarily exciting because the young Johnny Duhan was somewhere between Herman from the Hermits and Mick Jagger. They had that kind of slightly louche thing to look at them. They were the glamour band of the time without a doubt.

Pulled along by the mercurial musical currents of the late 1960s, a discernable folk influence began to seep into Granny's work, with songs by Bob Dylan and Tim Hardin finding their way into the set amongst the soul standards and newly birthed originals. An appearance on Telefís Éireann's *Twenty Minutes With...* in August, performing covers of songs by The Who, Frank Zappa and Tomorrow, received decidedly mixed reviews, with some viewers confounded and outraged by the group's outlandish attire and unconventional sounds, as this excerpt from a letter to the *RTÉ Guide* aptly demonstrates.

> *I have never written to a newspaper before, and didn't think that anything would ever move me to write. I regret that it should be annoyance and not satisfaction that motivates me. Last week's television programme, Twenty Minutes With Granny's Intentions was disgraceful. It should never have been transmitted on a national network. I am as partial as the next (I am only twenty) to pop music, but I would emphasise the word 'music' which is I presume what Granny's Intentions thought they were making in this programme*
>
> *In last week's programme I could hear neither words or music. The*

> *songs took second place to the gyrations of the lead singer in the intrusive, eccentric lighting of the set. Mind you, I am prepared to believe that the lighting man (or director) realised that Granny's Intentions were so bad they couldn't carry on the programme without gimmicks. What a pity.* (*RTÉ Guide*, 23 Aug 1968)

The group were back in RTÉ's studios that autumn, recording a slot for a brand new pop series, *Like Now*. They appeared on the show on Saturday 28 September, alongside Irish showbands The Dixies and The Riviera, as well as Beatle-esque English pop outfit, Grapefruit. This heightened exposure was about to coincide with the only commercial triumph of the group's lifetime. Having seen two psychedelic rock songs fare poorly on release over the previous twelve months Deram decided it was time to make an unabashed play for the top of the charts, and foisted upon the group the over-arranged, string-laden Wayne Bickerton composition, 'Never An Everyday Thing'. Fans in Ireland and England must have thought they were hearing a different group with an identical name when they dropped the needle on the record and were confronted with parping horns, a melodramatic orchestral arrangement and trite lyrics about finding that special love. If you strain your ears really hard it's just about possible to make out the sound of an electric guitar. Some people grumbled that it resembled teen-pop sensations of the moment, Love Affair. Worse still, others complained that it sounded just like a showband.

Granny's enjoying life. L-R: Johnny Hockedy, Greg Donaghy (new drummer), Jack Costello, Johnny Duhan, John Ryan

JOHN RYAN It was a real go for the mainstream. It was just a pop record. We were actually in the studio and we got a phone call saying Wayne Fontana was recording it, who was quite a big name. The session nearly got scrapped. The songwriters sold it to three people [and the singles] all came out in the same week.

JOHNNY DUHAN 'Never An Ordinary Thing' (as I like to call it) was the beginning of the end. It created new fractures in the band.

Over in Ireland the once-watertight seal that separated the showbands and beat groups was beginning to break. In a way, Granny's Intentions' new single was a timely demonstration of this. The showband phenomenon reached a peak in 1966, and two years later things were on a slide. No longer were showband managers able to sit back and watch punters dutifully file into ballrooms until they were filled to bursting point. Television, which was not commonly available at the dawn of the 60s in Ireland, had become widespread, the country had become more urbanised and less parochial in its outlook, and of course beat music, which had evolved into rock music, showed absolutely no signs of fading away as the entrenched entertainment industry had initially hoped. Going to hear live music in plush new lounge bars and cosy hotels that were permitted to serve alcohol rather than grotty, out-of-town halls that doled out nothing stronger than fizzy orange was becoming an attractive proposition to many. As the audiences for showbands began to shrink, cracks developed in the big bands. Established names like The Drifters and the Miami lost key members, who set up their own outfits after it was decided their pulling power was worth much more than the set salary being earned in co-operative bands at the time.

SMILEY BOLGER In the latter 60s managers were breaking up well established showbands. 'You form your one out there, we'll have another guy in this band here, we'll get a couple of lackeys in.'

> If there were two personalities in the band there'd be two showbands cloned out of them.

In order to attract a younger crowd to the showband gigs – replacing the one that was ageing, having families and deserting the ballrooms for other diversions – the managers began to form crossover type combinations, often made up of ex-beat group members but melded into a traditional showband-style seven man line-up. Around the same time that Granny's Intentions were releasing 'Never An Everyday Thing', a brand new band called The Real McCoy hit big in Ireland with 'Quick Joey Small', an infectiously hip tune with a driving rhythm, odd nasally vocals, prominent handclaps, and phased guitar. The lead singer of the outfit was Mike O'Brien, a ringer for Scott Walker who had served his time in lesser known beat groups The Gnumps and The Good Tymes. Drummer Dave Pennefeather had been around since the early days, performing with outfits such as The Semitones, The Inmates and The Earl Gill Showband. Sitting quietly amongst the other relatively anonymous musicians that had come from minor showbands was Liam McKenna of The Creatures, with newly shorn hair, looking respectable in pressed suit and dark tie. Listening to both Granny's Intentions and The Real McCoy's latest records it's difficult to identify which group had spent the previous sixteen months hanging out in the London rock star firmament or which had been thrown together by a conservative band manager looking to make a quick buck.

Big money also facilitated the launch of The Dreams, another group-cum-showband that were created in September 1968, fronted by John Farrell, who just two months previously had departed The Movement, a hugely popular beat group on the Dublin scene. After a lengthy delay and amid much anticipation, The Movement finally released one of the beat scene's most coruscating and spirited singles in January 1968, a version of Billie Davis' 'Tell Him' (renamed 'Tell Her' to suit the gender of the narrator). The record has become recognised as a classic in the genre known as 'freakbeat' (a peculiar amalgam of American soul and British beat), not least for its maniacal energy and blistering guitar break. *New Musical Express* in England were gushing in their praise for the record: 'The Billie Davis hit is revived in frantic style by The Movement on Pye. It has an earthy feel, a compulsive beat and a stimulating effect.' There were reportedly girls weeping dolefully at Farrell's last performance with the group at the Crystal Ballroom in June that year, and if the scene's more detached commentators didn't express their emotions in quite such dramatic terms, there was certainly a feeling that Irish rock music had lost one of its most promising singers to the lure of the professional showband circuit and all its potential riches. Fears of a creative neutering amongst the musicians in The Dreams (others included ex-Kingbees Jim Hudson and Dougie McIlwaine, as well as Eric Bell of Them) were seemingly well founded when BP Fallon accompanied the new entity on

The Movement, 1967. Lead singer John Farrell front left

some of their first live dates and found them playing old time waltzes and humdrum country 'n' western. Their debut disc was written for them by safe middle-aged favourites, The Tremeloes.

Poaching beat musicians to play in showbands wasn't an entirely new practice, although it accelerated towards the end of the decade. Paul Ashford and Fran Byrne had earlier been stolen away from The Chosen Few to join the Miami and Sands showbands respectively, at a time when their soul group's stock was at a high. Many beat groups' life spans were unfortunately cut short by departures and defections. It was one of the reasons why many promising groups never achieved long term success.

> **PAUL ASHFORD** We didn't really like showbands, because they were just playing other people's music. But they offered us huge amounts of money. I bought a house when I was seventeen and I couldn't even sign for it, I was under the legal age. But it was an opportunity as well to play every night. It broke up The Chosen Few. There's a quote in *Spotlight* where Phil [Lynott] says that Fran and I had become breadheads, 'they joined a showband, they sold out'. But the way we looked at it was we were actually working seven nights a week. That's all I ever wanted to do, play music. A lot of good guys came out of showbands. I didn't look at it like selling out, I just thought I'm gonna get really well paid for playing music seven nights a week and that's what I wanna do.

Some of their colleagues on the beat scene were not quick to forgive defectors to the dark side. Brendan Bonass, guitar player with a number of Dublin beat group during the mid-60s, recalls the high profile defection of Paul Ashford from The Chosen Few.

> **BRENDAN BONASS** Paul was being paid as much as a TD when he joined The Miami Showband. It was on the front page of the *Evening Herald*. He did very well, had a brand new Rover car and everything. But for us it was just a sell out. Because even though we didn't write our own tunes at the time we were digging deep into the record trade for the songs we did, rather than covering the Top 10, or country.

> **BP FALLON** Showband heads largely saw the beat group cats as silly riff-raff who were 'serious about their music, man' as they chortled to themselves about the big readies they were making all over Ireland at The Roseland and the This Land and the That Land, huge big sheds to pack in the punters at ten bob a head. So the beat groups were handy to pillage for fresh fruit to pervert, guys who'd been in groups stuck in cellars and tennis hops and no money and suddenly some geezer is saying, 'Sixty quid a week and you can sing some of the louder songs', and suddenly some poor fucker is sucked in and soon enough he's singing 'Simple Simon Says' and harmless shite like that; but after a while he loses his chops, his crusade is over.

With the radio friendly sounds of 'Never An Everyday Thing' blaring over transistors in Ireland and the single scoring a peak chart position of number

seven in this country, it is little wonder that the showband wolves came sniffing at Granny's Intentions' door. Connie Lynch, manager of The Royal Showband featuring Brendan Bowyer, wanted to bring in a brass section and turn the group into an eight-piece, guaranteeing the five permanent members a wage of £80 a week. The proposal was greeted with little enthusiasm.

JOHN RYAN There was a real war between showbands [and beat groups]. We used to see all our mates being picked off. It was always a bit embarrassing for them when they'd meet us because they'd have loads of money, but no credibility.

Granny's manager Brian Tuite had his own plans for his charges, scheming to take Greg Donaghy and Johnny Duhan out of the band to form a new pop supergroup with two members of psyche rockers The Orange Machine. Duhan wasn't keen on the idea and in the end just Greg departed for the new venture, with Jack Costello leaving the group soon after for other unspecified reasons. In spite of some positive noises emanating from *NME* about Granny's Intentions' new single, and a more concerted effort at promotion this time from Deram, the simultaneous release of three different versions of 'Never An Everyday Thing' ensured that no one would bring the song into the British hit parade (Wayne Bickerton finally hit pay dirt with his thrilling soul stomper 'Nothing But A Heartache' recorded by The Flirtations in 1969, and also later with The Rubettes' 'Sugar Baby Love' in 1974). Having been whittled down to three core members – keyboard player John Ryan, singer Johnny Duhan and guitarist Johnny Hockedy – and unhappy with the slick commercialism of their last single, Granny's Intentions changed their sound once again and set about recording their one and only full-length album.

JOHNNY DUHAN John Ryan introduced me to Tim Hardin at the height of the soul thing and I started leaning in a more folky direction after that. I got sick of trying to sound like a black man. Then I made the mistake of trying to sound like a country hick.

Some participants in the US music scene had grown tired of the flash and indulgence of the psychedelic scene by 1968. Already there was a feeling that the promise of a new society which the hippies had hoped to usher in was crumbling. Drug casualties were mounting, violence was escalating and a softer, more old-time rustic approach to music was being investigated by some musicians who only recently had been at the forefront of cutting edge innovation. Bob Dylan returned from his motorcycle crash with the bucolic *John Wesley Harding*, The Band released the hugely influential back-to-their-roots album *Music From Big Pink*, and even The Rolling Stones sought refuge in some country licks on *Beggars Banquet* after the misstep of psyche curio *Her Satanic Majesty's Request*. A few members of Granny's were revelling in the carefree atmosphere of the London music scene, soaking up the kaleidoscope of new sounds, hanging out with Irish ex-pat Phil Lynott and folk-rock group Dr. Strangely Strange and also indulging in the panoply of drugs widely available to them. John Ryan attests that The Byrds' seminal country rock opus *Sweetheart Of The Rodeo* had a major influence on the sound of *Honest Injun*, the album cut at irregular junctions by Granny's Intentions over the course of a number of recording sessions during the first half of 1969. Although a relatively poor seller at the time, The Byrds' record did feature regularly on the turntables of musicians and scenesters both in the US and across the pond in Britain after its release in August 1968. Indeed it was that very record that BP Fallon was encouraging The Dreams showband to draw inspiration from as he travelled with them on their tour bus. Someone else was definitely listening though. In December 1968 Pat Egan reported in *Spotlight* that Granny's Intentions 'have changed their music style and are now playing a type of country blues'.

With only three members now in the group, additional musicians were needed for the album's recording sessions. Enter Noel Bridgeman from Skid Row on drums and Pete Cummins, an ex-colleague of John Ryan's in The Circle, on bass. The two new members were unveiled to an Irish audience at the *Spotlight* Poll Winners gig in March 1969 (readers had voted Granny's number one 'beat' group of 1968, a categorisation that now sounded wholly inappropriate for the music of the day). Three tracks were laid down in London at the outset, but the curse of the group struck again and it wasn't long before Bridgeman left to be replaced by Pat Nash, who had drummed with Dublin soul men The Uptown Band. Additional guitar playing came courtesy of Gary Moore. As a young six string slinger who had come down from Northern Ireland to play with various combos on the Dublin beat scene, Gary Moore left a strong impression on everyone who witnessed his talent.

> **SMILEY BOLGER** When Gary Moore came to town for the first time it was to stand in for Dave Lewis in The Method, he was sick. He was probably fifteen and a half, sixteen. Skid Row were playing over in the 72 Club in Abbey Street, Wednesday night.

The Method were playing in the Club A Go Go on the same night. I don't know who came over and told us to get our pretty asses over there when the intermission came along. So we went over... Wow, that was something to remember. Because Gary had not been seen, no one knew who this guy was.

Gary Moore, 1969

Eight more songs were recorded with Moore's contributions (Ryan recalls that the Belfast teenager played tin whistle and also helped out on backing vocals at these sessions). A distinct rustic edge to the album reveals the influence of the new country rock movement, and the sound is light years away from the sterile orchestration of their previous single. The group's soul roots are not entirely left behind though. Side two opener 'With Salty Eyes, Dirty Lies' is resplendent with effervescent brass, and Johnny Duhan's voice still possesses the earthy growl that he developed singing James Brown and Otis Redding numbers in the Irish clubs. Song-writing is split between Duhan and John Ryan, the former taking much of his inspiration and ideas from the break-up of a teenage relationship.

JOHNNY DUHAN I was always very quiet and taciturn as a kid and I was lacking confidence. Writing gave me an opportunity to express my inner emotions in a way I couldn't with my tongue. I liked the way you could juggle with words until you found the right combination to express exactly how you felt. It was the most important discovery of my life.

Pete Cummins (back left) and Noel Bridgeman (back right) come on board to record Granny's LP

There is a certain tired-of-life weariness pervading the album, which, although not detracting from its overall impact, is hardly surprising considering what the group had been through over the last two years. However, it would not be uncharitable to describe this landmark Irish rock release as uneven. Recurring line-up changes and a sporadic recording schedule hindered any chances of a smooth gestation. Duhan was also experiencing problems with Wayne Bickerton, who was again on hand to produce *Honest Injun*, surprisingly perhaps after the bad feeling within the group over his previous work. The album is book-ended with two very strong hard rock numbers – particularly appealing is the arrogant strut of opener 'Maybe' with its killer Zeppelin-esque guitar hook. Quite a few of the songs were worked up by Granny's Intentions in the studio and while much of the writing is solid a few tracks suffer from a lack of development and polish. The album is certainly of its time – unfortunately nothing dates a record from the period more than the immoderate presence of a flute, and both the clumsily titled 'Fourthskin Blues' and 'Nutmeg, Bitter Sweet' are marred somewhat by its inclusion. All things considered, under the circumstances, the album still showed a lot of potential for the future and was well received on its belated release in March 1970.

> **JOHNNY DUHAN** It was a good starting point, but unfortunately things started going downhill. Communication in the band was poor. More line-up changes. More arguments. More drugs. More confusion.

Deram hardly threw their weight behind the record, having long abandoned Granny's Intentions to concentrate on other priorities. Indicative of their lack of interest was the fact that the final cover design was a cheap photo of the group superimposed over the actual *sketch* that John Ryan submitted to the label's art department to show what he had in mind for the finished sleeve. Brian Tuite, the group's manager since 1966, went back to Ireland to concentrate on the domestic scene and was replaced by John Gee, an eccentric character from the old school of London club management.

> **JOHN RYAN** John Gee at one stage wanted to change the name [to Hunky Dory] and start again. It was just chugging along. You had a few gigs and you had enough to pay for your flat. Nobody really had a long term plan.

When Johnny Hockedy, another stalwart since the early days, lost interest and drifted away after *Honest Injun* was released, a talented young slide guitarist called Ed Deane was drafted in to replace him. An attempt was made to reinvigorate the group in a rented cottage in Killala, County Mayo, but the divisions already apparent between various group members manifested themselves more strongly there. Just one more single was issued, another country-rock composition called 'Take Me Home', which was not included on the LP. In August 1970 Granny's 'New' Intentions headlined a number of shows at the Marquee and later an offer was made to record a second album. Duhan had worked up some new songs but his colleagues were not impressed by their quality and after a year of treading water the group slowly spluttered to a halt in early 1972.

> **JOHHNY DUHAN** I often think that we used up most of the energy in breaking into the Dublin scene. Had we gone straight to London with the powerful energy we had to begin with we might well have cracked the London scene in the way we did Dublin. Rory Gallagher did that. But that's all water under the bridge. The bottom line for me is that we let ourselves down. We had no clear musical direction; we allowed ourselves to be manipulated. We weren't honourable to one another. We were young, foolish, frightened, hungry, drugged-out. Bad management didn't help, but we really had no one but ourselves to blame. The one album shows potential. But it was just a starting point, and the real energy was left behind with the string of intentions that got lost along the way. But I have no regrets whatsoever. Life is for learning.

Around the same time that Granny's Intentions moved to London in the summer of 1967 another Irish group found themselves primed for success in the British capital after being taken into the management stable of Chas Chandler, the ex-bass player for The Animals who had recently brought Jimi Hendrix over from America. Eire Apparent was the new awkwardly punning

The People, 1966. Clockwise Top L-R: Ernie Graham, Henry McCullough, Chris Stewart, Davey Lutton

name that Chandler had given to The People, a group hailing from County Antrim who had spent the previous year establishing a reputation in Dublin's beat scene. Before that, they had tasted the heady rock 'n' roll lifestyle in Blackpool, after taking the boat across the water to follow fellow countrymen The Wheels, who had been gigging in the seaside resort for a number of months. The People existed meagrely through a Sunday afternoon residency in a pub on the main street of the Lancashire town which earned them just £5 per gig. They were condemned to share a small bedroom in a dilapidated house that contained one solitary creaking bed. Despite the discomforts the group's soul-inflected sound went down very well in the north west – a point The Wheels were not slow to pick up on, poaching keyboard player Eric

Wrixon, who had also played with Them, from the ranks of the rival group. Henry McCullough, a supremely gifted blues guitarist who was tired of endless ballroom engagements with popular Northern Ireland showband Gene and the Gents, brought the compliment back up to four. Ernie Graham was the lead vocalist, Davey Lutton played drums and Chris Stewart rounded out the foursome on bass guitar.

It was McCullough who convinced the rest of the group in Blackpool that there was more money to be made in Dublin's thriving beat scene. He had been travelling regularly back to Ireland to visit the wife he had married before joining The People, and was told by Liam McKenna of The Creatures that a four-piece could pocket up to £50 a night in basement clubs in the capital.

Chris Stewart remembers the impact of the newly arrived group in Dublin: 'We were doing a lot of old R&B material, a lot of stuff people had never heard of, so they probably thought it was our material. But it was older blues and rock 'n' roll. We got records from here, there and everywhere. We would take songs that were completely unknown. Ernie, the singer, would jump on top of my amp and swing a microphone round his head and sing these really simple three chord songs, getting the crowd going. They liked the approach, the energy, the excitement.'

Despite rapid success in Ireland, The People felt they had outgrown the scene by May 1967 and just like Granny's Intentions deemed it necessary to move to England to try their luck in a bigger pond. Erstwhile manager Dave Robinson, who would later set up influential punk label Stiff Records, booked a few gigs for the group in some of their old haunts in Blackpool along with a handful of club dates in Liverpool and London. Life was tough for the adventurous four-piece in the English capital, particularly for The People's lead guitarist who not too long before had been experiencing the generous financial awards available to musicians of a showband persuasion.

> **HENRY McCULLOUGH** We were sleeping in the van and there was a hole in the top. We had to live under a bridge in Camden Town so the water wouldn't come in. We were broke as anything. We used to change down at Trafalgar Square if we were doing any sort of gig.

It was there in London on 16 June, after a 5am slot at an all-night gig in the ultra-hip underground UFO club on Tottenham Court Road, headlined by Procul Harum, that Chas Chandler offered the group a personal management contract in conjunction with his business partner Mike Jeffery. Although Chandler's name was hot at the time, having stunned British audiences with the outrageous talent of his new guitar hero from Seattle, McCullough soon became wary of the management duo's attempts to mould the band.

HENRY McCULLOUGH They said you'll have to brighten yourselves up. Ernie had his hair permed, [like] Hendrix and Clapton. I was told I was standing wrong playing the guitar. I had to stand wide legged and thrust slightly forward. I said I can't fucking play a chord if I'm concentrating too much on getting my legs right. They dressed us up in velvet, and furry boots and hats and all the rest of it. What [Chandler] tried to do with Eire Apparent he actually got done with Slade.

The group was sent out to Majorca to knuckle down to some serious song-writing, their managers hoping for at least an album's worth of material. The sun evidently went to everyone's head as they re-appeared after a three month engagement in Chandler-owned Spanish clubs with just one song, 'Here We Go Again'. The relaxing break was followed by a more arduous series of dates on a phenomenal package tour of the UK, playing with Hendrix, The Move, Amen Corner, Pink Floyd and The Nice (the itinerary included a 'homecoming' date in Belfast on 28 November). Their debut single 'Follow Me', written by a trio of session musicians connected to Chandler, and released in January 1968, was a weak song in search of a decent groove that failed to adequately demonstrate the talents in the group.

CHRIS STEWART Chas Chandler took us into the studio and he produced. This was the song he suggested. It was our first time in a real studio, I think it was Olympic in Barnes, and we more or less did what was asked, because we didn't know how to make records. And that was the result. After a bit of contemplation we thought, 'What was that all about?!' So we didn't do that again.

On the B-side was the group's souvenir from Spain, an impressive effort written together by all four members, finding Eire Apparent dabbling in psychedelic hard rock shades. Widely respected Irish pop DJ Larry Gogan, reviewing the week's single releases in *Spotlight*, appeared more fond of 'Follow Me' than the band were: *Definitely under the influence of Jimi Hendrix, Eire Apparent get a great sound on their first disc. Lead singer has a very distinctive voice and with a bit of a push this could easily make the charts.*

HENRY McCULLOUGH I didn't think it was any good at all. The B-side should have been the single. But we were going along a railway line and these boys had started the train. We didn't know what to do. If we had got off we'd be back home in Ireland, so we went along with everything.

With the blessing of Hendrix ringing in their ears (he was quoted in *Melody Maker* in customary laconic style, 'That group the Eire Apparent are

Eire Apparent, 1967. L-R: Davey Lutton, Chris Stewart, Ernie Graham, Henry McCullough

really good') the band were whisked away to North America before they could do any promotion at home for the single, backing up Eric Burdon and The Animals on a sixty-date tour. Henry McCullough sent a postcard to Pat Egan at *Spotlight* wishing all the readers well and updating him on the band's progress. After The Animals' tour had finished the Irish quartet decided to stay in the US and go on another tour, this time with The Jimi Hendrix Experience, Soft Machine and Vanilla Fudge. The sunny greetings in McCullough's missive masked a darker reality however. The lead guitarist was arrested for drug possession in Canada, in a hotel room he was sharing with Ernie Graham.

> **HENRY McCULLOUGH** I got fired from the group. I got busted for a joint of marijuana. That was the perfect excuse for Chas Chandler and Mike Jeffery to fire me. I would wonder why we didn't have any money after a particular night after the gig being packed. 'Don't worry, it'll all go into your offshore account, Henry.' Dave Robinson woke me one morning and gave me a one-way ticket home, and I was in Dublin before the rest of the band knew I was fired. It's all very well now for musicians to have a little bit of puff, but in those days it was bad for the image.

Speaking to journalist Trevor Hodgett before his death in 2001, Ernie

Graham was annoyed at the inconvenience that his guitar player had caused the band.

> **ERNIE GRAHAM** Henry had the knack of mixing with shady characters. I'd warned him, don't involve me. But he had people in our shared room, smoking dope, and they attracted the attention of the house detective. I got back and found three policemen there. I was arrested for doing nothing and held overnight, before Henry gave a statement I wasn't involved and I was released. But for the rest of the tour, every time I heard footsteps I imagined people coming to arrest me.

Mick Cox, an English guitarist who had played with Belfast beat merchants The Alleykatz and had recently completed some work with the solo Van Morrison in London, was hired to fill the vacancy created by McCullough's sacking. He had previously met his new cohorts as The People in Dublin, where his own short-lived group The End had done some support slots with them. Cox was an accomplished player who was influenced by jazz greats such as Django Reinhardt and Charlie Byrd as much as by blues masters like Big Bill Broonzy and Sonny Boy Williamson. This eclecticism would manifest itself on some of the intricate guitar work and complex arrangements on Eire Apparent's debut album.

> **MICK COX** I literally got the call, I was over in a week and I was straight into the studio recording, because I was a songwriter and they didn't have any other songwriter apart from Ernie. The first day I came in to do a track, before we did anything at all, [Hendrix] said, 'Have a listen to this.' And he put on 'All Along The Watchtower'. No sounds had ever sounded like that. Then he said, 'Okay, do you wanna go out and do your thing?' So I went out and started laying down the rhythm track for 'Yes, I Need Someone' and he said, 'Do you mind if I put a bit of guitar on that? I've got an idea.' So he took my guitar, which is right handed, turned it over the other way, bunged it in the amplification system I had, turned it up absolutely full... You've gotta remember he's been up all night mixing 'All Along The Watchtower' and he's taken a few chemicals and a few bits and pieces. In fact he's completely out of it. He [asks engineer] Eddie Kramer to play the track that we had just done backwards through the cans. He just started making these noises along with this track being played backwards. This feedback noise stuff is nearly breaking the windows in the studio. We just thought, 'Well, okay, you have to indulge Jimi, he's flipped a bit.' And then when he came back into the studio he said to Eddie, 'Now

> play it forward', and there's this perfect soundscape on 'Yes, I Need Someone'. That was my introduction [to Jimi Hendrix].

Back in Ireland, Henry McCullough's career was about to take an interesting diversion. Two years before, after arriving in Dublin from Blackpool, he had become friendly with Johnny Moynihan of legendary folk outfit Sweeney's Men.

> **HENRY McCULLOUGH** He taught me a lot, gave me stuff to listen to that I always had a great love for but [was] never able to find, traditional stuff, unaccompanied singing. I turned him on to John Lee Hooker and that end of it, blues and rock 'n' roll. The folk players would have drank in a particular pub and the rock 'n' rollers would have drank in another. Not to keep away from anyone, it was just the way it was. But at that time when The Beatles and Stones and long hair [was coming in] they started visiting each other's pubs.

Andy Irvine, a young British actor turned musician, was leaving the folk trio to travel to Eastern Europe in order to study that region's forms of indigenous music. In the increasingly fluid and mutually influential music scene in Ireland it didn't seem a particularly strange proposition for Johnny Moynihan to invite the ex-Eire Apparent lead guitarist to sit in on some informal jams with Sweeney's Men. On 17 May 1968, Terry Woods, Moynihan and McCullough appeared on stage together for the first time, comprising the new line-up of one of Ireland's most illustrious folk ensembles. Many people in both the trad and beat scenes were surprised by the replacement of Andy Irvine with the Northern Ireland blues man, and unsure of the wisdom of the decision. How would a rock 'n' roller fit into such a resolutely traditional folk band? In an interview with BP Fallon the trio made light of the situation, Moynihan pointing out that he had previously harboured desires to work with Henry McCullough and that the coincidental timing of Irvine's departure and the troubles within the Eire Apparent camp couldn't have been more serendipitous. In the same article, McCullough laid bare the problems he had been having in his old group, discreetly skirting the issue regarding the discovery of the illicit drugs.

> **HENRY McCULLOUGH** I loved the pop tours, like the British tour and the American tour with The Animals, but I hated everything going on around The Eire Apparent. We were told what to play – we had to play Beatle numbers like 'Magical Mystery Tour' – and it even got to the point where we were told what to wear on stage. I had the same argument with Gene and The Gents, but I thought in a group this had been done away

> with. Our managers just wanted a straight corny pop group and I wouldn't accept this any more. We all thought 'Follow Me' was crap and didn't want it to be released, and the only good piece on the record Chandler cut out 'cos he thought it was too like Hendrix. (*Spotlight*, Vol. 1, No. 52, 28 May 1968)

Sweeney's Men were hoping to forge a new sound by mixing traditional Irish strains with each individual member's idiosyncratic tastes – American country and folk in the case of Terry Woods, time-honoured Celtic sounds from Moynihan and the rustic blues that was dearly loved by McCullough. Other groups in Britain were trying similar experiments and achieving more widespread and lasting acclaim than the Irishmen – The Incredible String Band and Pentangle being two of the more notable examples. A tantalizing performance at the Cambridge Folk Festival and a now-erased appearance on RTÉ's *Twenty Minutes With...* have contributed to the semi-mythical standing afforded the McCullough/Moynihan/Woods line-up.

Sweeney's Men, summer 1968. L-R: Terry Woods, Henry McCullough, Johnny Moynihan

HENRY McCULLOUGH It was always of interest to me to use the guitar in a drone situation, like the [uillean] pipes. Use it with traditional instruments, the bouzouki, the banjo, acoustic guitar. It did work and we had a great time but we took it to the point where we didn't know what to do next. It was strange, [Terry on] acoustic guitar, Johnny on bouzouki and me on electric guitar with a small amp. We played down the country a

> few times and I'll tell you I was glad to get out of it and the people were glad to see us gone as well!

McCullough was certainly bullish at the time about the prospects of his new innovative group: 'Sweeney's Men will have to change musically, because I'm not capable of doing Andy's job. Anyway, we're all interested in making a change – gradually.' Four months later, Henry was in Joe Cocker's Grease Band! Sweeney's Men were staying in the Madison Hotel in London, renowned for the continual stream of rock 'n' rollers and counter-cultural icons that flooded its corridors. Brian Tuite, manager of Granny's Intentions, who were staying there at the same time, introduced McCullough to a young lad with a voice like sand and glue who had just come down from Sheffield and was on the lookout for a new guitarist. By his own admission, Henry was feeling the need to be 'a bit more tribal' once again and craved the company of pumping bass guitar and thunderous drums. McCullough would later go on to join Paul McCartney in Wings. During his extensive career he has worked with Marianne Faithful, Scottish soul legend Frankie Miller and with the ensemble who played on the original recording of Jesus Christ Superstar. Furthermore he has the unique distinction of being the only Irishman to play at the seminal Woodstock Music And Arts Festival in Bethel, New York in August 1969. McCullough is the one playing guitar and supplying high pitched backing vocals during Joe Cocker's earth-trembling rendition of 'With A Little Help From My Friends'.

> **HENRY McCULLOUGH** At that time there were a lot of festivals going on. Half the bands would have done the same festivals; there was a core of Johnny Winter and Joe Cocker and The Grease Band and others. So Woodstock was just like another festival. And it wasn't until days before it, when this influx of people starting moving, [that] there was a huge vibe about it. It sort of got out of hand a little bit. Most of the bands stayed at the Holiday Inn, about twenty miles out. Because of the amount of people all the bands were flown in by helicopter, maybe two at a time. You hung around for an hour, did your gig, hung around for another hour, got into the helicopter, got taken back to the hotel and the following day you were off on tour again. It was just another gig with a clatter of gigs around it. The myth of Woodstock just gets bigger and bigger. Joe Cocker and The Grease Band surpassed themselves that particular day. It was brilliant to watch the footage back but it didn't have that same feel on stage. We were just looking out on a bunch of people.

The Record Plant, New York, May 1968: Ernie Graham, Davey Lutton,

Jimi Hendrix works on the Eire Apparent LP as Mick Cox and Chris Stewart look on

Chris Stewart and new boy Mick Cox are busy laying down the tracks for *Sunrise*, the debut album by Eire Apparent. Sessions were conducted at the same time that Hendrix was putting together his universally renowned masterpiece *Electric Ladyland*. According to the fanzine *Jimpress* (Issue 46, Apr 1996), apart from the Eire Apparent record there is only one other album that bears Jimi Hendrix's name as producer, an obscure LP called *The Street Giveth…And The Street Taketh Away* by little known roots rock band Cat Mother and The All Night Newsboys. It contains no prominent guitar work from its sonic sculptor. Conversely, rock's most charismatic axeman sprays his psychedelic space dust liberally across the *Sunrise* album, peppering the grooves with wah-wah freakouts, acid soaked fills, trills and feedback drenched wails. The songs derive mostly from the pens of lead vocalist Ernie Graham and guitarist Mick Cox. Only two tracks out of ten are not produced by Hendrix and have no input from him whatsoever – 'Captive In The Sun' on side two and the iridescent instrumental '1026' that closes the record and serves as the album's come-down. They were both taped in a studio in Los Angeles, where Robert Wyatt of Soft Machine and Noel Redding of The Experience were at hand to supply vocals to the wordless chorus on '1026'. Stylistically varied, commendably bold and unashamedly elaborate, *Sunrise* is a seductive *mélange* of psychedelia and pop, astutely conveying the excitement and hunger of a group who two years previously had been entertaining kids in Dublin's Club Arthur and Club A Go Go and were now working with rock music's hottest property in one of the best studios money could hire. The members of Eire Apparent all had a warm and productive relationship with

Hendrix, and their management team was happy to indulge the group financially in the studio, supplying orchestras and arrangers to bolster various songs.

> **MICK COX** Jimi's input was track by track. He didn't have a concept of a theme for the whole thing, that was left to the band. He was very much an encouraging type of person but he was shy of stamping his mark on it. It's great to have somebody who was very sympathetic to what we were doing. Jimi liked the band, he liked Irish music. It was just one of those bizarre scenes where he got on with all of us and we loved him, he was a lovely man. [Later] he gave me his Flying V, money to record in a studio...he didn't have to do all that stuff, he was an absolute gentleman.

> **CHRIS STEWART** Hendrix was brilliant. He was very patient with us, he did a marvellous job. His technique in the studio, sound-wise, was brilliant. At the end of the day he would come in and put a lot of guitar on, help fill it out, a couple of solos here and there.

If there is one area in which the album falls short, it's the vocal department. Ernie Graham had a distinctive nasal whine which doesn't always do justice to the material, and the vocal takes with Mick Cox are similarly under-developed. Not everyone in the group was satisfied with the completed product. There had always been unease with the direction The People/Eire Apparent had been coaxed into taking and some felt the songs on the album didn't reflect the foursome's true nature.

> **CHRIS STEWART** I was quite happy with the production, but the material was quite bad, the musicianship and the group I wasn't impressed with at all. I think Jimi Hendrix did a great job patching up something that wasn't too good. Compared to what The People was, it just didn't compete. Ernie's strength was his showmanship, not his vocals, which we didn't realise until we got into the studio!

Little of *Sunrise* was performed live, the group opting to stick with more straightforward rock and blues. In a Peel Session for the BBC in April 1969 they performed Dylan's 'Highway 61 Revisited', Van Morrison's garage rock classic 'Gloria' and just one song from the new album, the buoyant lead off 'Yes I Need Someone'. At the end of 1968, Eire Apparent returned to England, free of one half of the management team that they had never felt comfortable with. It seemed Mike Jeffery had mysteriously disappeared.

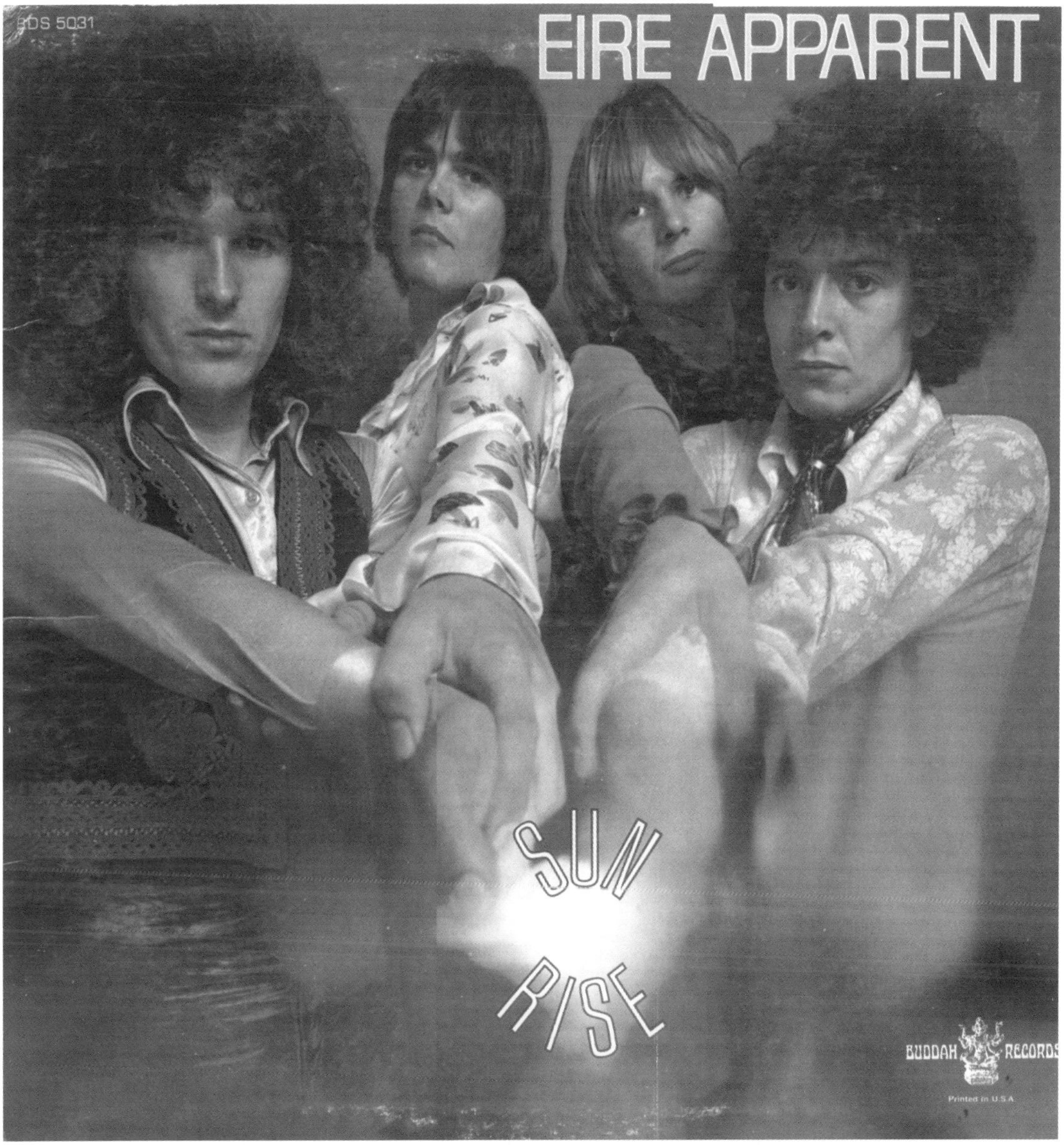

There were unsavoury rumours floating around concerning shady business associates; someone even falsely claimed he had drowned. In truth, he had probably decided to concentrate all his energies on steering the career of Jimi Hendrix, after buying Chas Chandler out of the management partnership. One thing was certain – the group decided they were much better off without him. Mick Cox, who had contributed so much to the *Sunrise* recording sessions, also departed shortly after completion of the album. Ernie Graham has claimed it was because the guitarist's playing was not up to scratch. The Dagenham-born musician, who re-united with Van Morrison in Boston to work on the demos for *Astral Weeks* during a short break from recording at the Record Plant, refutes this.

> **MICK COX** I brought my wife over [to America]. There was a disagreement about women being part of the group and on tour. We had an argument and they said she had to go back. It was a combination of very silly things, and things that were said at the wrong time and in the wrong place. And the next thing Dave Robinson said I was out of the band. I was quite happy with it. I'd written a lot of stuff that they didn't like, it probably wasn't Eire Apparent music.

Cox was replaced by Belfast guitarist Tiger Taylor who had actually been in an early incarnation of The People before their Dublin days. The album's British and Irish release was delayed, finally hitting the shops in May 1969. Reviews were mostly supportive. BP Fallon, writing a column about the London scene for *Spotlight*, rather uncharitably described *Sunrise* as a 'mixture of good luck and poor bubblegum'. His view is largely unchanged today.

> **BP FALLON** *Sunrise* isn't Eire Apparent at their magic height, when the wonderful Henry McCullough was playing guitar in the band, the band that toured America with The Jimi Hendix Experience and Eric Burdon and the New Animals and The Soft Machine, psychedelicising their way through freak-flag America. Henry's the great unsung hero of Irish rock 'n' roll – The Skyrockets and Gene and the Gents to The People and Eire Apparent to the electric Sweeney's Man – what an AMAZING group, Henry and Terry Woods and Johnny Moynihan doing stuff together that no one had done before and no one's done since – to Joe Cocker and the Greaseband and Woodstock and Wings with McCartney – Henry was Paul's Lennon, stubborn with a heart of gold but all soul, and what a guitarist!

A tour of Germany was organized for Eire Apparent and a new single was released, the Stones-y 'Rock 'n' Roll Band', cut afresh in London and again featuring a solo by Jimi Hendrix. Polydor Records had the group on its books in the UK (the LP was put out by Buddha in the US) and there was some talk of a second LP. Despite this various group members were becoming increasingly disillusioned. The success that was expected of them after recording with Hendrix and touring so extensively in the US and UK had not materialised. An inability to recreate the album's heavily arranged songs in a live situation probably hampered sales and wider recognition.

> **CHRIS STEWART** We came back and it was pretty tough. At that point the band started to disintegrate a bit. We lived in a house together which was OK. Then we got a couple of different guitar players in and we tried to continue and do the odd gig

> here and there. But I could see the writing on the wall. When Henry went, to me it lost a lot. When Mick Cox came in it lost quite a bit. Nothing detrimental about Mick but it started to go in a different direction, more story songs as opposed to rock 'n' roll. I started to switch off then and it gradually went down and down for me personally. I think Davey and Ernie didn't know which way to turn anyway so they were prepared to hang in there. But I could see the end of the road and I started looking around. I got a few offers to go and eventually I went.

Eire Apparent finally called it a day in May 1970.

Back home on the domestic scene in the late 1960s many musicians in Irish beat groups were happy to continuously update their set-lists of soul standards, Beatles covers and pop faves, and there was always a healthy proliferation of non-professional combos to keep dancers happy in the clubs. Other more talented players who decided that the vagaries of life within a beat group were too unpredictable and volatile found themselves enticed by the promise of a steady wage in an established or newly created showband. As is evident in the case of both Eire Apparent and Granny's Intentions, those few individuals with the ability and the driving ambition (not forgetting the financial backing) to succeed were able to grow out of humble beginnings on the domestic scene and achieve varying degrees of eminence in international markets. They certainly became the trailblazers for a legion of indigenous acts that came after them. By 1968 numerous universally loved groups such as Bluesville, The Action and The Next In Line were now defunct and tearfully missed, but with the musical climate changing at such a breakneck speed there were plenty of other names to take their place in fans' affections.

The Kingbees had returned to Ireland after their German adventure came to an end in December 1967. Unable to sustain momentum with a compromised line-up and aware that a lot of new groups had stolen their thunder on the Dublin scene whilst in exile, Ditch Cassidy put together his next band, The News, in early 1968. The line-up was very fluid over the next couple of years, with a rotating cast of drummers and guitarists making up the ranks, including at one point the Skid Row luminaries, Gary Moore and Noel Bridgeman. American adventurers The Creatures had split up by this point, two of their members having been poached by the predatory showbands. Frank Boylan (bass) and Ray McDonald (drums) from The Creatures chose to stick with rock music and drifted into the initial line-up of The News. Regular trips were made to Germany for six week stints, backing up big name acts such as Ben E. King, Joe Tex, Clarence 'Frogman' Henry and The Temptations. As befitting these support slots, the group's

Ditch Cassidy and The News, 1968

repertoire became even more soul oriented, and the addition of two go-go dancers went down a storm with the American GIs. These infatuated fans would mop Ditch Cassidy's brow with silk handkerchiefs in a gesture of ostentatious appreciation. After a star-making turn at home performing the Wilson Pickett hit 'Land of 1,000 Dances' on *Like Now*, bookings for Ditch and The News shot up, and there was a lot of chatter at the beginning of 1969 about a possible solo contract with CBS Records. After a couple of months movement seemed to have stalled on the proposed deal. When another offer to hit the big time was presented to The News by Phil Solomon – in the form of a showcase gig in front of potential labels at famous London club Blaises in March 1969 – the group leapt at the chance. Unfortunately the night descended into a farcical calamity. A handful of unidentified pills had been passed around on the evening of the gig to calm nerves and bolster confidence. Unbeknownst to everyone half the band had swallowed uppers and the other half had ingested downers – so their timing was a *little* off!

> **BRIAN HARRIS** It was the worst gig we ever did. Willie [Behan, new drummer who had replaced Ray McDonald] was playing drum fills and he was playing *in between* the drums. He was losing time and it was kind of embarrassing, I kept kicking him and he'd be all right for a while. At one stage I was holding him by the collar, hoping the attention would be on Ditch out front.

The gig was cut short and Phil Solomon, a serious businessman with a fiercely anti-drugs philosophy, was furious. He gave the group their boat fare home and never had any further dealings with them again. The News were not a permanent fixture on the club scene in Ireland during 1969, spending large chunks of time touring in Germany. Their musical vision began to change as well, this time partly prompted by a new found drug of choice, LSD. The psychedelic sounds of Jimi Hendrix and the hard rock leanings of Iron Butterfly began to replace the soul standards, puzzling some of the people who had known them in a very different incarnation on the German scene, including the manager of the Casino Club in Augsburg.

> **DITCH CASSIDY** The bossman couldn't understand us anymore, we had gone from being semi-clean cut guys, wearing the same suits, to hippies with the hair down to here and beards. We didn't drink with him anymore…stoned all the time.

Their newly acquired uniforms of kaftans, sandals, and flared jeans soon got them into a serious spot of bother with the French *gendarmerie*. On 1 December 1969 Ditch Cassidy and guitarist Frank Boylan decided to take a well-earned short break to Nancy in the south of France. Two local GIs offered them a ride in their enormous shiny Cadillac, which was eagerly

One of Ireland's finest soul singers, Ditch Cassidy, 1969

accepted by the Irish musicians (originally they were planning to slum it in their beat-up van). One of the GIs had brought back a big bag of 'serious, lethal' grass from his tour of duty in Vietnam and all parties indulged gleefully in the hallucinogenic herb as they cruised through the countryside. By the time they reached the German/French border the driver was in no fit state to continue, so the mellow travellers pulled into the parking lot at the railway station in Mulhouse to catch some shut-eye. At 8am the next morning the Irish rockers and the American conscripts woke up to find the car surrounded by armed police. A customs man on his way to work had seen the US registered vehicle with two GIs and two hippies slumped in the interior and alerted local law enforcement. As they were being escorted to the police station Ditch Cassidy tried to persuade his army buddy to get rid of the incriminating evidence, but the soldier was reluctant to dump the top gear, as it was the only thing he had managed to bring back from Vietnam, apart from endlessly recurring psychotic nightmares. At the station, the car, the military men and the bearded freaks were all methodically stripped and searched and the illicit substance uncovered.

> **DITCH CASSIDY** The hippies were the scapegoats. We were taken away to what you would only describe as a dungeon, a very, very old French prison. Now the French were never renowned for their penitentiary facilities. They beat us, and they kept at us to confess and say, 'Yeah, we did it.' Then after a day or two when they couldn't get anything they broke us up and put us into cells with murderers and rapists and all kinds of headcases.

The Irishmen were kept under lock and key for a total of nine days and dragged to two 'tribunals'. Adding further to the humiliation the warden of the jail arranged for their long hair and beards to be chopped off. Frank Boylan put up a feisty struggle, only giving up when pressure was applied to his neck with a fistful of keys. Ditch's reaction was altogether more bizarre.

> **DITCH CASSIDY** When they came to me, something happened, I've never felt anything like this… this language came out of me. It was like Romany or something like that… it was a curse. I was actually putting a curse on the head screw. It was unintelligible, it wasn't like any language I had ever heard, but it was a feeling that came from way down, pure hatred.

The next day, 10 December, the incarcerated were released. Ditch's father, perturbed by the salacious reporting of the whole incident splashed all over the front pages of the Irish newspapers, had been playing golf with the brother of the Irish Ambassador to France and convinced him to pull some strings. The ex-cons stumbled bleary-eyed out of the French prison on a bitterly cold morning to find two feet of snow on the ground, the car battery dead, no money in their pockets, no hair on their heads, and very little dignity left. With the help of the GIs, they eventually got the car working again and drove back to The Big Apple Club in Augsburg where the group (who had changed their name by this stage to Chillum) had been performing their acid-inspired jams prior to the aborted vacation. The locks had been changed on their apartment, their manager didn't recognise them with their shaved heads, and to make matters even worse German police were still looking for them because the case had not been satisfactorily closed. Gathering together some army regulation survival gear the musicians took off into the forest and camped out under the stars for a couple of weeks, before cold and hunger forced them back to the city. Ditch's father wired money to the Irish consulate in Bonn so his son could buy a plane ticket back to Ireland. The plan was for Chillum's lead singer to write the real story of events upon his arrival in Dublin and sell it to the newspapers in order to raise cash to get the rest of the group home. Of course, sticking by the old adage that facts get in the way of a good story, none of the papers wanted to know Ditch's account. The rest of the group staggered back to Ireland one by one as soon as they were able to scrape together the required funds.

Despite their once high profile on the Dublin scene, very few promoters and club owners wanted to know about Ditch Cassidy and his band after they all eventually limped back from Germany. The only person who gave them a helping hand was John Ryan, manager of Club A Go Go (not the same John Ryan of Granny's Intentions fame). He had a good working relationship with bass guitarist Frank Boylan, and agreed to take over management duties of the group in 1970. There were various incarnations of different groups featuring Ditch Cassidy, 'the white singer with the coloured soul' (*Hitsville* magazine, July 1968), over the next few years, mostly based in England and Germany – Ditch eventually got a £10,000 deal with Decca to release a full-length album, but the tracks recorded were never released. Just one single, a version of Leon Russell's 'Pisces Apple Lady', appeared in 1971. The potential shown by The Kingbees and The News never quite metamorphosed into long-term success, something Ditch looks back on with a tinge of disappointment and resignation.

> **DITCH CASSIDY** We were all looking for the one thing – we wanted fame and success and money. But then you look back at The Small Faces and how much did they get? £20 a week, the rent paid for, clothes allowance. The guys who are left are still looking for their money; they're fighting court cases on this.

The lack of decent pay, certainly in light of what the showbands were making, may still have been a contentious issue for beat groups in Ireland, but fame was beginning to slowly materialise for some, albeit confined to the domestic scene on a relatively limited scale. Not only was there still a hive of activity down the metal staircases in the subterranean clubs, and a flourishing scene out in the suburban tennis pavilions, but bigger concerts were being promoted in places like the National Stadium, the Mansion House and the Crystal Ballroom, where audiences were measured in the thousands, not hundreds. Liberty Hall on Eden Quay played host to a particularly mouth watering line-up on Monday 11 March 1968. On the bill that night were soul survivors The Uptown Band, pop sensations The Strangers and blues quartet Sugar Shack, who had recently come out of nowhere to score a hit with a version of Tim Rose's portentous nuclear holocaust ballad 'Morning Dew'. Even The Creatures reformed especially for a one-off performance.

Increased media coverage was encouraging as well. *The Showband Show* had helped spur The Greenbeats on to nationwide fame back in 1964, widening their appeal beyond the confines of the capital city and ensuring great receptions in country ballrooms up and down the land. Since then, however, there had been very little publicity of the beat group scene on Irish television. It was still an underground happening, centred around a closely bound community of musicians and fans. With the launch of RTÉ's *Like Now* programme in October 1968, that all changed. Suddenly a vivid blast of Irish rock was beamed into family living rooms all across the country and the scene was truly unveiled for the first time. Three years earlier, when the domestic broadcaster tried to introduce a contemporary slant to a new series of *The Showband Show* by constructing a studio set modelled on a typical cellar club, there was an outcry amongst mainstream pop fans. A full page editorial in *Spotlight* derided the brave format and slammed the inclusion of 'long haired, weird, agony music'. The Action's appearance on one of the programmes even prompted a heated debate on *The Late Late Show*.

> **SHAY HEALY** One of the things that happened during the showband period was that girls used to get up and jive together at the dances. On *The Showband Show* the girls would get up and dance together on the television live and they used to get

these irate letters into the *RTÉ Guide* saying how disgusting it was. Then when *Like Now* came along and you saw these fellas waggling their heads there was outrage!

Like Now, hosted by club DJ Danny Hughes and taped in the Top Hat Ballroom in Dún Laoghaire, had a broad and democratic philosophy, fitting in fashion items, Irish showbands, a chart rundown and British rock groups as well as home-grown beat talent into a thirty minute allotment. The Movement from Dublin, The Gentry from Northern Ireland, Limerick's Granny's Intentions and Manfred Mann from England were some of the featured acts on the first two broadcasts. Honorary Irishman Ian Whitcomb even paid a brief visit to the city where his music career began, showing up for the third instalment in the series. The theme music for the programme was written and performed by The Uptown Band.

Dublin pop band Stop Press on the set of Like Now

DANNY HUGHES *Like Now* changed everything. It was ninety per cent beat groups, ten per cent showbands. Everybody got a fair chance, it didn't matter if you were starting off, once you could do the business when you got there. We also had David Bowie and Cat Stevens live. We would have video clips of some of the English bands, The Kinks, whatever. So the kids down the country in Killarney were seeing the fashions for the first time. They were seeing a boy and girl dancing, wearing bell bottoms.

> This was a very exciting time. At that time RTÉ had maybe one hour or half an hour a week for playing pop music and that would be censored.

As well as additional exposure on the airwaves, the beat scene got a magazine of its own when *Hitsville* appeared on newsstands in April 1968. A twelve-page fanzine-type publication, coverage was strictly limited to rock and pop music. There was no need to take meek second billing to the showbands like the groups did in national entertainment bible *Spotlight*. Even Pat Egan, who had done much to further the cause of the beat scene through his weekly column, found the freedom refreshing, moonlighting as an anonymous columnist in the new periodical. These developments were a shot in the arm for Ireland's home-grown scene, which some felt was becoming stale and predictable only three or four years after The Greenbeats, Bluesville, The Strangers *et al* had kick-started it all. Lack of originality and a lack of education on the part of the audience were seen as the main causes of this sterility. 'The scene is dead now' was the dramatic announcement by John Ryan of Granny's Intentions in an interview given to *Spotlight* in June 1968. 'I'm glad we went to England because The Creatures lasted at the top for over a year before becoming over-exposed and we reckoned if we stayed we'd be lucky to last that long.' Speaking in the same issue Brush Shiels, who had formed Skid Row eight months previously, bemoaned the dearth of innovative groups on the scene. 'There's not enough excitement or original progression – too much imitating. Yet if everyone played just pop, the clubs would be full. There's never been a progressive group on the Irish scene – except maybe Bluesville. We need someone to come along and blow the scene open again.' 'Most groups play what the punters want,' added Skid Row's vocalist, Phil Lynott, 'not what they themselves want, and that defeats the purpose of being in a group, which is to create your own individual sound.' (*Spotlight*, Vol. 2, No. 4, 22 June 1968) Lynott had impressed everyone with his charisma, ambition and determination ever since he began to create a name for himself at sixteen years of age, singing with Crumlin rockers The Black Eagles. Ted Carroll remembers booking the precocious group to play at his club, The Bastille, in Dalkey.

> **TED CARROLL** They changed in the van and when it was time to come on stage suddenly the back doors of this Transit van opened and out leapt these guys – Brian Downey, Phil, who I had never seen before, plus three other guys and they had mod type shirts and pale blue bell bottom flared jeans with these little bells sown down [the side]. They came jingling out!

One of many groups of the time doing covers of Small Faces, Yardbirds and Stones material, The Black Eagles ground to a halt in 1967. The group's rhythm guitarist, Frank Smyth, wasted no time in putting together a new outfit with the controversial name of Kama Sutra, who specialised in Tamla Motown pop. Lynott lasted only three months with the band before moving on and to gain even more plaudits in his next position as lead singer of Skid Row. Brush Shiels, a mischievous and individualistic presence on the group scene, had grown tired of playing popular soul tunes to the club crowds with The Uptown Band, and put together his own progressive outfit in October 1967. Sensibly rejecting the bizarre short-lived name of My Father's Moustache, Skid Row quickly leapt to prominence on the back of some inimitable live shows (with extravagant stage projections created by lighting man 'Ashtar', who had worked with Pink Floyd), and a forward looking approach to sculpting sound. Freelance showband and beat group photographer Roy Esmonde was taken aback by their fresh approach and soon became the group's first manager.

> **ROY ESMONDE** They were more dangerous, more off the wall. Brush was always a very interesting, clever guy. I remember him doing demo tapes and playing stuff that had strange jazz rhythms, interesting bass lines. Very unusual, it wasn't mainstream. But he knew how to do a gig and get the punters [going]. And then he had Philo who was a big draw and could sell it well.

On stage in amongst the fast intricate guitar solos Lynott could be seen hunched over an echo box, screaming into it, fiddling with the dials and manipulating the device to create a collage of other-worldly frequencies. Initially influenced by the West Coast sound of The Byrds, The Doors and the peace and love phase of The Beatles, Skid Row morphed into a much more complex and experimental beast as the 1970s dawned, mixing musical styles, employing complex time signatures and frequently emphasising virtuosity above accessibility. Brush Shiels has freely admitted that the recruitment of Phil Lynott for the group was as much to do with his exotic appearance and popularity amongst female fans as his ability to hold a note. After one particular appearance on *Like Now*, when Lynott murdered 'Strawberry Fields Forever' by warbling wildly off-key, Brush decided something needed to be done about his vocalist's limitations.

> **ROY ESMONDE** Philip couldn't sing that well. I told Brush to get rid of him numerous times. By that stage I was involved with a singer and I became very conscious of keys and that kind of stuff. I realised that Philip wasn't singing on key and I couldn't stand it then. I'm very fond of Philip, I did lots of photographs of [him], we were great mates but I thought the band needed a better singer. Brush kept saying to me, 'Yeah, but he has

fantastic appeal, look at the women, the crowd around the stage,' Anyway it used to come up so often and it came up again one day and Brush said, 'Come to the next gig, he's had his tonsils out and now he's singing on key,' I went along and he was! It makes no sense to me but it's true!

Skid Row, late 1968. L-R: Phil Lynott, Gary Moore, Brush Shiels, Robbie Brennan

Brush had sent Phil over to Manchester in March 1969 for an operation on his throat. While he was away the remaining Skid Row members found themselves performing adequately as a Cream-style trio. Gary Moore was on guitar and Noel Bridgeman had taken up permanent residence on the drum kit after a brief sojourn to Germany with ex-Action frontman Colm Wilkinson and a sabbatical helping out Granny's Intentions (Robbie Brennan had replaced him during this time). On Lynott's return, despite his new-found vocal prowess, the singer was deemed surplus to requirements. Evidence of Lynott's tenure with the band can be found on Skid Row's first record, 'New Faces, Old Faces / Misdemeanour Dream Felicity', which was recorded in Eamonn Andrews' studio and put out on the small Song label, run by Dublin solicitor Joe Colgan and folk musician Donal Lunny. The group he left would achieve solid success in Britain and America in the early

1970s without quite managing to emulate the simultaneously spectacular exploits of their discarded vocalist. Tours of America with The Allman Brothers, Jethro Tull and The Grateful Dead kept Skid Row's name alive in progressive rock circles. Two LPs were released on the CBS label, but Brush Shiels' unorthodox approach to making records (the first album reportedly took eleven hours to cut, the second one 34 Hours, hence its title) and his casual disdain for the music business in general possibly scuppered Skid Row's chances of ever making the big time.

Legend has it that the very same bass guitar which Robert Ballagh had discarded – in the corner of his room when he quit The Chessmen – in favour of painting, was sold to Phil Lynott shortly after his Skid Row exit. Brush Shiels, the very man who had dismissed him from that group, charitably gave Phil lessons on the four-stringed instrument. A call was made to old Black Eagles' band mate Brian Downey, who had been drumming in Sugar Shack, about forming a new group. Pat Quigley, previously of The Movement, was recruited as bass player, Lynott still in the process of developing his own skills. Quigley also brought in a lead guitar player called Joe Staunton, but in truth the line-up of this new group, called The Orphanage, was fairly elastic and subject to intermittent guest appearances. The music reflected the fact that Lynott was spending more and more time mixing with musicians from outside the beat scene, including poetically-inclined folk ensemble Tara Telephone. Occasionally Terry Woods from Sweeney's Men could be found sitting in on Orphanage gigs.

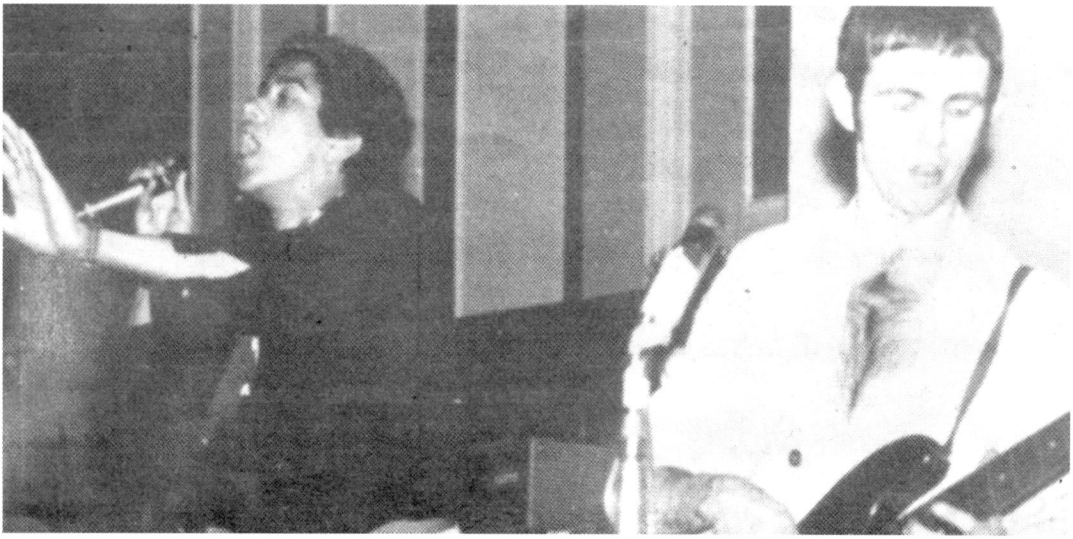

Phil Lynott and Brush Shiels on stage

Interaction between the more receptive side of the folk scene and the liberally-minded rock crowd was becoming more commonplace as the decade wore on. In 1969 a new weekly club night called the Ghetto was established in the 5 Club, where musicians from the beat scene would mingle and play experimental sets accompanied by poets, acoustic folk players, painters and any other artistically inclined people who dropped by. Out in Sandymount on the south coast of Dublin, Phil Lynott, Gary Moore and other beat heads were hanging out with eccentric acid-folk band Dr Strangely Strange, in a large house affectionately nicknamed The Orphanage (a name appropriated for Lynott's new band). Ireland's premier 'folk rock' crossover act of the time, Dr Strangely Strange signed to Joe Boyd's Island Records after sharing a bill in Carlow with Skid Row and local beat group The Word. Robin Williamson of the UK's Incredible String Band was in attendance with Boyd, having invited the American-born producer over to Ireland to check out the new act.

> **BP FALLON** Ah, strangely strange but oddly normal. The whispy trio of Tim Goulding and Ivan Paul and Tim Booth danced in the clouds spun across the water by The Incredible String Band – who were Scottish, fellow Celts – and had a hippied, stoned, cosmic vibe fuelled by some of the finest hash around. Lovely cats, weaving tapestries of sound on wheezing organic instruments that when they weren't entirely in tune or in time were entirely in tune with the times.

Peter Fallon, brother of BP, came together with future Horslips' drummer Eamonn Carr to form modern poetry collective Tara Telephone, other regular attendees at the Ghetto. Such a fertile meeting of minds and cross-pollination of ideas and influences would help Irish rock music and Irish folk music move steadily forward into the next decade as the initial flowerings of the beat scene began to wane. One particular musician who successfully infiltrated the folk world in the late 60s and became one of Ireland's most famous and successful singers in both the rock and folk idioms over the next few decades, started his career off in the rough and tumble environment of Dublin's packed basement clubs before moving on to greater international acclaim.

Paul Brady came to the Irish capital in the autumn of 1964 from Strabane, County Tyrone on a scholarship to study Irish and French at University College Dublin. Not all that interested in his studies, Brady would regularly drift into town to see what was happening on the local music scene. He soon came in contact with the acorn-sized beat scene just taking root.

> **PAUL BRADY** I remember seeing a poster somewhere on Stephen's Green for a blues extravaganza or something in the Crystal Ballroom. There would have been four bands on the bill. I went to see that gig and was totally blown away by the experience. I'd never seen anything except a showband before that and I'd never really seen bands playing the kind of music that I really liked to listen to – Jerry Lee Lewis stuff, which John Keogh was playing with The Greenbeats; Jimmy Reed stuff, which was being played by Bluesville. It was a huge eye-opener

> to me and I immediately knew that I wanted to play in a band in Dublin as soon as I could.

Included on the bill for that R&B Spectacular on Monday 12 October was a group called The Inmates, who Paul approached after the gig to see if they needed a guitar player. Up to then the young Tyrone man had little outlet for his musical passions, keeping his Hoffner Club 60 guitar tucked under his bed in digs he shared with four agriculture students from Kerry. After some persistence on his part Brady procured a phone number from Inmates guitarist Brendan Bonass and shortly after attended an audition in a neighbourhood tennis club.

> **BRENDAN BONASS** We were rehearsing one day in Belvedere Tennis Club and Paul walked in. I think he had called into a couple of gigs before that. Anyway he got playing and Paul was a terrific guitar player, a very exciting rhythm 'n' blues singer. We recognised that even then.

Brady soon took over lead vocal duties with the group, who changed their name to The Kult, but not before they cut a version of Bob Dylan's 'She Belongs To Me' with original singer Ronnie Stewart. However, Bonass recalls that the new member from Northern Ireland brought the song to the group as a devotee of the American bard and sang on the track.

> **BRENDAN BONASS** Paul was a fan of Bob Dylan. We went in with acoustic guitars and recorded in Eamonn Andrews Studios on Henry Street. John Paul Jones was the producer. What he added to the day was he was playing a record rack with a screwdriver. I though it was really good. It was pressed as a 45 on a red label, the Sound City label.

Brady's recollection is different, insisting the record was sung by the group's original vocalist and claiming that Dylan was not a major interest of his at this point: 'We recorded it above the GPO in Henry Street. It was a Sunday morning I remember. Ronnie Stewart sang.' Whoever sang or whatever name the record came out under (was it The Inmates or The Kult?), the 7" single is rarer now than rocking horse droppings and remains a lost curio of Paul Brady's career and a buried treasure of the early beat scene. Towards the end of 1965 The Kult disintegrated when drummer Dave Pennefeather joined The Earl Gill Showband ('He took the King's shilling!' Brady recounts with a chuckle). Paul then fell in with a band called Rootzgroop, who hailed from the Seapoint area of south Dublin, and started to play more regularly on keyboards than on guitar, developing a predominantly soulful sound with his new associates.

Rootzgroop, 1966. Paul Brady second from left

PAUL BRADY Soul music was coming in that summer of '65 like Otis Redding, Wilson Pickett, Junior Walker and the Allstars. All that kind of music was finally coming through Ireland and I started moving away from the Muddy Waters, Howlin' Wolf blues thing into more of the Ray Charles, Ike and Tina Turner, Marvelletes kind of [thing].

Soul music was wildly popular amongst club goers in mid-60s Dublin, probably for the simple reason that it was just great to dance to. Although plenty of punters went to the basement venues expecting to hear the latest Kinks, Stones and Beatles hit from the charts, Tamla Motown and Atlantic soul were hugely appreciated by Irish kids, and both DJs and groups scrambled to keep up with the latest imports from the US to satisfy their thirst.

SMILEY BOLGER You could say people were mimicking what was happening in Liverpool and in the British scene to a certain degree but I think our musical influences were nearly all American. Tamla Motown was huge. There was something about it that connected more with us, same with the soul music. It seemed to have more of an earthy feel than say Gerry and the Pacemakers which was all very nice but it wasn't our cup of tea.

BP FALLON Soul music is for dancing and sex. Those records by Otis and Aretha and Sam and Dave and Wilson Pickett and Solomon Burke and Joe Tex – all that brilliant Atlantic Records stuff – they pump like mothers, y'got t'shake a tailfeather when the bass and drums hit you and the horns lift you higher and the singer's testifying about waiting till the midnight hour… they're

> hot records, and tougher than Motown. Ray Charles shakin' out the achin' with 'What'd I Say', The Raelettes wailing… my God!

'Sweet Soul Music' by Arthur Conley, 'The Happening' by The Supremes, 'All I Need' by The Temptations and 'Ain't No Mountain High Enough' by Tammi Terrell and Marvin Gaye – these are just a small selection of the records from black US singers given extensive turntable time by top club DJ Pat Egan throughout 1967. Paul Brady's tenure in Rootzgroop didn't last very long, as he deserted them in May 1966 to join the more serious and dedicated Rockhouse, who were being managed by Ted Carroll. Again the emphasis was on soul music, with hot tunes like Ray Charles' 'What I'd Say' and Aretha Franklin's 'Every Little Bit Hurts' featured in the group's set, mixed with contemporary stuff from The Spencer Davis Group. For someone who is mostly associated with folk music and adult contemporary rock it is perhaps surprising to discover that the songs of black America were the ones that made the most impression on the young Paul Brady.

DJ and journalist Pat Egan, 1968

> **PAUL BRADY** I was aware of traditional music in the background. It wasn't something that I was really madly interested in. It was something that I took for granted; it was part of the cultural backdrop. Where I came from [there] was quite a lot of trad music around, but I was mainly interested in pop music and R&B.

Although rock 'n' roll was Brady's first love, his promising career in beat groups would be abruptly terminated by the intervention of his parents, concerned that their son was squandering his education to play wild jungle sounds with long-haired louts.

> **PAUL BRADY** I had been a disaster as a student. I hadn't been going to lectures at all and I conned my way through first Arts and [for] second Arts I got to a doctor and got him to fake a medical cert. University didn't even know where I was so they sent a letter to my home address in Strabane and my mother, incredibly, opened the letter. It was one of these letters from the Registrar saying, 'Dear Mr. Brady, unless you shape up you're out!' I was completely squandering my time at university. I was in total denial. I didn't feel like I was a student, I just wanted to be a musician.

With the departure of their talented lead singer Rockhouse imploded. Brady went home and spent the Christmas holidays sheepishly kicking his heels. Returning to Dublin in January the following year, he was unable to give up his beloved music and, unbeknownst to his parents, began to gravitate towards the folk clubs. Staying in a flat in the same building as Paul in Ranelagh, just outside the city centre, were Mick Moloney and Johnny Morrissey of The Emmet Folk Group. Strains of traditional folk music would waft up to Brady through the floorboards when they rehearsed in the rooms below. Paul would also be forced to listen to Bob Dylan's early acoustic records when he partook in all-night poker games with his gregarious neighbours.

> **PAUL BRADY** I didn't really have an awful lot of time for the ballads. It all seemed kind of self-conscious to me. Why are all these people singing all this shit from two hundred years ago? It was all a bit fake to me. Of course I really didn't understand it at the time, I didn't get it.

That would soon change. Slowly, the young rocker began to develop an appreciation of those less flamboyant and more introspective tunes. He was encouraged to get up and do some short acoustic blues sets in places like the

95 Club on Harcourt Street, playing old American songs written by Mississippi John Hurt and Leadbelly. This led to a revised opinion of contemporary US folkies like Dylan and The New Lost City Ramblers, which inevitably led him to the songs and traditions of his native land.

> **PAUL BRADY** Before long I was being offered support slots to The Johnstons in the Embankment or the Old Sheiling. Then I'd be asked to play guitar with somebody like James Keane, who was the accordion-playing brother of Sean Keane, the fiddle player with The Chieftans. Bit by bit I came around to folk music.

The conversion was complete when in June 1967 Brady joined The Johnstons, an established folk act with a number one hit single under their belt. Their popularity and proven achievements gave him enough ammunition to convince his parents that his future lay in music and he quit college to concentrate full-time on playing guitar and singing. Brady's interest in Irish folk music deepened rapidly as a member of The Johnstons and it would be a long time before he returned to rock music, eventually releasing his first solo album in that genre over a decade later, in 1981.

Paul Brady, 1967

> **PAUL BRADY** Vocally the folk scene was more interesting than the rock scene. In the rock scene you were largely trying to sound like the records you were covering. Whereas in the folk scene in the mid-60s something was actually being born in Ireland that we were all part of. It was exciting although we didn't really know what we were doing at the time. It was more challenging, more interesting, you were making something that hadn't been there before. I know the *songs* were there before but the approach to arranging them and performing them was a whole new thing that came in on the back of The Clancy Brothers.

Paul Brady's big successes would come in the 1970s with The Johnstons and also with hugely popular folk group Planxty, as well as throughout the 1980s and beyond as a highly acclaimed international solo artist. He certainly wasn't the only Irish musician to learn his trade on the domestic beat scene and use it as a springboard for greater things in the ensuing decades. The intermingling of the rock and folk scenes gave birth to Phil Lynott's collective Orphanage, but its casual nature was not conducive to long-term existence. Their lead singer would soon find fame and fortune with quite a different set-up.

> **BRIAN DOWNEY** Orphanage were together for about eight or ten months and then one night we were playing at the Countdown

> Club where we were spotted by Eric Bell. He was working with John Farrell and The Dreams at the time, but wanted to get into something else. That's how Thin Lizzy started. (Mark Putterford, *Phil Lynott: The Rocker*, pp36-37)

Eric Bell had become tired of chugging along on the showband steamboat. Lucrative as it undoubtedly was, the conservative world of the big bands was creatively stultifying for a man who had briefly been in a line-up of Them (what Northern Irish musician wasn't?) and who was a true rocker at heart. Phil Lynott had been trying out his song-writing skills while he was in Orphanage and was now keen to take up duties on bass guitar in a different group, feeling he had mastered the instrument after his crash course with Brush Shiels. With Downey on drums, Bell on guitar, Phil on bass and another ex-Them man Eric Wrixon on keyboards, Thin Lizzy were unveiled to an excited public in February 1970. Great things were expected from Phil and his band. And great things ensued.

The golden age of Ireland's beat group scene could probably be bracketed within the period between 1964 and 1968. This was when the first combos playing the new sounds came to prominence throughout the country, capturing the hearts and minds of the young Irishmen and women who thronged the cellar clubs, suburban tennis pavilions and local cinemas to see their favourite acts (cinemas such as the Apollo in Dundrum and the Apollo in Walkinstown regularly had multi-band R&B extravaganzas in their auditoriums in the mid-60s). As the 1970s hovered into view circumstances on the domestic music scene changed significantly. The innocent and carefree days of the beat scene were drawing to a close and many musicians had to make a tough choice between struggling on or giving it up for a regular job and a steady wage. As we have seen, quite a number of beat scene players realised that the best way of performing music six nights a week and earning good money was to join a showband. Although it was not entirely clear at the time, even that lucrative scene was past its commercial peak and some of the seven-piece line-ups that the so-called 'bread heads' joined didn't last all that much longer than the beat groups they had deserted. Of course, music in general was progressing and changing and different groups were playing radically contrasting music to increasingly differentiated audiences. In the riverside dungeons of Sound City or in the stuffy confines of the No. 5 Club during 1965 all the kids danced in one delirious swirling mass to a mixture of pop, beat, soul and rhythm 'n' blues. Now the more discerning listener was hunting down progressive rock, hard rock, or psychedelic rock while those that were ostracised by these new offshoots still packed the halls to hear bands play note-perfect covers of radio-friendly hits. The original beat fans were growing up and moving into different stages of their lives. A new legion of fans quickly followed on from them, more informed and judicious in their tastes.

Along with Skid Row and Granny's Intentions on the more 'progressive' side of the musical landscape, one of Ireland's most distinctly idiosyncratic groups of the late 60s was The Orange Machine, who are probably deserving of the title – 'Ireland's first psychedelic group'. Although formed in late 1966 the group didn't make a huge impression on the scene until they broke the domestic charts with their playful Brit-psyche single 'Three Jolly Little Dwarfs' in the summer of 1968, taken from UK group Tomorrow's eponymous LP. The B-side of the hit was a hard-rocking mindwarp from the same record called 'Real Life Permanent Dream'. To many ears the sound of this new amalgam was wilfully uncommercial, influenced strongly by the heavy blues of John Mayall and also that peculiar childlike brand of English toy town psychedelia typified by Tomorrow, The Move and their contemporaries. This was starkly illustrated as The Orange Machine's reputation grew rapidly in the aftermath of their chart success.

> **JIMMY GREELEY** (drums, The Orange Machine): Inadvertently we were getting gigs down the country in showband bastions. I can remember the look of shock and horror on everyone's face as they stood at the back of the hall with this racket on stage and the manager in dementia trying to get us out of there as fast as possible. They thought they were getting something safe from the charts. They'd never heard the record. They just knew we were in the charts so we must be a showband!

Dressing up in tailor-made orange suits and frilly orange shirts clearly didn't endear the group to the rural crowds. Their first hit was followed with a Dave Mason (Spencer Davis Group) number, 'You Can All Join In', released in February 1969. This time the B-side was a self-written track (by guitarist Robin Crowley and drummer Jimmy Greeley) called 'Dr. Crippen's Waiting Room', a gloriously eccentric piece of whimsy with a wonderfully propulsive fuzz guitar riff. Unfortunately the promise and talent on display in the first two singles was never properly harnessed. *Melody Maker* in England gave the thumbs up to 'You Can All Join In' but Pye Records didn't have an adequate distribution system in place to exploit the situation. Managers came and went with frustrating regularity and the group's efforts to break out of the home market were thwarted.

> **JIMMY GREELEY** Nobody had broken it in England at that stage. It was difficult for an Irish band to do that. The first thing you had to do was find the money to live abroad. Very few people went across. If you were serious about really making it you had to get out of Ireland because there was no infrastructure here apart from the showband scene. We would have had a very severe inferiority complex about what we were doing, because it

> was hard to get work outside of the cities, Dublin, Cork and Belfast. Nobody ever mentioned an album. Because that would have been for people in England. There was no such thing as an album deal anyway [in Ireland]. That's why we were always going into this dead end.

Before ending up in the proverbial cul-de-sac The Orange Machine was forced to alter its line-up when impresario Brian Tuite (who was managing the band at the time) decided to put together what he hoped would be his Irish pop supergroup Blue, coaxing two members away from the psyche

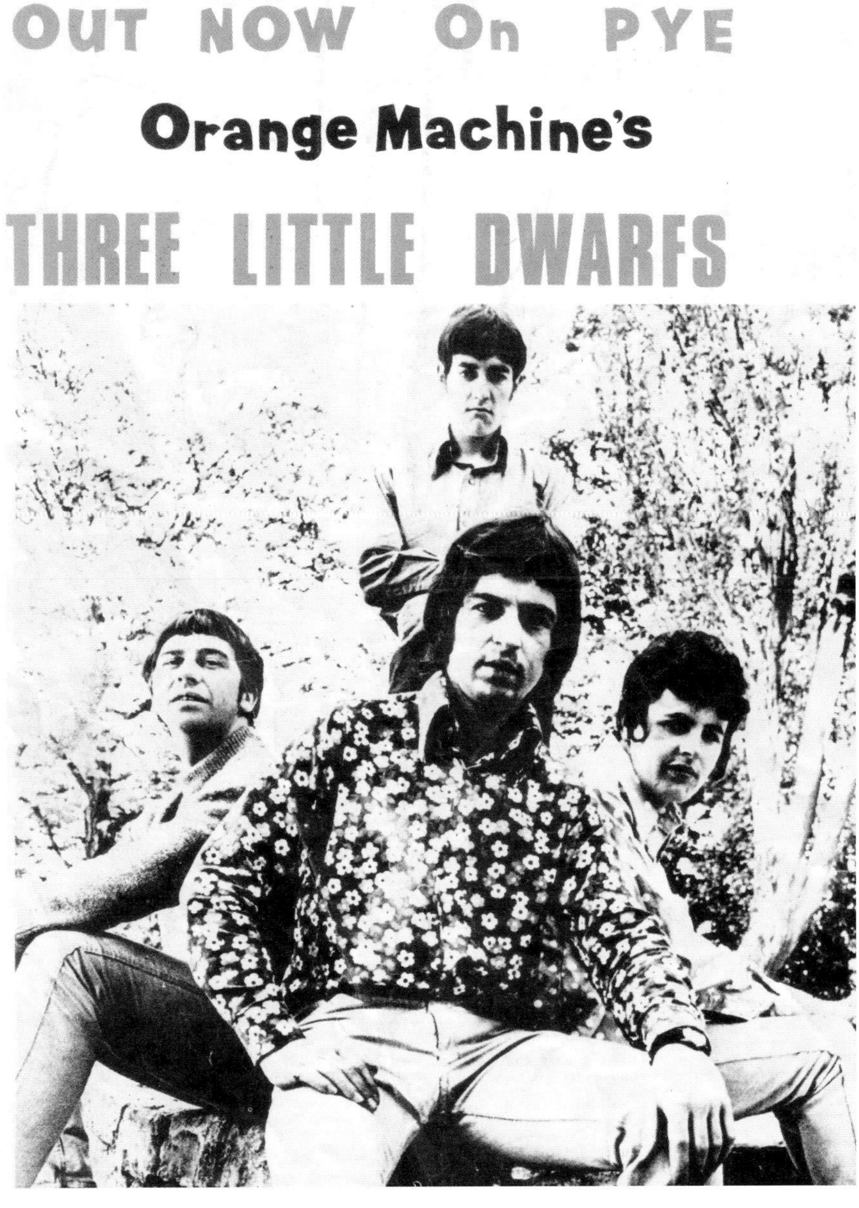

Press ad for The Orange Machine's debut 7"

pioneers in the process (singer Ernie Durkin and bassist Tommy Kinsella). Karen Byrne, a rare female presence on the beat group scene and previously a member of Northern Ireland's Soul Foundation, was asked to join a new look Orange Machine, along with fiddle player Joe O'Donnell. The group's new sound was even more abstruse than before.

> **JIMMY GREELEY** It was a mad sound. There was a band called East of Eden which is the nearest thing I can think of that we sounded like. We had long guitar solos followed by long fiddle solos, quite good but it had a limited appeal. It was so uncommercial that I don't think we were getting a second [chance].

Karen Byrne temporarily joins The Orange Machine, second from left

It was all too much for Byrne as she left just three months after joining the band, claiming 'the group no longer found me musically acceptable' (*Spotlight*, Vol. 1, No. 9, 2 Aug 1969). Frustratingly there were precious few choices available for beat group musicians – either take a chance and head to the UK, eek out a living on the domestic scene or accept the showband payout. There was a robust supply of new groups coming through to entertain audiences in Dublin and other big towns, but the fervent atmosphere of a few years previous was dissipating.

> **JIMMY GREELEY** What was left was very pop-oriented. [Those groups] were successful. You might have in the same venue a rock-oriented Wednesday and a pop Sunday. These things fell into place. The Bye Laws would have a specific routine. They were a good little dance band and [played] popular songs of the day. I think they used to do medleys of really old songs.

At the opposite end of the spectrum to The Orange Machine were polished pop groups like the aforementioned Bye Laws and The Others, who followed on from their ideologically similar predecessors The Strangers and The Vampires by performing tight, disciplined versions of everyone's favourite tunes. There were no 5/4 time signatures or sitar solos in their music – sleek pop covers and recognisable crowd pleasers gained both groups huge audiences as the decade came to a close.

The Bye Laws, who formed during the summer of 1967, rivalled Skid Row and Granny's Intentions as Ireland's most popular group in the latter part of the decade, despite being cut from a very different cloth. In fact, a sort of friendly rivalry developed between fans of Granny's, the trendy Limerick rock group, and the smartly dressed popsters from Ballyfermot (on the cover of one particular issue of *Hitsville* magazine the five members are nattily decked out in tuxedos and bow ties). Despite their lack of original tunes, and their seeming disregard for contemporary developments in the music world, The Bye Laws built up a massive following in the cities (particularly amongst girls), on occasion necessitating the intervention of local police to safely escort them away from venues surrounded by hysterical fans. Original drummer Maurice Walsh, who by force of personality soon became the group's lead vocalist, quickly ended up with Joe Dolan and The Drifters (after a short detour in pop band Purple Pussycat) and was replaced by heart-throb Pat Morris, who remained The Bye Laws' singer until their demise. Walsh features on the group's first record, which paired 'Then You Can Tell Me Goodbye', an American hit for clean-cut crooners The Casinos in 1967, with the similarly smooth 'Come On Over To My Place' which was associated with another middle-of-the-road outfit, The Drifters. Similar to that debut, The Bye Laws' crisp 1969 release 'Run Baby Run', with Pat Morris this time commandeering the microphone, sounded like it could have been released years earlier, resonant as it was of classic Merseybeat archetypes. In 1971, after

The Bye Laws featuring second vocalist Pat Morris, left, 1968

the group had dissolved following a permanent move to Canada, their singer acknowledged the restrictions he felt the group had imposed on themselves in an interview conducted by new underground rock magazine *Gun*.

> **PAT MORRIS** The scene will go on and on as it has for the past five or six years. It is not sufficient to do cover versions of other people's material anymore. The main fault with most groups, and indeed the big factor regarding the failure of The Bye Laws, was lack of originality. Every group needs a revolutionist, as with say Lennon in The Beatles. One radical to open up the ideas and bring the others in.

Another very well-received pop group were The Others, from Dublin's prosperous Southside who built up a strong local following at Stella House in Mount Merrion during 1968 before moving on to play more demanding city centre clubs. They would frequently be in competition with The Bye Laws to see who would be the first to play a faithful rendition of the latest smash.

> **PAT WHELAN** (bass, The Others): We always worked off the charts, the hits of the day, Ken [Tubbert, guitar] being such an avid collector. The advance copies would be sent to the DJs in the stations by the record companies only a week or so before the release date and so a lot of people wouldn't have heard enough of the song [to be familiar with it]. We'd have the record and we'd learn two or three songs every Saturday. We'd be playing songs that we would think will be hits and then [the fans] would hear the original. We prided ourselves on our ability to recreate.

The Others were firm devotees of the magic that three minutes of pop music can produce – a cursory listen to their 1969 single 'Lovely Loretta' is ample evidence of this. It has the kind of naggingly insistent refrain that requires no more than one spin on the turntable to lodge itself firmly in your brain. Later on the group cleverly picked up on 'Ring Ring' by ABBA, a year before the Swedish group exploded internationally via exposure on *The Eurovision Song Contest*. The Others were also a particularly attractive proposition for the businessmen who were opening up new types of clubs in Dublin as the decade drew to a close. These new establishments (Sloopy's and Zhivago being two of the most popular) were more sophisticated and urbane than their grotty predecessors and placed a distinct emphasis on atmosphere, comfort and style as much as on music.

> **SMILEY BOLGER** As always the money men take over. There was an original group of people running the beat clubs, the coffee

shops, avant-garde little get togethers, all ad-hoc, in places that wouldn't get away with it now. No fire escapes. There were places in Parnell Square, up the back lanes of Leeson Street, where they had wine and people would be sitting around reading poetry and playing acoustic guitars, really freaking out and being hippies. Probably smoking a bit of dope. They were half-legal [places]. Because they were little cafés, they could serve wine...and that probably gave people ideas, if you have food you can serve wine. The ante went up, and they could go late night, and then the whole thing became business. They were basically discotheques. They were still using bands during the week, [but] Thursday to Sunday they just had DJs. There was more of a sheepish crowd going to them. They were taking [punters] from the showband scene. To play [these clubs] you had to clean yourself up a bit. Someone like Thin Lizzy would die a death, and they did. The Bye Laws would have got loads of work.

Alan Dee's Watchtower play the TV Club, Harcourt Street

The irrepressible Alan Dee, who had formed a new group called The Watchtower in March 1968 after disbanding his post-Chessmen beat group The Light, also saw the writing on the wall. Although still dressed up in outlandish clothes and initially leaning in a heavy blues direction, his new group gradually started to change their sound and incorporated more accessible material in their sets to appeal to the new crowds.

> **ALAN DEE** We started getting a bit 'cabaret' actually. The clubs were beginning to wane and the discos were coming in, Zhivagos, Club Picasso, the Countdown Club on Mary Street. It wasn't beat-oriented, the music was getting a bit bland.

Groups began to discover that they weren't as much in demand as before. A DJ was cheaper, more reliable and less unpredictable. 'I hated DJs,' adds Dee, 'because I saw DJs as competition that would ultimately ruin the scene, and that's exactly what happened.' Rumours of the imminent closure of the No. 5 Club spread like wildfire in April 1969. Ted Carroll, a crucial instigator of the beat scene back in 1963 when he operated the Rhythm 'n' Blues Club at Longford Tennis Club, bemoaned the dearth of suitable venues for rock groups to *Gun* magazine, when he took a trip back to his native land as manager of Thin Lizzy in 1971 (he had moved to England in 1968).

> **TED CARROLL** There was a great scene going here three or four years ago. There was a whole round of clubs for groups to play and a lot more healthy competition. Now it's becoming increasingly difficult for groups to get gigs in Dublin, so much so that the scene appears to be moving to other cities like Cork and Galway.

The changing club situation was not the only indication of a *malaise* within the beat scene. By 1968 the era of the album had definitely arrived. Just three years previously Irish beat groups were struggling to cough up a couple of hundred pounds to cut a single in ill-equipped studios with unsympathetic producers. Pye Records were far too busy producing platters for the big name showbands to bother too much with rock 'n' roll.

> **KEVIN DUNNE** Pye didn't promote anything. They pressed the things, put them in the bags and distributed them to the shops, that's all they did.

Even if a beat group did achieve substantial sales of their 7" there were many people who felt unfair practices would prevent the record from ever assuming its rightful position in the Irish charts. A growing appreciation of albums as the true expression of an artist's worth meant that those groups without the means to invest in such a costly venture were sidelined. Even if a group could find one person to stump up the cash and another to guide them musically, it was doubtful whether the end product would shift enough units in Ireland to justify the investment in the first place. An alternative to recording in Eamonn Andrews Studios finally emerged in the summer of 1968 with the opening of Trend Studios, run by young engineer John D'Ardis, who remains boss of the still-functioning operation to this day.

Trend marketed itself as a studio that was much more sympathetic to beat groups' needs, as Brian Tuite noted when he recorded 'Three Jolly Little Dwarfs' with The Orange Machine there – 'the relaxed atmosphere definitely helps the heads to exploit their talents to the full'. (*Hitsville*, Vol. 1, No. 6, Oct 1968). Although it was always fully booked (popular groups who laid down their sound on tape there included Skid Row, The Bye Laws, The Movement, and The Magazine), technically there was not a huge improvement in Trend Studios on what was already available elsewhere. Whatever about the equipment, even having the qualified personnel on hand proved to be a major challenge.

> **ROY ESMONDE** The facilities were limited, there was two track recording in Eamonn Andrews Studios. But out of that Ian Whitcomb and Bluesville produced really innovative stuff and they had a very good engineer, Bill Somerville-Large. He was more than an engineer, he often produced. I don't know if there were any producers in the sense in which you would expect somebody to be a producer now – someone with a vision of how a band should sound or what new ground they should break. With more of them we probably would have had a more distinct sound. But with a lot of [bands] records were seen as promotional vehicles and not as end products in themselves. So you had a local industry built around Pye Records. Getting signed to Pye nobody expected a penny back. You just got 'Hey, we have a record; it's out in the shops!'

> **BENNY WHITE** (singer with hard rock group Elmer Fudd): If you were a pop band you could go into Trend Studios, or Eamonn Andrews Studios. The Television Club used to have a recording studio in that building [as well]. You could do an itsy-bitsy pop number no problem. But if you wanted to do a serious rock album you'd definitely have to go abroad because there weren't enough experts here for that. There was nobody with that kind of expertise because they were just used to recording either solo artists or showbands.

To give them their due, at the very end of the decade, Pye Records did release a full-length compilation LP of Ireland's beat groups, with the defiant title *Paddy Is Dead And The Kids Know It* emblazoned across its sleeve.

> **PAT EGAN** *Paddy Is Dead…* was my idea. I approached John Woods and told him about the various beat groups who had sizeable followings. I felt an album would sell. The idea behind the title was the ballad groups and showbands were old hat and

the kids knew it. It sold about six thousand copies.

What should have been a victorious declaration of Irish beat groups' superiority over the staid ballroom and trad folk scenes poignantly turned out in hindsight to be a eulogy for the death of the whole beat scene itself. Recorded during various sessions at Trend Studios, the album sounds tired, flat, sludgy and distinctly amateurish. Six groups were asked to contribute two songs each. Side one kicks off with the supper club schmaltz of Purple Pussycat who wade through an instantly forgettable version of Brenda Holloway's 'You Made Me So Very Happy'. Why no one advised them against attempting an execrable version of the Phil Spector masterpiece 'River Deep, Mountain High' as their second offering is hard to fathom. Right from the off they manage to drain the song of every ounce of the pomp and passion that made Ike and Tina Turner's original such a breathtaking tour-de-force. County Meath beat merchants The Pan Pipers fare little better with a timid rendition of The Beatles' 'Back in the USSR'; worse still is their entirely superfluous run-through of 'Blue Suede Shoes'. Other dismal offerings from Mitch and The Editions, Northern Ireland five-piece Taxi (a flute-drenched instrumental of Gershwin's 'Summertime'), scene veterans Some People and the highly professional Bye Laws (who should have known better) round off what must have seemed like clear confirmation to the showband establishment that there was never anything to worry about from the beat groups after all.

In January 1969 there had been talk about releasing a live album of Irish groups, showcasing the gifts of The Movement, The Vampires and The Orange Machine amongst others. A concert setting would have impressed that the featured groups were at least awake, unlike the somnambulant recordings on the *Paddy Is Dead* LP. In truth, a full-length album displaying the talent and verve of the Irish beat scene should have been put out three years sooner – when The Action were thrilling fans with previously unheard exotic blues and jazz; when cool cat Peter Adler was stalking devilishly around stages; before The Creatures sadly split up, and when the country's clubs were teeming with scores of soul bands, R&B aficionados, and pop pretenders.

Of course rock music in Ireland didn't die at the dawn of the 1970s. Far from it! University campuses became increasingly receptive to nationally touring groups like Elmer Fudd, Alyce and Iron Horse and a budding festival scene further helped spread the word amongst non-urban dwelling folk. Even though a lot of beat clubs went 'disco', the tennis club circuit survived on the sidelines, attracting relatively small crowds but offering a lifeline to bands that didn't have the clout to fill the National Stadium. Most musicians knew that fame and fortune lay outside Ireland, and the very best of the talent sought it out. It will always be the way with this small island. Deke O'Brien, who had served his time playing with Bluesville and The Chosen Few, took his invaluable experience and loyal musical partner Mick Molloy over to London where they hooked up with old Trinity College jazzman Ruan O'Lochlainn and formed Bees Make Honey. Along with Eggs Over Easy this no-nonsense roots rock group kick-started the pub rock scene in London during 1971 and 1972, playing fading jazz venues like the Tally Ho in Kentish Town and the Hope & Anchor in Islington. This wasn't the only link that Ireland's beat scene had with the punk rock movement of the late 70s. If the spirit of punk is driven by a rejection of accepted societal constraints, an attitude of self-sufficiency and a rebellion against the prevailing orthodoxy, then the group scene's dogged survival in the face of a showband/showbusiness system that all but tried to sabotage it means that the 1960s struggling beat musicians can be seen as ideological predecessors to groups like The Boomtown Rats and The Radiators From Space, who were still surrounded by anaemic pop dross in Ireland almost a decade later.

The massively popular showband scene was a phenomenon in 60s pop music, unique to this country, and a suffocating presence for innovative musicians who constantly fought against (and occasionally succumbed to) its entrenched ways. To their credit many beat participants managed to prevail against the odds, and the fact that Bluesville, The Creatures, Granny's Intentions, Ditch Cassidy, Them and their ilk were able to lay the solid foundations of Irish rock music has to be recognised as a considerable achievement. The ubiquitous presence in the twenty-first century of some of the biggest names from the fabled showband era (Dickie Rock and Brendan Bowyer are still touring) means that the story of Irish popular music in the 1960s has been told through their particular experiences and via their perspective, and subsequently validated through their fans' reminisces. It's high time that this imbalance was redressed. The smaller but no less significant beat group scene and its influential contributors are long overdue some hard-earned credit and recognition. Shay Healy, a dedicated folkie at the time, acknowledges the importance of the beat scene's influence on what was to be Irish rock, not just musically but in cultural terms as well.

> **SHAY HEALY** I think the beat scene was the first emerging culture that was not specifically Irish, it was borrowing very heavily from foreign influences. They were ploughing a furrow that a lot of us didn't understand at the time, or were not particularly interested in. It was a breakaway scene from what we were used to. It was new and probably slightly threatening to a lot of people. This was a left turn for a lot of the young Catholic boys to be going off playing that jungle music! Certainly that kind of music was the first sign that we were emerging from being an insular society, that we were taking a load of stuff on board. It was just a pity that nobody knew how to exploit it enough, to sell it to people. But it was the beginning of our rock identity.

Beat scene camaraderie. L-R: DJ Pat Egan, Mike O'Brien (The Good Tymes), DJ Jon Hodges, DJ Lee, Phil Lynott, Maurice Walsh (Bye Laws), Paul-Paul (Deep Set), Mick Roche (The Vampires), Jimmy Fanning (The Strangers), DJ Tony Johnston

Scores of kids, who got their pop music fix via safe family entertainers like Cliff Richard, or through neutered renditions of chart favourites when the showband hit the stage in their local hall, were inspired to set up their own rudimentary groups by the explosion of British beat and the discovery of exotic black American sounds. Instigated and nurtured by bold club owners, determined promoters, indefatigable managers and brilliant musicians, and championed unceasingly by journalists like Pat Egan in *Spotlight*, the beat scene provided Irish youth with a first taste of rebellion, a first taste of real live rock 'n' roll and a reason to reject the strictures and iron-clad certainties of their parents' generation. Many of the first participants in the scene were still active in the music industry well into the next couple of decades, both on the business and artistic sides of things and indeed many continue to play a role in Irish popular music today.

PAUL BRADY I thought it was a very important scene. Out of the beat scene in Ireland came Rory Gallagher, Phil Lynott, Van Morrison. That period was a very influential [one] and a lot of seeds were sown in that era which maybe didn't bear fruit until later.

Of course, regardless of the beat scene's importance in the story of Irish rock, and the nurturing role it played in teasing out the talents of our greatest musicians, one must not also forget the pleasure and joy that it brought to thousands of kids throughout those heady times. After all, it was fun – a lot of fun.

> **BP FALLON** Back in those early 60s years and nights and daze... listening to Muddy Waters on Pye Records or The Pretty Things on Fontana or The Velvelettes on Oriole, or going to The Club A Go Go off O'Connell Street to catch the magnificent Next In Line or going to The No. 5 Club in Harcourt Street to lurk in its Cavern Club-like cellars and get to shake it and maybe make it with girls with black fringes and short, short skirts and tongues hotter than a volcano... electric guitars and rebel guys growing their hair long and jukebox-tan teen girls looking like art school Mary Quants... the sound of untamed youth and the fantastic fumblings of one's first freedom...

BIBLIOGRAPHY

Boyd, Joe, *White Bicycles: Making Music in the 1960s*, Serpent's Tail, 2006

Clayson, Alan, *Beat Merchants – The Origins, History, Impact and Rock Legacy of the 1960s British Pop Groups*, Blandford Press, 1995

Clayton-Lea, Tony and Taylor, Richie, *Irish Rock: Where It's Come From, Where It's At, Where It's Going,* Gill & MacMillan, 1992

Duhan, Johnny, *There Is A Time*, Brandon, 2001

Harper, Colin, *Seaside Rock*, North Down Borough Council, 2003

Harper, Colin and Hodgett, Trevor, *Irish Folk, Trad & Blues: A Secret History*, The Collins Press, 2004

Gogan, Larry, *The Larry Gogan Book of Irish Charts Hits*, axwell, 1987

Heylin, Clinton, *Can You Feel The Silence? Van Morrison, A New Biography*, Viking, 2002

Keogh, Dermot, O'Shea, Finbarr and Quinlan, Carmel, *Ireland in the 1950s: The Lost Decade*, Mercier, 2004

Larkin, Colin, *Virgin Encyclopedia of Sixties Music*, Virgin Books, 2002

O'Keefe, Finbar, *Goodnight, God Bless and Safe Home*, The O'Brien Press, 2002

Power, Vince, *Send 'Em Home Sweatin'*, Mercier Press, 2000

Prendergast, Mark, *Irish Rock – Roots, Personalities, Directions*, The O'Brien Press, 1987

Putterford, Mark, *Phil Lynott: The Rocker*, Omnibus Press, 2002

Rogan, Johnny, *Van Morrison – No Surrender*, Secker & Warburg, 2005

Smiley-Childs, Marti and March, Jeff, *Echoes of the Sixties*, Billboard Books, 1999

Smyth, Gerry, *Noisy Island: A Short History of Irish Popular Music*, Cork University Press, 2005

Strong, M.C., *The Great Rock Discography*, third edition, Canongate Books, 1996

Whitcomb, Ian, *Rock Odyssey: A Chronicle of the Sixties*, Hutchinson, 1983

RECOMMENDED LISTENING

VARIOUS ARTISTS

Irish Rock: Ireland's Beat Groups 1964-1969 *Sequel NEX CD 262*

A 25 track compilation drawn exclusively from the archives of Pye Records. As a result, it omits wildly popular groups such as The Creatures, The Kingbees, and Granny's Intentions, whose releases appeared on other labels. Still, it is an admirably eclectic set, featuring the pristine pop of The Strangers and The Vampires; the psychedelic rock of The Orange Machine and a handful of lost nuggets by The Movement, Mitch Mahon and The Editions and scene pioneers The Greenbeats. Although quite what DJ Danny Hughes is doing on there with a cover of Jeff Beck's 'Hi Ho Silver Lining' is anyone's guess.

This is the only CD to date which has attempted to gather together singles produced during Ireland's golden period of beat. It was issued by Sequel Records in 1993 and is now deleted. To hear other recordings by Irish beat groups of the 1960s, try logging onto ebay armed with a sturdy credit card and a deep well of patience. There weren't an awful lot of copies sent out to the record shops in the first place, and good quality 45s command serious prices amongst collectors today. Happy hunting!

IAN WHITCOMB

You Turn Me On! Ian Whitcomb's Mod Mod Music Hall *Sundazed SC 11044*

Ian Whitcomb and Bluesville's compelling US chart hit, 'You Turn Me On', is the lead track on this 'twofer', which couples the group's first Dublin-recorded album with Ian's second record, the distinctly non R&B 'Mod Mod Music Hall'. Other singles, 'Nervous' and 'This Sporting Life', are featured as well. In order to hear the very first Bluesville record that Jerry Dennon released on his Jerden label in late 1964 – 'Soho' b/w 'Bony Maronie' – you'll have to track down Varese Sarabande Records' *You Turn Me On: The Very Best of Ian Whitcomb* (VSD-5897), a selected overview of the Englishman's career stretching from the 1960s to the 1980s. Listen closely and you might be able to hear an ashtray smashing to the floor on the test pressing version of their most famous song, tagged onto the end of the CD as a bonus track.

THEM

The Angry Young Them (aka Them) *Deram 844 924-2*
Them Again *Deram 844 825-2*
The Story Of Them Featuring Van Morrison *Deram 844 813-2*

The re-mastered sound on these re-issues is revelatory. Listen to one of the finest examples of 'British' R&B of the mid-60s, powered by the surging soulful vocals of Van Morrison, who would never again sound so feral and unfettered. The kids who went to see Them play those legendary gigs at The Maritime will tell you that the group's raw sound was never properly captured on wax. However, turn these CDs up loud and you can almost imagine yourself back there at that illustrious club in the spring of '64, feeling the sweat rolling down your forehead and the sticky condensation trickling down the walls.

The debut is the stronger of the two albums, Morrison demonstrating that he was miles ahead of his contemporaries on the 'mainland' with the inclusion of six of his own compositions, one of which is the stone cold classic, 'Gloria'. Although the 14 track LP is rounded out with a few blues standards from the likes of John Lee Hooker and Jimmy Reed, they never once make the album seem flabby. The solid playing and stunning vocals lift these versions above the mundane. If follow-up, *Them Again*, sacrifices some of the wild R&B of the first album, it makes up for it in achieving a more far-reaching and all-encompassing mix of ambitious styles: jazz elements are to the fore in 'I Put A Spell On You', folk rock on Dylan's 'It's All Over Now, Baby Blue', soul is represented by Ray Charles' 'I Got A Woman', and if Van Morrison claims he was never a singer in the 'rock' genre then it must be a different vocalist spitting out the mocking words on the violent punk gem, 'I Can Only Give You Everything'.

Completists are directed to the 2-CD release, *The Story of Them Featuring Van Morrison*, which sweeps up practically everything the group ever recorded for Decca, including the two big hits, 'Baby Please Don't Go' and 'Here Comes The Night', which don't feature on the debut record, as well as some alternate takes, although the compilation jettisons the original running order of both LPs.

VARIOUS ARTISTS

Belfast Beat Maritime Blues *Big Beat CDWIKD 152*

With a nod to the venue that started it all, this compilation takes eight songs that were released on the 1966 LP, *Ireland's Greatest Sounds: Five Top Groups From Belfast's Maritime Club*, and adds nineteen more cuts of prime beat, R&B and pop from Northern Ireland's fertile scene; however, for some reason, The Alleykatz' 'Friendly Undertaker' and The Bats' 'People Like You' failed to make the transition across the decades. The track-listing is heavily weighted towards The Wheels, and why not, as their eleven contributions included here amply illustrate the elevated status in which they were held amongst Belfast's and Blackpool's beat cognoscenti. Them are represented by early recordings, 'Don't Start Crying Now' and 'Philosophy'. The People and The Mad Lads also feature.

TASTE

Taste *Polydor 841 600-2*

On The Boards *Polydor 841 599-2*

No frills releases of Rory's first two albums with his power trio Taste, before big European festivals and international stardom took him miles away from his showband and beat scene beginnings. Intricate blues guitar fretwork is the name of the game on the eponymous debut, with follow up *On The Boards* revealing tantalising glimpses of the Donegal man's love of jazz.

THE COUNT FIVE

Psychotic Revelation – The Ultimate Count Five *Big Beat CDWIKD 230*

A one-stop shop for the San Jose garage punks (everything they officially released is here, and more), lovingly compiled by Alec Palao with a generous amount of photos and memorabilia included in the liner notes. Also features extensive interviews with band members and other notable participants involved in the group's fleeting moment of stardom.

THE BEAU BRUMMELS

Introducing The Beau Brummels *Repertoire REP 4697*

The Beau Brummels produced four more LPs after the departure of Irishman Declan Mulligan, but their most famous songs appeared on their debut in June 1965, on which the Tipperary native played guitar. This ground-breaking folk-rock record preceded The Byrds' 'Mr.Tambourine Man' long player by two months. Repertoire's re-issue from 1998 adds twelve additional tracks to the original running order.

DAVID MCWILLIAMS

The Days of David McWilliams *RPM Records RPM 225*

The best available introduction to the Belfast singer-songwriter, this single CD contains twenty-two tracks drawn from his first three albums, with two B-sides dating from 1968 and 1969. The original albums themselves remain un-issued on compact disc.

NIRVANA

The Story Of Simon Simopath *Island IMCD 301*

All Of Us *Island IMCD 302*

To Markos III *Island IMCD 303*

Delve into the magical chamber pop world of Waterford-born Patrick Campbell-Lyons and Greek native Alex Spyropolous with these crystal clear re-masters from Island Records. There's not much to differentiate the three albums, although *All Of Us* is perhaps the strongest overall, containing as it does their finest moment, 'Rainbow Chaser'. Additional tracks are included on the first two CDs. Nice artwork, too.

GRANNY'S INTENTIONS

Honest Injun *Lemon CD LEM 39*

The liner notes make much of the fact that Gary Moore played on this LP, the first album recording sessions he was ever involved in. Its important place in the history of Irish rock confers a much loftier significance on the record, however, and the songs contained within showcase the promising talents of youthful singer Johnny Duhan and gifted organist John Ryan. It's a real pity that the three singles released between 1967 and 1968 are not tacked on as bonus tracks, as they clearly demonstrate how Granny's evolved from an innocent psyche pop delight to a down-trodden, bone-weary, country-rock beast in the space of a couple of years. Duhan continues to write and record to this day, but in an alternate universe somewhere, that second album was completed and Granny's enjoy the same status as those other Irish rock pioneers, Thin Lizzy.

EIRE APPARENT

Sunrise *One Way Records OW 27734*

'Glorious failure' is probably an apt description of this Irish psychedelic rock treasure. You won't find mention of it in many Jimi Hendrix biographies, most writers deciding its status doesn't even warrant a footnote. But it's a fascinating document of its time, not always successful, but never less than intriguing. A beefed-up remaster would be greatly welcomed, the sound on this CD version coming across as slightly reedy and thin. The group's first single, with Henry McCullough, is missing as well.

ANDWELLA'S DREAM

Love And Poetry *Vinyl Japan ASKCD 144*

This limited edition CD was released to satisfy Andwella's Dream's legion of fans in the Far East, growing year by year. It's a nice package, too: the sound is good and lyrics are included for all songs. At the time of writing, the label Lightning Tree is planning a more widely available re-issue of the album on CD, along with bonus tracks. They have also issued a 180g vinyl pressing.

SKID ROW

Live And On Song *Hux 075 (Australia)*

A 2006 compilation with seven tracks. The group's early period is represented by their first two singles which were put out on Song Records, and produced at Eamonn Andrews Studios by Donal Lunny, then a member of folk-popsters, The Emmet Spiceland. The bucolic, West Coast sound on these cuts is in stark contrast to the elongated jazz-influenced workouts on 'Christian Brother Blues' (warning: contains 10 minute drum solo!) and 'Felicity', taped in January 1971 for BBC's *Live In Concert*, and included here along with the mercifully truncated track 'Un Co-Op Showband Blues', also recorded at that session.